D1068629

DISCARDED

THE COMPLETE ILLUSTRATED GUIDE TO
ISLAM

Sugar Grove Public Library
125 S. Municipal Dr.
Sugar Grove, IL 60554
(630)466-4686
sgpl.org

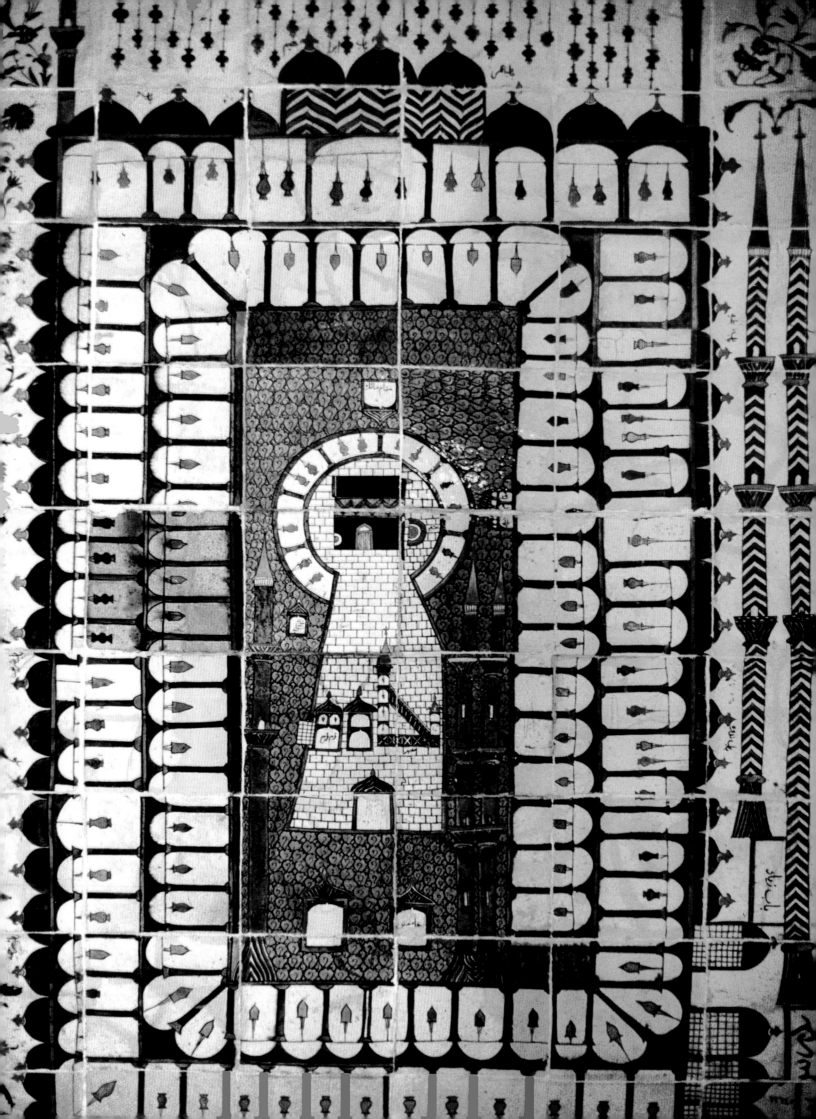

THE COMPLETE ILLUSTRATED GUIDE TO
ISLAM

A COMPREHENSIVE GUIDE TO THE HISTORY, PHILOSOPHY AND PRACTICE OF
ISLAM AROUND THE WORLD, WITH MORE THAN 500 BEAUTIFUL ILLUSTRATIONS

RAANA BOKHARI • MOHAMMAD SEDDON • CHARLES PHILLIPS
CONSULTANT: DR RIAD NOURALLAH

HERMES
HOUSE

CONTENTS

Above A candlestick from the 13th century, decorated with scenes from daily life.

Above An interior view of the dome in the Great Mosque of Córdoba, Spain.

Above The mihrab (arched niche) of the Tanjal Mosque, Tripoli, Lebanon.

Above Detail from a Persian carpet of a warrior surrounded by flowers and animals.

Above A 16th-century manuscript painting in the Mughal style.

Above 'No Conqueror But God', an inscription from the Alhambra Palace, Spain.

Above The minarets of the Sultan Hassan Mosque, Cairo, Egypt.

Above Suleyman the Magnificent, Venetian woodcut, 1540–50.

INTRODUCTION

Islam is believed to be the world's second largest religion, behind Christianity. It has more than 1.3 billion followers making up about a fifth of the global population. The meaning and message of Islam is one of peaceful submission to the will of one God, who is referred to in Arabic as 'Allah'.

Arabic is the language in which the Quran – according to Islam, a divine revelation – was disclosed to Muhammad, the 'Prophet of Islam', in 610CE in Makkah. Muslims believe that what followed over the next 23 years was a series of revelations to guide and instruct people to lead deeply spiritual, moral and upright lives, with God at the centre as sacred creator, and men and women seeking to live in peace through worship.

Above Verses from the Quran, believed by Muslims to be divine revelation, the very words of God given to Muhammad.

Below The maghrib *(sunset) prayer offered at the Prophet's Mosque in Madinah, Saudi Arabia.*

Within 100 years of Muhammad's death, the faith that had transformed Arabian society had extended as far as what is now Spain in the West and China in the East. The spread of Islam heralded a great time in Muslim civilization, marked by many mosques, forts and gardens that still stand today in Andalusian Spain, Moghul India and Abbasid Baghdad.

THE PROPHET OF ISLAM

Muslims consider the Quran to be the direct word of God and so do not challenge its authenticity, but a critical science of interpretation developed around the text over the centuries. Islam teaches that people cannot lead Godly lives through personal search and obedience to rules alone, but that they must depend on guidance from their

creator. This guidance, Muslims believe, came through prophets who were selected by God and sent to every nation: Adam is considered the first of these prophets and Muhammad the last.

Muhammad is central to Islam, which holds that there can be no belief in God without belief in Muhammad as his messenger. Known by Muslims as the Prophet, Muhammad is viewed not as the founder of a new religion, but rather as the restorer of monotheistic belief as practised by Ibrahim (Abraham), Moses, Jesus and others. Islam claims to be the culmination of Judaeo-Christian monotheism. The Prophet's life, as narrated in hadith (collections of the Prophet's sayings) and biographies, is the exemplary model that all Muslims aspire to follow.

ISLAM AS A WAY OF LIFE

The prescriptive and binding nature of Islam touches every aspect of life. Therefore, a Muslim's life is regulated by discipline. The five pillars of faith – declaring belief, prayers, giving alms, fasting and pilgrimage – give a ritualistic form to worship, but many Muslims believe that such observances should be imbued with inner spirituality.

Great scholarly activity after the death of Muhammad saw works in theology, philosophy, spirituality and law, as well as in the arts, sciences and medicine, being produced by independent scholars to ensure that people knew how to apply Islamic teachings to their lives.

HOW THIS BOOK IS SET OUT

Because the Prophet and his teachings are so central to Islam, this book begins with the story of the life of Muhammad, and the importance of the revelations he received, his teachings (hadith) and his life example (sunnah) to Muslim belief. The second chapter continues the story of the development of Islam, and the spread of Islamic civilization, beginning after the Prophet Muhammad's death and leading up to the present day.

The next three chapters examine theological beliefs, ritual worship practices and Muslim life. Chapter six explores issues of morality and ethics and the law, including controversial topics, such as medical bioethics and 'just war'. The final chapter reviews the unity and division among the Muslim community worldwide, for while all Muslims claim to be part of the global *ummah* (community), there are many points of difference, notably between Sunni and Shiah.

Each chapter also includes special themed spreads, highlighting particular issues, people and places of importance in Islam.

A great variety of pictures have been used to illustrate the beauty and breadth of Muslim life. Islam may forbid the depiction of Muhammad in art, but Islamic history is full of vivid depictions of places and people. As it is a sensitive issue regarding the Prophet, he is generally portrayed either without facial features, veiled or surrounded by divine light.

A NOTE ON ARABIC TERMS

As Arabic is the literary language of Islam, Arabic terms have been used and explained throughout the book, and a glossary of the major words appears at the end. Spellings considered to be correct by the wider Muslim academic community have been adopted: for example 'Makkah' and 'Muslims' rather than 'Mecca' and 'Moslems'. It is customary for peace and salutations to follow the names both of Islamic prophets and of Muhammad's companions, but these have been omitted in this book.

Below Pilgrims circumambulate the Kaabah in the Sacred Mosque in Makkah, the holiest site in Islam.

THE GLOBAL ISLAMIC COMMUNITY

SINCE THE EARLIEST PERIOD OF ISLAMIC HISTORY, MUSLIMS HAVE MIGRATED AND TRAVELLED TO NEW AREAS, AND COMMUNITIES OF MUSLIMS NOW LIVE ON EVERY CONTINENT IN THE WORLD.

The phenomenon of migration is perhaps at the heart of understanding the establishment of the *ummah*, or universal Muslim community. Muhammad's migration (*hijrah*) from his home city of Makkah to Madinah in 622CE was the turning point for his message in the creation of an Islamic citadel and the first Muslim community. The Muslims of Madinah were ethnically different from the first Muslims and religiously pluralistic.

DIVERSITY AND UNITY
Today, Muslims are truly global and extremely diverse – ethnically, culturally, theologically, socially, geographically, economically and politically. Across the Muslim world, Islam is reflected in the geo-cultural expressions of its varied adherents, the most noticeable differences being in the way people dress, speak and eat, and the ways in which they celebrate their rites of passage. There is, therefore, no single way that one can think of a Muslim.

Muslim diversity is seen as a cause for celebration in the Quran, which states 'O Mankind! Verily We have created you from a single male and female and made you into tribes and nations so that you may know each other. Indeed, the best of you with God are those who attain piety. Surely God is all-knowing, best-aware' (49:13).

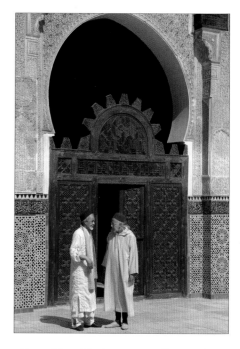

***Above** Two Muslim men talk outside the gates of a madrasa in Fez, Morocco. Islam encourages fraternity, teaching that all Muslims are brothers in faith.*

***Below** This demographic map illustrates the percentage of the Islamic population around the world. Muslims total more than one-fifth of the world's population.*

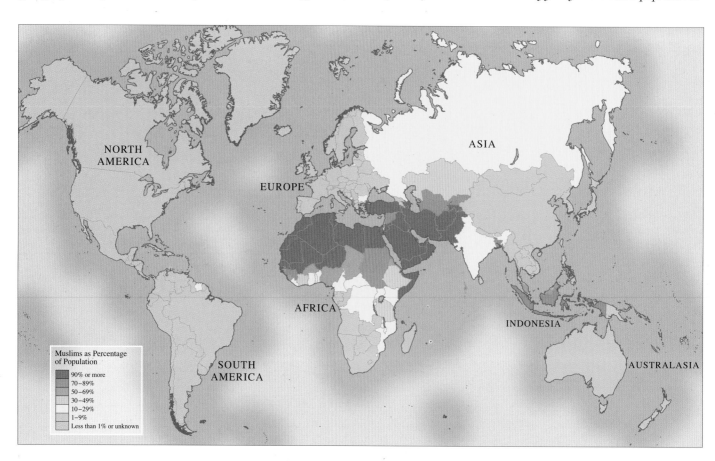

Muslims as Percentage of Population

- 90% or more
- 70–89%
- 50–69%
- 30–49%
- 10–29%
- 1–9%
- Less than 1% or unknown

NORTH AMERICA

SOUTH AMERICA

EUROPE

AFRICA

ASIA

INDONESIA

AUSTRALASIA

Left The Quran is preserved and recited in its original Arabic by Muslims throughout the world and is believed by all Muslims to be the sacred word of God as revealed to Muhammad.

The global Muslim community can be understood best through its beliefs and practices. Much of the Western scholarship on Islam has represented the faith as harsh and indignant, but for the majority of Muslims worldwide, the overarching characteristics of God are his endless mercy and immeasurable compassion. Their attitude to him is, therefore, one of grateful worship rather than fearful obedience.

Yet, despite their incredible diversity, Muslims are unified by their core Islamic beliefs and practices. For example, believers in every mosque from Beijing to Boston and Moscow to Makkah worship the same God, offer the same congregational prayers, read from the same Quran and loyally follow the teachings of the same prophet, Muhammad. Muhammad once declared that 'the Muslim *ummah* is like one body. If the eye is in pain then the whole body is in pain and if the head is in pain then the whole body is in pain.'

CHANGE AND CONSTANCY

Muslim contributions to human civilization and scholarship in the fields of science and technology have all been inspired by the religion of Islam. Although Muslim societies are constantly evolving – as are all human societies – the fundamental beliefs of Islam have remained constant since the time of the Prophet Muhammad, more than 1,500 years ago.

Right Muslims offering Friday prayers in Kuwait. Community life in Islam is centred around the mosque as a place of ritual prayer and social interaction.

TIMELINE

THE FOLLOWING TIMELINE LISTS SOME OF THE MAJOR EVENTS IN ISLAM'S RICH AND CULTURALLY DIVERSE HISTORY.

- 570 Muhammad is born.
- 610 Muhammad receives his first revelation from Archangel Jibril.
- 613 Muhammad begins preaching.
- 622 Muhammad leads the *hijrah* (migration) to Madinah.
- 629 Muhammad leads a pilgrimage to Makkah, where thousands are converted to Islam.
- 630 Muhammad takes control of Makkah and rededicates the *Kaabah* shrine to Islam.
- 632 Muhammad dies.
- 632–4 Abu Bakr rules as the first caliph or successor to Muhammad.
- 634–4 Umar ibn al-Khattab rules as second caliph and calls himself *amir al-mumineen* ('Commander of the Faithful').
- 635 Muslim troops capture Damascus.
- 636 Muslims defeat the Byzantine army in the Battle of Yarmuk.
- 638 Muslim troops take Jerusalem.
- 642 A crushing victory over the Persian Sasanian army at the Battle of Nahavand delivers Persia into Muslim hands.
- 643 Muslim troops capture Alexandria in Egypt.
- 644–56 Uthman ibn-Affan rules as third caliph.
- 651 Islam is introduced to China: Muhammad's uncle Saad ibn Abi Waqqas travels as an envoy to Gaozong, emperor of Tang dynasty (618–907).
- 656 Uthman's assasination sparks civil war in the Muslim world.
- 656–60 Ali ibn Abu Talib rules as fourth caliph.
- 661 Ali ibn Abu Talib is murdered, ending the period of rule by the four 'rightly guided' caliphs.
- 661 Muawiyah I establishes the

Above *An Ottoman manuscript depicts the first Muslims building the Prophet's Mosque in Madinah in 622.*

Umayyad caliphate (661–750).
- 680 Muawiyah's son Yazid succeeds as caliph. Ali ibn Abu Talib's son Hussein ibn Ali and followers are killed in the Battle of Karbala on 10 October.
- 711 Tariq ibn Ziyad leads the Umayyad conquest of the Iberian Peninsula. Muhammad ibn-Qasim leads the Umayyad invasion of Sindh.
- 749 Hashimiyyah rebels capture Kufa and proclaim Abu al-Abbas caliph.
- 750–1258 Abbasid caliphate.
- 756 Umayyad prince Abd al-Rahman I (reigned 756–88) establishes the emirate of Córdoba in Spain.
- 762 The second Abbasid caliph, al-Mansur (reigned 754–75), founds Baghdad as capital for the caliphate.
- 836–92 Abbasid caliphs move their capital from Baghdad to Samarra.
- 909 Ubayd Allah al-Mahdi Billah establishes Fatimid rule in Tunis.
- 929 Abd al-Rahman III (reigned 912–61) declares himself caliph of Córdoba in Spain.
- 945 Shiah Buyids take control in Baghdad, although the Abbasid caliphs remain in nominal control.
- 969 Fatimids conquer Egypt and build a royal capital at Cairo.
- 1055 Seljuk Turkish leader Toghrul Beg takes effective power in

Above *The Dome of the Rock in Jerusalem was built in 687–92 by the fifth Umayyad caliph, Abd al-Malik.*

Baghdad. The Abbasid caliphs are still in nominal control.
- 1050 The Muslim Ghana empire in West Africa is at its height.
- 1090 Yusuf ibn Tashfin establishes Almoravid rule in Spain.
- 1099 European crusaders on the First Crusade (1096–99) capture Jerusalem from the Fatimids.
- 1100 The Christian Kingdom of Jerusalem is established.
- 1143 The Quran is translated into Latin for the first time.
- 1160s The Almohads invade Spain from North Africa and take power from the Almoravids.
- 1171 Saladin ends the Fatimid caliphate, establishing the Ayyubid dynasty (to 1250).
- 1187 Saladin recaptures Jerusalem.
- 1193 Muslim Afghan ruler Muhammad of Ghor captures Delhi, India.
- 1206 Qutb-ud-din Aybak declares himself Sultan of Delhi. Delhi sultans rule in India until 1526.
- 1212 Almohad leader Muhammad III al-Nasir is defeated by a Christian army in the Battle of Las Navas de Tolosa.
- 1236 King Ferdinand III of Castile captures Córdoba.
- 1248 Ferdinand III of Castile captures Seville.
- 1250 Izz al-Din Aybak founds the Mamluk sultanate in Egypt.
- 1258 Mongol army under Hulagu

Kahn loots Baghdad. The Abbasid caliphs take refuge in Cairo.

- 1258–1324 Osman I founds the Ottoman state in Anatolia.
- 1291 Mamluks capture Acre and drive European Christian powers from the Holy Land.
- 1327 The African Muslim Mali empire is at its height.
- 1398 Mongol ruler Timur raids Delhi. The sultanate never recovers.
- 1453 Ottoman sultan Mehmed II (reigned 1444–6 and 1451–81) captures Constantinople, renames it Istanbul and makes it the empire's capital.
- 1492 Nasrid sultan Boabdil surrenders Granada, Spain's last Muslim territory, to the Spanish monarchs Ferdinand and Isabella.
- 1502–1722 The Shiah Muslim Safavid dynasty rules Iran.
- 1517 Ottoman sultan Selim I (reigned 1512–20) defeats the Mamluk sultanate in Egypt; the final Abbasid caliph, al-Mutawakkil III, is taken to Istanbul as a prisoner. On his death, the title of caliph passes to the sultan.
- 1526 Afghan ruler Babur defeats the last Delhi sultan, Ibrahim Lodhi, and founds the Mughal dynasty.
- 1632–54 Mughal ruler Shah Jahan builds the Taj Mahal in India.
- 1740 Muhammad ibn

Abd al-Wahhab founds the Wahhabism movement. He makes an alliance with the House of Saud.

- 1744–1818 The first Saudi state dominates Arabia.
- 1824–91 The second Saudi state rules a smaller part of Arabia.
- 1839–76 In the Tanzimet period, Ottoman sultans attempt modernizing reforms.
- 1876 First Ottoman constitution is introduced but suspended in 1878.
- 1908 The revolution of Young Turks forces Sultan Abdulhamid II to abandon absolute rule and accept a constitutional monarchy.
- 1918 After the Ottoman defeat in World War I, Istanbul is occupied by British and French troops.
- 1919–23 Mustafa Kemal leads Turkish nationalists to victory in the Turkish War of Independence.
- 1923 The Republic of Turkey is proclaimed, with Mustafa Kemal Ataturk as president.
- 1924 Mustafa Kemal Ataturk abolishes the caliphate.
- 1932 The kingdom of Saudi Arabia is established by King Abdul Aziz ibn Saud.
- 1947 Pakistan is established as a Muslim-majority dominion in the Commonwealth of Nations.
- 1948 The creation of the state of Israel in Palestine.
- 1956 The kingdom of Morocco gains independence; Pakistan is

declared an Islamic republic.

- 1971 East Pakistan secedes from Pakistan to form Bangladesh.
- 1979 The Islamic Republic of Iran is established.
- 1980–8 War between Iraq and Iran.
- 1990–1 Iraqi forces invade Kuwait.
- 1991 Western-Muslim alliance drives Iraq from Kuwait.
- 1996 The Islamic fundamentalist Taliban regime comes to power in Afghanistan.
- 1998 Osama bin Laden and Ayman al-Zawahiri, leaders of the Islamic terrorist organization al-Qaeeda, issue a *fatwa* calling on Muslims to expel foreign troops and interests from Islamic lands.
- 2001 The USA declares a 'war on terror' after al-Qaeeda terrorist attacks on New York City and Washington on 11 September kill over 2,900 people. US-Western troops invade Afghanistan in search of Osama bin Laden and others, and to oust the Taliban.
- 2005 Muslim leaders and scholars from 50 countries agree the Amman Message, stating that no declarations of apostasy may be made against a Muslim.
- 2007 One of the founding members and a senior theologian of al-Qaeeda, Sayyid Imam al-Sharif, publishes a repudiation of *jihad* violence from his prison cell in Egypt.

Above Pupils flocked to learn from Persian-born polymath Ibn Sina or Avicenna (980–1037).

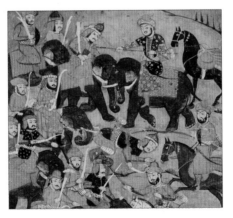

Above A scene from the Shahnameh *by Firdawsi (c.934–1020), who worked mostly under the Samanid rulers of Iran.*

Above Mughal Emperor of India, Shah Jahan (reigned 1628–58) built the Taj Mahal to honour his wife Mumtaz Mahal.

CHAPTER 1

MUHAMMAD: MAN AND PROPHET

To make sense of the religion of Islam, it is essential to gain an understanding of Muhammad's life and the early medieval Arabian society in which he lived. Before Muhammad's prophethood and the advent of Islam, Arabia was divided into hostile tribes who worshipped many gods. Their religious effigies were housed in and around the *Kaabah*, an ancient temple attributed to the prophet Ibrahim (Abraham) in Makkah, the city where Muhammad was born.

During Muhammad's early life, Makkah was established as the site of religious pilgrimage for the polytheist Arabian tribes. Muhammad the man became God's prophet, and the divine revelations he received, known as al-Quran, 'The Recitation', proclaimed him the 'Seal of the Prophets' (33:40). Within a generation, he united his tribal society and established a belief system based on absolute monotheism that eventually gave rise to one of the world's most influential religious civilizations.

Opposite The Prophet Muhammad's mosque at Madinah. The green dome is situated directly above the original site of Muhammad's house, in which he is buried.

Above The 'Mountain of Light' outside Makkah houses the cave where Muhammad is said to have received the first revelations of the Quran from Archangel Jibril (Gabriel).

ARABIA BEFORE ISLAM

UNTIL THE ADVENT OF ISLAM, ARAB CIVILIZATION HAD LITTLE IMPACT ON NEIGHBOURING ROMAN AND PERSIAN EMPIRES. THE PRE-ISLAMIC ERA WAS MARKED BY POLYTHEISM AND TYRANNY.

The city and desert dwellers of Arabia were traditionally two distinct peoples, who were shaped and conditioned by their different surroundings. Historically, the Arab Bedouins roamed the desert plains, living in territorial regions that were loosely held together by tribal codes and agreed treaties (*assabiyah*). Sedentary Arabs were originally grouped together in tribes, but in the urban setting, tribal divisions were generally social rather than geographical.

In pre-Islamic Arabia, the life of the Bedouins was romanticized by urbanized Arabs as pure, chivalrous and unrestricted. The desert Arabs were considered to embody all the noble characteristics of the Arab peoples. As a result, city children were often temporarily fostered with nomads to learn aspects of traditional Arab culture, such as the pure Arabic language, desert living, camel rearing and goat herding.

THE CITY OF MAKKAH

While the deserts of 6th-century Arabia and their inhabitants were largely overlooked by the powerful neighbouring empires of Abyssinia, Byzantium and Persia, the oasis city of Makkah was already an important Arab metropolis. It had long been established as a trading nexus between Arabia and Africa to the west, Yemen and India to the south and Egypt and Syria to the north. Trade brought wealth and status to Makkah's ruling tribes, increasing their power and influence way beyond the city.

The leading Makkan tribe of the Quraysh, the bloodline descendants of the prophet Ibrahim (Abraham),

Above The arid deserts of the Arabian Peninsula provided a breathtaking backdrop for the desert's unique people and their journey to Islam.

were the religious custodians of the ancient temple, the *Kaabah*. This square stone structure was originally built by Ibrahim, and the Quran asserts that the *Kaabah* was the first place of worship dedicated to Allah (God) (2:15–127). Elements of religious monotheism still existed in the minority communities of Jews in Yathrib (Madinah) and among

Below For thousands of years, caravans wound their way along the ancient trade routes, cutting through the oasis towns.

ORAL TRADITION

From as early as the 5th century BCE, the Arabs, originally a largely illiterate people who were proud of their tribal genealogies and histories, developed an incredibly descriptive and rhythmic language. This was achieved mostly through the custom of memorizing oral narratives from generation to generation. As the ancient nomadic cultural traditions were lost as a result of urban settlement, they were recaptured in the collective consciousness through the art of poetry and story-telling. These unique tribal narratives included genealogies of their ancestors and the extensive pedigrees of their prized camels and thoroughbred horses.

Left Bedouin Arabs socialize as they drink coffee. This is the time when they can enjoy their ancient customs of story-telling and poetry recital.

individual Arab Christians living in Makkah. However, the religion taught and practised by Ibrahim had long since been replaced by polytheism, and by the time Muhammad and his followers eventually conquered the city in 630CE, it was filled with no less than 360 statues and other images of devotion.

Below Antar, the 6th-century Arabian poet and warrior, epitomized the noble qualities of pre-Islamic desert Arabs.

BELIEFS AND SUPERSTITIONS

Polytheism prevailed in the pre-Islamic era – a period referred to in Islam as *jahiliyyah*, or 'the days of ignorance' – and every pagan Arab tribe possessed its own idol housed in the *Kaabah*. People believed that these devotional images would act as intercessors between humans and Allah (literally 'the one God'), and that by offering sacrifices and making pilgrimages to the idols they would ultimately earn God's grace and favour.

A few of the rites from the time of Ibrahim had been preserved – circumambulation, pilgrimage and animal sacrifice, for example – but they existed alongside superstitious beliefs and the worship of images. Omens, amulets, astrology and divination (by the casting of arrows) were important practices in deciding serious matters, such as when to travel, marry or go to war.

TRIBALISM AND SOCIETY

Social and tribal hierarchies also meant that the pre-Islamic period was marked by oppression, tyranny and racism. The conflicts between dissenting tribes led to continuous hostilities and strife. Slavery was a common practice, as was female infanticide, and while ownership of slaves was perceived as a sign of great wealth and power, daughters were often seen as an expensive liability. Women, whether married or not, as well as slaves were treated as personal property that could be sold or exchanged, and polygamy (the practice of marrying more than one woman) was common in pre-Islamic Arabia.

But Muhammad's prophetic call to Islam would soon transform Arabian society into a new civilization based on absolute monotheism, social egalitarianism and a fraternity of faith.

MUHAMMAD'S CHILDHOOD

WHILE MUHAMMAD WAS STILL A CHILD, AND INDEED EVEN BEFORE HE WAS BORN, THERE WERE INDICATIONS THAT THIS BOY WOULD TRANSFORM THE ARABIAN SOCIETY IN WHICH HE LIVED.

Muhammad is said to have been born in 570CE, a year that became known as the Year of the Elephant. According to a chapter of the Quran entitled 'The Elephant', Abyssinian Christians, led by army commander Abraha al-Ashram, invaded Makkah in an attempt to eradicate polytheism and destroy the ancient temple, the *Kaabah*.

Terrified, the inhabitants fled the city. But before leaving, their tribal leader, Abd al-Muttalib (who was later to become Muhammad's grandfather), dared to ask the Abyssinian general to return 200 camels that had been taken from him. When Abraha expressed surprise that Abd al-Muttalib was more concerned with the camels than the religion and its shrine that he had come to destroy, Abd al-Muttalib replied, 'I am the lord of the camels, and the temple likewise has a lord who will defend it!' According to the Quran, the Abyssinians were miraculously bombarded by huge flocks of birds, forcing them to retreat before they could even approach the *Kaabah*.

The retreat was seen as a miracle by the Arab tribesmen, who believed they had witnessed Allah's divine intervention to protect the *Kaabah* after their abandonment of it. The Quraysh, the ancient custodians of the *Kaabah*, interpreted the attack as an omen, a precursor to a possible future event connected to the temple that had been built by Ibrahim to honour the one God.

MIRACULOUS CHILDHOOD

Later that year, Muhammad ibn Abdullah, grandson to the former tribal *shaykh* (teacher) of the

***Above** Abraha's elephants attacking the* Kaabah. *This event reputedly occurred in the year of Muhammad's birth.*

Quraysh, Abd al-Muttalib, was born. Muhammad's father, Abdullah ibn Abd al-Muttalib, had unfortunately died some months earlier.

In his infancy, Muhammad was given to the care of a nursemaid, Halimah. He was fostered with her, staying with her tribe, Banu Sa'd, intermittently for the first five years of his life. The custom of foster-mothering their newborn with the Bedouins was common among the Quraysh, who wanted to imbue their children with the traditional Arab customs and pure language of the nomad Arabs.

According to a Hadith narration of Muhammad, it was during Muhammad's stay in the desert as a child that Archangel Jibril (Gabriel) came to him while he was playing with other boys. The angel allegedly held him down and split open his chest. Taking out his heart and removing a clump, he said 'this was Satan's portion of you'. He then washed Muhammad in a basin of

***Left** During the 5th and 6th centuries, Abyssinian Christianity and civilization ruled over most of the south of the Arabian Peninsula.*

Right Muhammad, cradled in his veiled mother's arms, is presented to his grandfather, Abd al-Muttalib, while the inhabitants of Makkah look on.

gold, with water from the sacred Well of Zamzam in the *Kaabah's* precinct, before sealing his chest. The boys then ran to Halimah, shouting, 'Muhammad has been killed'. When they approached the boy, they found him pale and in a state of shock.

BAHIRA THE MONK

Muhammad's mother died when he was only six years old. The boy's paternal grandfather, Abd al-Muttalib, took charge of him, but unfortunately, he, too, died only two years later. Thereafter, Muhammad was raised by his father's younger brother, Abu Talib, a merchant and a leader of the Quraysh tribe. Muhammad benefited from the love and kindness that his uncle bestowed upon him and he would occasionally accompany him on his caravan trading trips.

When he was about 12 years old, Muhammad travelled with his uncle to Syria. Reaching the town of Busra, they met with a Christian monk called Bahira, who, unusually and for no apparent reason, insisted that they dine with him. The young Muhammad did not at first join the guests, remaining behind with the caravan's camels, perhaps to keep watch over valuable merchandise. But when Bahira saw that the boy was absent from the invited party, he asked Abu Talib to fetch him.

When Muhammad arrived, the priest immediately began to ask him a series of questions. As a result of the answers that Bahira received, he asked for permission to inspect a birthmark between Muhammad's shoulder blades. He then advised Abu Talib to take good care of his nephew, who, he declared earnestly, would become a great leader of

men. Upon receiving this counsel, Muhammad's uncle concluded his business and immediately returned with his nephew to Makkah.

Although Abu Talib intuitively knew that Muhammad was special, as the Christian monk had confirmed, he could not have realized that Muhammad was, in fact, destined to become a fulfilment of Ibrahim's prophetic promise to the people of Makkah and beyond. As later asserted in the revelations of the Quran: 'and remember when Ibrahim raised the foundations of the House (*Kaabah*) with Ismail, supplicating, "Our Lord! Accept (this service) from us: for you are the All-Hearing, the All-Knowing... Our Lord send amongst them (Ismail's progeny) a messenger of their own, who will rehearse Your signs to them and and instruct them in wisdom and purify them: for You are the Exalted in Might, the Wise." ' (2:127–129)

MUHAMMAD'S IMPACT ON SOCIETY

MUHAMMAD'S EXEMPLARY CHARACTER, CARING NATURE AND WISDOM WERE RENOWNED IN THE CITY OF MAKKAH, AND HE WAS OFTEN CALLED UPON TO RESOLVE DISPUTES.

Muhammad was born into a family of noble lineage that belonged to the tribe of Banu Hashim of the Quraysh, who claimed descent from Ibrahim's son Ismail (Ismael). Pre-Islamic Arab society was based on tribal hierarchy, in which a tribe could be led to extinction in defence of its honour and that of anyone under its agreed protection.

Muhammad's family had been the ruling tribal family of Makkah at the time of his grandfather, Abd al-Muttalib. Muhammad's father, Abdullah, was the youngest and most loved son of Abd al-Muttalib but soon after marrying Aminah bint Wahb, Abdullah left with a trading caravan to Syria and never returned. The caravan came back with news of his sickness on the return journey through Yathrib (Madinah), where he eventually died. His son was born a short time later and was named 'Muhammad', meaning 'Praiseworthy', by his grieving grandfather. As Abd al-Muttalib later explained, 'I wanted Allah to praise him in heaven and mankind to praise him on earth.'

THE 'ALLIANCE OF VIRTUE'

As Muhammad reached maturity under the gentle care of his loving uncle, Abu Talib, his virtuousness earned him the title of al-Amin, 'the Trustworthy', among the inhabitants of Makkah. As a result, people would often entrust their valuables to him for safekeeping, and consult him to resolve their

Above Two Bedouin women playfully carry their children, a scene that has changed very little since the Prophet Muhammad's era.

problems and disagreements. Even as a young man, Muhammad showed commitment to issues of social justice, regardless of tribe.

A religious practice adhered to faithfully by the pagan Makkan tribes was observance of the sanctity of the month of pilgrimage, *Dhul-Hijjah*, which included a complete prohibition of hostilities. When Muhammad was 15, however, war broke out between the Quraysh and the tribe of Hawazin, which involved four years of protracted violence and bloody revenge.

The senseless bloodshed caused great loss and hardship to many people from both tribes, but as a result of their common suffering, a spirit of goodwill slowly began to prevail. Finally, another of Muhammad's uncles, al-Zubayr, took the initiative to find a

Left Pilgrims surround the Maqam Ibrahim in the al-Haram Mosque, Makkah. This shrine contains a stone that is believed to hold the permanent footprint of the prophet Ibrahim.

Above The shahadah − *'There is no God but God and Muhammad is His Messenger' − adorns the Topkapi Palace in Istanbul, Turkey.*

resolution to the conflict. He called for a meeting of representatives from both tribes, in which a charitable foundation, *Hilf ul-Fudul* ('Alliance of Virtue') was established to address the needs of the needy, poor and oppressed.

Muhammad was present, and joined the foundation, stating years later, 'I witnessed an alliance with my uncles at the house of Abdullah ibn Jadan and I would not wish to exchange it for the choicest luxuries. If I were called in Islam to participate in it I would respond.'

THE BLACK STONE

On another occasion, after a flood destroyed the *Kaabah* and repairs had been completed, tribal elders were having difficulty in deciding which nobleman should replace the decorative corner piece, *al-Hajar al-Aswad*, or the 'Black Stone'. (According to tradition, this ancient relic was sent from the heavens to adorn the *Kaabah*.) As the task was one of great honour, there was much dissent. Finally, exhausted

from arguing, the elders agreed that the first person to enter the *Kaabah's* precinct would decide. When Muhammad entered, the elders were delighted, as he was renowned for his fairness and honesty. He advised them to place the stone on to a cloth to be held at each corner by a tribal elder, and he himself then placed the stone into position. Muhammad's wise and peaceful resolution to the problem averted bloodshed and united the various tribes of Makkah.

There was little doubt that Muhammad was not only a noble tribesman of great intelligence and integrity, but also that he was very generous and kind-hearted. In addition, his honesty was without question, and his ability to resolve serious problems and feuds was widely accepted. However, his rejection of the beliefs of his tribal peers, as well as his sudden claim to be an appointed prophet of God, was soon to test both the trust and the loyalties of the people of Makkah.

Right After the Kaabah *was rebuilt, arguments arose about who should have the honour of replacing the Black Stone. Muhammad's diplomacy averted tribal bloodshed.*

MUHAMMAD AND ORPHANS

Muhammad received much love and attention from his uncle Abu Talib after he was orphaned when only six years old, but he realized that the plight of most orphans did not reflect his own stable and protected upbringing and that many suffered from neglect and abuse.

Islam reflects Muhammad's concerns regarding orphans, and the Quran enshrines rights and protective measures: 'Give unto orphans their wealth. Exchange not the good for the bad (in your management thereof) nor absorb their wealth into your wealth' (4:2). And 'Come not near the property of orphans except to improve it, until he attains the age of strength (adulthood), and fulfil every agreed promise for every promise will be enquired into' (17:34).

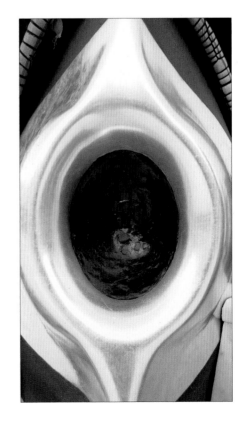

MARRIAGE TO KHADIJAH

MUHAMMAD'S WIFE, KHADIJAH, WAS A CAPTIVATING WOMAN AND 15 YEARS HIS SENIOR. SHE ENCOURAGED HER HUSBAND'S CONTEMPLATIVE LIFE AND ACCEPTED HIS MISSION AS A PROPHET.

The Quraysh tribesmen were accomplished merchants, and Muhammad's uncle Abu Talib was a wealthy businessman who encouraged his adopted nephew to become a trader. Muhammad's good character and reputation for honesty made him an ideal partner.

At the age of 25, Muhammad was employed by Khadijah bint Khuwaylid to trade for her in Syria. Khadijah was a highly successful businesswoman who employed men to work for her for an agreed percentage of the profits. After hearing of Muhammad's great honesty, she offered him a higher percentage than others in order to secure his employment. She also sent her trusted servant, Maysarah, to assist him on the long caravan.

MARRIAGE PROPOSAL

Muhammad's trading in Syria was extremely profitable, and Khadijah was pleased with both his business acumen and his outstanding moral behaviour, as observed by her servant on the trip. After discussing the matter with her close friend, Nafisah bint Munabbah, Khadijah expressed her wish to marry Muhammad, and Nafisah was asked to approach him with a proposal of marriage on her friend's behalf.

Khadijah was known for her beauty and intelligence. Many prominent men had asked for her hand in marriage, but she had consistently refused their proposals. She had been widowed and then later divorced for a number of years from her second husband, Abu Halah, and at the time of her proposal to Muhammad, she was 40 years old, some 15 years his senior.

Khadijah was a respected and wealthy woman, admired for her integrity and independence, and, like Muhammad, she was from the ruling Quraysh tribe. Muhammad willingly accepted her offer of marriage and asked his uncles, Abu Talib and Hamza, to make all the necessary wedding arrangements. As a part of the marriage dowry, Muhammad presented Khadijah with 20 pedigree camels. A modest wedding ceremony was conducted by Abu Talib at the bride's home.

MUHAMMAD'S CHILDREN

The couple lived happily until Khadijah's death at 65. His wife was a source of great comfort to Muhammad and they were blessed with two boys, al-Qasim and

Above A 14th-century manuscript painting depicts Muhammad with his wife Khadijah behind him. The third figure, on the left, is Muhammad's young cousin Ali ibn Abu Talib.

Abdullah, and four girls, Zaynab, Ruqqaya, Umm Kulthum and Fatimah. Sadly, all Muhammad's sons died in their infancy, including Ibrahim, born to a later wife, Maria, a Coptic Christian from Egypt who later converted to Islam. Even after the death of his first-born son, al-Qasim, Muhammad was known by his *kunya* (a respectful but intimate Arab way of describing someone as 'the father of ...') Abul Qasim.

In a society that prized sons and denigrated daughters, Muhammad's loss of his male progeny became a point of ridicule among the Arabs. They mocked his prophetic mission by proclaiming, 'what we are involved in [polytheism] is more lasting than what the amputated *sunburn* [a date palm whose roots are broken] is involved in', meaning that Muhammad had no heirs to continue the propagation of Islam.

Left Ruins remain of the 14th-century Mosque of Fatimah, Busra, Syria. It was named for Muhammad's daughter Fatimah.

THE *HUNAFA*

Throughout his union with Khadijah, Muhammad continued the life of contemplation and seclusion that he had chosen before his marriage. He kept away from the adultery, drinking, gambling, and rivalries of pre-Islamic Makkan life and shunned the polytheism of his people. At the same time he successfully conducted his business activities and cared for the less privileged from his society.

Ibrahimic monotheism had not been completely abandoned in Arabia, and there existed a small group of people there who, like Muhammad, rejected the pervading polytheism of their tribal peers. These individuals were referred to collectively as *hunafa* (singular *hanif*), meaning 'one who follows the primordial belief in a single deity'. One such *hanif* was Zayd ibn Amr ibn Nufayl, who was known to proclaim, 'O Quraysh! By God none of you is following the religion of Ibrahim but me.'

THE REVELATION

Like Zayd, Muhammad was a *hanif*, and he would regularly visit a remote mountain cave outside Makkah to retreat in prayer and contemplation. Khadijah accepted and encouraged these retreats as a devotion that her husband had observed before their marriage.

It was during one such retreat in the month of Ramadan in 610 that Muhammad is believed to have received a visit from the Archangel Jibril, who revealed to him the first few verses of the Quran (81:22–3, 96:1–5). He returned home shaken, where he was comforted by Khadijah, who thereafter accepted her husband as a prophet. This event signalled the beginning of Muhammad's prophetic mission, the religion of Islam.

Below The 'Mountain of Light' is found on the outskirts of Makkah. Muhammad frequently made spiritual retreats on the mountain and it was here he received the first Quranic revelations.

Above Archangel Jibril is depicted in a handwritten Persian text dated to around the 14th century. According to Islamic tradition, Jibril often appeared to Muhammad in human form.

THE SIGNIFICANCE OF MAKKAH

MAKKAH IS HISTORICALLY IMPORTANT AS AN OASIS ON THE CARAVAN TRADING ROUTES ACROSS ARABIA, AS THE SITE OF THE ANCIENT TEMPLE, THE *KAABAH*, AND AS THE BIRTHPLACE OF MUHAMMAD.

Makkah is located in the Hijaz (literally 'barrier') region in the modern-day Kingdom of Saudi Arabia, a narrow tract of land punctuated by the Tropic of Cancer that runs some 1,400km (875 miles) north to south on the eastern side of the Red Sea and the chain of Sarat mountains. Between the volcanic peaks of the Sarat and the busy entrepot coast, there are sweltering barren deserts and desolate sandy passes. The landscape is both breathtakingly expansive and fiercely uninhabitable except by the hardiest of nomadic Arabs.

As the desert plains slowly rise toward the mountains, they give way to a series of arid, sun-baked rocky valleys. In one such valley is located the ancient city of Makkah with its temple and Well of Zamzam, which Muslims believe appeared miraculously in the desert. Makkah is also known to the Arabs as Wadi Ibrahim ('the valley of Ibrahim').

EARLY FOUNDATIONS

The moon-like terrain of this region is linked to a number of ancient Biblical characters. In a long prophetic hadith, Adam and Eve are said to have reunited on the plains of Arafah, just outside Makkah, after having been separated on their descent from heaven. The hadith

Right Muhammad's grandfather, Abd al-Muttalib, and al-Harith, rediscovered the sacred Well of Zamzam in the precinct of Ibrahim's ancient temple, the Kaabah, in Makkah.

recounts that Adam placed the foundation for Ibrahim's later temple, and states that Adam was buried near Makkah and Eve in nearby Jeddah. Muslims also believe that Noah's son Seth lived in the Hijaz and that Noah's Ark was constructed at Mount Budh, India, and was carried northward across the flooded plains to its resting place at Mount Judi (11:25–49).

THE WELL OF ZAMZAM

The story of the ancient Well of Zamzam that gave importance to Makkah as an ancient oasis and trading centre is associated with the patriarch Ibrahim, his wife Hajar and their baby, Ismail.

According to a hadith, Ibrahim brought his family from Egypt to the desert plains of Arabia before resting under a thorn tree in the valley of Makkah. The place was isolated and totally uninhabited. Leaving Hajar and Ismail with only a bag of dates and a leather water carrier, Ibrahim marched onward alone. Hajar cried after him,

Above The harsh rocky landscape surrounding Makkah, with its mountain peaks overshadowing narrow valleys passes, has changed little since the time of the Prophet Muhammad.

'Ibrahim, where are you going leaving us in this desert where there is no one and nothing? Is it by God's command?' When Ibrahim confirmed it was, the desperate Hajar replied, 'Then he will not let us go to waste.'

After the dates and water were finished and Hajar's breast milk was exhausted, both mother and child became thirsty. Hajar fretted as Ismail lay crying and writhing. In desperation, she ran to the top of a nearby hillock (Safa) and looked down over the valley for help. Seeing no one, she ran across the short plain to another hill (Marwa), again searching for assistance. Seven times she ran between the two hills beseeching God's mercy. Then an angel appeared, striking the ground with his wing at the midway point between the hills, at which a spring gushed forth. The infant cried 'Zamzam' (which is said to mean 'abundance'), and the well was established with this name.

IBRAHIM'S *KAABAH*

A prophetic hadith recounts that when Ibrahim and Ismail were beginning the construction of their temple, a wind entered the Makkan valley, swirling violently around a particular site. They dug deep into the ground to reveal Adam's foundations, then began to collect huge stones, assembling them into a cube shape. When the walls reached the height of a man, Ismail brought a stone block for his father to work from. A stone, complete with Ibrahim's footprint, remains a holy relic in the *haram* ('sacred') precinct. At the corner of the building, an ornate stone, *al-Hajar al-Aswad* (the 'Black Stone') was inset to mark where circumambulatory rites begin.

Ibrahim's humble edifice – the only 'house of God' in its time – was eventually surrounded by colossal pyramids and monumental towers constructed to celebrate pervading polytheistic beliefs, yet it was Ibrahim's simple 'cube' that was to permanently change the course of religion in the region.

Above This 16th-century painting depicts Ibrahim about to sacrifice his son Ismail as an angel brings a substitute lamb. The Makkan tribes claimed descent from Ismail.

THE CITY TODAY

Makkah is Islam's primary religious centre, the spiritual heartland to 1.3 billion Muslims around the world, who all face in the direction of the *Kaabah* as a part of their five daily prayers. More than two million Muslims make the annual pilgrimage (*Hajj*) to Makkah. Yet this barren and remote desert valley city would not even exist but for the story of Ibrahim.

Below Muslims congregate from around the world to make pilgrimage and to offer ritual circumambulations around the Kaabah in Makkah, just as they believe Ibrahim did in ancient times.

CALLED AS A PROPHET

THE QURAN RELATES THAT, FROM THE AGE OF 40, MUHAMMAD RECEIVED MANY ANGELIC VISITATIONS. THE QURAN WAS DICTATED TO HIM AND HE WAS COMMANDED TO CALL PEOPLE TO ISLAM.

Before Muhammad's call to Islam, the dominant religious beliefs and practices in Arabia were polytheistic, but there were also a number of minority groups from different monotheistic traditions.

THE MONOTHEISTS

As the religious centre of pre-Islamic Arabia, Makkah was a focus for polytheism and the *Kaabah* housed many statues and devotional images within its precincts. In contrast to the regions of Yathrib and Najran, communities of Christians and Jews were largely absent from Makkah. In this almost universally polytheistic society, they were generally prohibited from the *Kaabah* and were permitted to live – as slaves or servants – only on the outskirts of the city.

As a *hanif* (one who followed the original teachings of Ibrahim), Muhammad would have been one of the few religious monotheists living in Makkah itself. Another such man was Waraqa ibn Nawfal, a devout Christian and Khadijah's elderly cousin.

MUHAMMAD'S RETREATS

Muhammad is thought to have regularly observed spiritual retreats in a cave in the mountains on the outskirts of Makkah. Here he would spend weeks at a time in fasting, prayer and contemplation, grieving over what he saw as the erroneous religious practices and excessive lifestyles of his people. He also lamented the grave social injustices of the society in which he lived, which were often based on racial and tribal hierarchies: infant daughters were buried alive, women were traded and bartered like chattel, and slaves were treated no better than livestock.

RECEIVING REVELATIONS

According to prophetic hadith, Muhammad's many prayers and devotions to God were rewarded at the age of 40 by an unexpected angelic visitation. The story tells that Archangel Jibril appeared before Muhammad in every direction in which he gazed and that he was surrounded by a blinding light.

Above Jibril, accompanied by a group of angels, visits Muhammad. The artist has obscured Muhammad's face as a sign of respect for the Prophet.

Then, gripping Muhammad so tightly that he could barely breathe, the angel ordered him to 'Read!' Muhammad replied, 'I cannot read!' Jibril repeated the command, and on receiving the same reply, directed Muhammad to 'Read in the name of thy Lord who created, Created man from a clot, Read: and thy Lord is the Bounteous, Who teaches man with the pen, Teaches man that which he knows not' (96:1–5).

Ibn Ishaq's 8th-century biography of Muhammad, *Sirat Rasulillah*, relates that after his traumatic experience, Muhammad quickly returned home, frightened and confused. Khadijah hurriedly called for Waraqa, her Christian cousin, who, upon hearing Muhammad's encounter, concluded, 'This is the

Left Pilgrims visit the Hira cave on the 'Mountain of Light' overlooking Makkah. It was here that Muhammad is said to have received the revelations of the Quran from Archangel Jibril.

angel that God sent to Moses. I wish I were younger to witness your people exile you!' Muhammad cried 'Will they drive me out?', to which Waraqa replied, 'Anyone previously who came with something similar to what you have brought was treated with hostility: if I were to live until that day of rejection, I would strongly support you.'

THE PUBLIC CALL TO ISLAM

A lengthy period of time passed before Muhammad received further revelations, but eventually he was instructed to call his people to submit to God's will.

He began by inviting those nearest to him, starting with family and friends. After Khadijah, the first to become a Muslim was Zayd ibn Harithah, a freed slave whom Muhammad had adopted as his son. They were followed by his young cousin, Ali ibn Abu Talib, and his intimate friend Abu Bakr.

In the beginning, Muhammad's public call to Islam was merely scorned by his tribesmen, who claimed his new religion appealed only to the young, elderly and slaves. However, as the popularity of Islam spread and conversions increased, his enemies began to apply brute force and torture against its adherents.

MIGRATION TO ABYSSINIA

To relieve the oppression faced by many of his followers, Muhammad permitted a small band of Muslims to migrate to the Christian kingdom of Abyssinia. They received welcome and support from the Abyssinian King (Negus) and his subjects, despite pressure from the pagans to return them to Makkah.

They remained under the protection of the Christian king for almost two decades, living as loyal Muslim citizens, before returning to Arabia to join the burgeoning Islamic community at Madinah.

Below Muhammad's claims to have received angelic visitations and his call to the religion of Islam provoked much discussion among the tribal leaders of the Quraysh of Makkah.

Above The Prophet Muhammad and his trusted friend Abu Bakr are depicted taking refuge from the pursuing pagans in a cave during the migration (hijrah) to Madinah.

EXILE FROM MAKKAH

FEARING THAT THEIR PAGAN BELIEFS AND SOCIAL HIERARCHIES WERE UNDER THREAT FROM ISLAM, TRIBAL ELDERS BEGAN TO PERSECUTE AND TORTURE MUSLIMS AND TO PLOT MUHAMMAD'S ASSASSINATION.

The first exile of Muslims from the mounting hostilities of the Makkan pagans occurred around 615, when Muhammad sanctioned the migration of around 80 Muslims to Abyssinia. His public call to Islam was beginning to compromise the very fragile tribal allegiances and protection extended to him and his increasing number of followers. Muhammad's message of absolute monotheism (*tawhid*) and social equality was an anathema to the Makkan establishment.

PERSECUTION OF MUSLIMS

At the beginning of the fourth year of Muhammad's prophetic mission, the polytheists carefully aimed their persecution of Muslims at those unprotected by any tribal bonds. This meant that those already most vulnerable were targeted. When it was found that this strategy was having little impact on stemming conversions to Islam, leaders began pressuring anyone from their tribe found to be Muslim.

One of Muhammad's fiercest enemies was his uncle Abdul Uzza ibn Abd al-Muttalib, known as Abu Jahl ('the father of ignorance'). Abu Jahl worked relentlessly to undermine Islam, persecuting and torturing many Muslims. A few were even killed for their beliefs.

DELEGATIONS TO ABU TALIB

In an effort to prevent conversions to Islam, a delegation of Quraysh leaders visited Muhammad's uncle Abu Talib. They complained that Muhammad was mocking their religion, cursing their gods and finding fault with their way of life. However, although Abu Talib managed to pacify the angry tribesmen, Muhammad continued to proselytize. According to Ibn Ishaq's biography of Muhammad, he told his uncle, 'if they put the sun on one hand and the moon in the other [as a reward for abandoning his mission], I would not leave it until Allah has made me victorious or I perish.'

Above A Muslim cavalryman with lance and shield rides his camel into battle, much as the Muslims would have done against the Makkan Arab pagans.

Left Abu Jahl, Muhammad's uncle and arch-enemy, is depicted attacking the Prophet as he offers his prayers at the Kaabah.

Realizing that Muhammad would not end his preaching and that Abu Talib would not forsake his nephew, Muhammad's enemies increased their oppression and torture, even plotting to kill him. On one occasion, a group led by Abu Jahl set about Muhammad while he was praying at the *Kaabah*.

When the news of Muhammad's persecution reached another of his uncles, Hamzah, an accomplished huntsman and warrior, he was so outraged that he immediately approached Abu Jahl and his accomplices. Ibn Ishaq records that, striking Abu Jahl violently across his back with his bow, he declared 'Ah! You have been abusing Muhammad: I too follow his religion and profess whatever he teaches!' The surprise conversion of Hamzah was a real blow to Muhammad's enemies.

THE YEAR OF GRIEF

A protracted series of negotiations, boycotts and plots followed in the next few years, until, in 619, Abu Talib died. Then, within a few months, Muhammad's beloved wife Khadijah passed away. These two painful events added to his trials: he had lost not only his protector but also his greatest love and spiritual companion. The pagans took advantage of this misfortune and increased their hostilities.

Muhammad is said to have suffered even greater humiliations when he visited nearby Taif to invite its people to Islam. There, the citizens set their children on him, chasing him from the city and pelting him with stones.

THE TREATY OF AQABAH

During the pilgrimage season in 621, Muhammad approached a group of pilgrims from the Khazraj tribe of Yathrib (Madinah). They were aware of the Judaeo-Christian

Below This building outside Makkah marks the site where pilgrims from Yathrib (Madinah) accepted Islam.

Right According to Islamic tradition, Muhammad was taken on a night journey to heaven on a winged horse, al-Buraq, a year before the migration (hijrah) to Madinah.

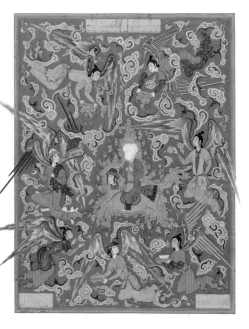

claims of a 'promised prophet' and had heard of Muhammad back in Yathrib. Muhammad explained the teachings of Islam and recited parts of the Quran to them, with the result that they were persuaded to convert to Islam.

A year later, these pilgrims returned to Makkah, along with a delegation of Muslim converts from Yathrib, and invited Muhammad and his followers to settle in their city. Muhammad ordered his followers to emigrate in small groups to avoid detection by the Quraysh, before leaving himself.

This migration, known as the *hijrah*, became a turning point for Islam. Muhammad went on to establish an Islamic community in the city, where he initiated a series of important treaties with some neighbouring tribes of both Arabs and Jews, and entered into a number of marriages with women from noble families and important tribes. The *hijrah* now marks the beginning of the Islamic calendar.

THE MADINAN COMMUNITY

THE MIGRATION (*HIJRAH*) OF MUHAMMAD AND HIS FOLLOWERS TO YATHRIB (MADINAH) TO ESCAPE PERSECUTION WAS TO BECOME PIVOTAL FOR ISLAM AND ITS SPREAD IN THE ARABIAN PENINSULA.

The persecution of Muslims in Makkah had intensified almost to the state of civil war. The two pledges that had been agreed at Aqabah between Muhammad and the Yathribite pilgrims, who had converted to Islam after their first meeting with him, became a lifeline for his prophetic mission.

Muhammad's enemies from the Quraysh were plotting a cunning assassination that would include a youth from each of the four major clans, thus avoiding any subsequent tribal bloodletting and feuding. However, when the youths attacked Muhammad's home intent on murdering him, their plot was frustrated. They found only his cousin Ali present; Muhammad had already departed from Makkah a few days earlier, and was heading for Yathrib, along with his trusted friend Abu Bakr.

Above *A late 16th-century Ottoman manuscript painting shows early Muslims building the Prophet's Mosque in Madinah in 622.*

ARRIVAL AT YATHRIB

After the first agreement at Aqabah, Muhammad had sent his envoy Musab ibn Umayr with the Yathribites to teach them the doctrines of their new faith and to help them propagate Islam among their fellow citizens. Musab was so successful in this mission that by the time the Yathribites returned to Makkah the following year, there was hardly a house in Yathrib without a Muslim.

The migration of many Muslims from Makkah came at considerable personal cost. Not only were most of them forsaken by their families and tribe, but their hasty exile meant that they left with virtually nothing. However, the Yathribites were generous, sharing their homes, businesses and belongings with the Muslim migrants.

Left *A plan of the Prophet's Mosque in Madinah showing his pulpit, date orchard and house. It was both a religious building and political institution.*

Eventually, Muhammad arrived in the city, after an eventful and dangerous journey in which he was forced to hide in a cave from the persuing Makkans. The Yathribites had been awaiting his arrival with great anticipation, and many broke out in song when they saw him on the distant horizon.

After Muhammad's migration to Yathrib, the city was renamed Madinat un-Nabi, 'City of the Prophet', in his honour.

THE ISLAMIC CITADEL

The Quranic revelations that Muhammad is believed to have received at Madinah are markedly different from those said to have been revealed to him in Makkah. While the Makkan verses concentrate on the main Quranic themes of divine unity, the coming resurrection and judgement and righteous conduct, the Madinan ones are concerned with social and political issues. These range from social relations between Muslims and others to verses communicating Shariah (divine law). Treaties and agreements between Muslims and confederate pagan-Arab and Jewish tribes are also mentioned.

These 'Madinan revelations' formed the basis of all social and political interactions and the regulating of Muslim society, state formation and Islamic dominance in the region. Muhammad was firmly established as Prophet-ruler of a virtual Islamic state within the heartlands of pagan Arabia.

Muhammad encouraged a spirit of brotherhood between the Madinite Muslims, known as *al-ansar* ('the helpers'), and the Makkan migrants, or *al-muhajiroun*, and developed a multicultural and religiously plural city-state. This was achieved by a pledge between the Christian and Jewish communities, who wished to retain their faith but pledged allegiance to Muhammad.

Right Muhammad's followers suffered a demoralizing defeat at the Battle of Uhud in 625. The prophet planned and organized his military campaigns from Madinah.

DECISIVE BATTLES

As the *ummah* began to establish itself under Muhammad's guidance at Madinah, his Makkan enemies continued in their determination to destroy Islam. This led to a number of decisive battles, some of which were won and some lost by the Muslims.

In 624, at wells of Badr near Madinah, the Muslims gained a notable victory, despite being heavily outnumbered by their opponents. However, their resilience was severly tested at Uhud, a mountain at the city boundary. In the battle here, Muslims broke their ranks, which led to a serious defeat.

Madinah was in danger of capture by 10,000 Makkans in 627 when they laid siege to the city for more than two weeks. However, the construction of a series of defensive ditches (*khandaq*) around Madinah kept the invaders at bay, eventually forcing a retreat.

BLOODLESS VICTORY

Two years after the Hudaybiyah treaty with the Makkans, which granted the Muslims permission to make pilgrimage, Muhammad marched upon Makkah with 10,000 followers. However, he did not take the city by force: instead, he granted a general amnesty. This peaceful gesture resulted in reciprocal goodwill and a mass conversion to Islam, and thus helped establish the city as the religion's spiritual centre.

Left Muhammad is flanked by angels on his triumphant return to Makkah, some eight years after the migration (hijrah) to Madinah.

ISLAM IN THE PENINSULA

BY FORGING USEFUL LINKS WITH NEIGHBOURING KINGDOMS AND TRIBES, MUHAMMAD TRANSFORMED THE ARABIAN PENINSULA WITH HIS PROPHETIC MESSAGE AND ISLAM SOON DOMINATED THE REGION.

Having established what was effectively an Islamic state at Madinah, Muhammad was able to send emissaries to surrounding tribal leaders and sovereigns. In the process he gained some important adherents, whose influence was essential to the successful long-term Islamization of the region.

TREATIES AND ALLEGIANCES

The early covenant between the Makkan Muslims and the Yathribite pilgrims at Aqabah provided an opportunity for Muhammad's message to flourish in the peninsula through the agreed migration (*hijrah*) to their city. The Yathribite tribes of Aws and Khazraj were neither Jews nor Christians, and the treaty was a useful experience for the Muslims in building alliances and propagating the doctrines of Islam to less hostile tribes in Arabia.

Once he had established Muslim ascendancy in Madinah, Muhammad quickly forged strong links with neighbouring communities. In order to accomplish his mission to promulgate Islam, it was necessary to create the right conditions for religious dialogue. To this end, Muhammad's envoys travelled to the nearby rulers of Abyssinia, Egypt, Persia, Syria and Yemen.

THE NAJRAN CHRISTIANS

Around 630, Muhammad received a delegation of some 60 Christian clergy and leaders from Najran in Yemen. They were orthodox Trinitarians who were under the protection of the Byzantium empire, and Muhammad allowed them to use the mosques to offer their Christian worship. He also took the opportunity of their visit to invite the Jews of Madinah to a tripartite religious dialogue.

During the congress, Muhammad criticized both faiths, accusing them of compromising their monotheism and tampering with their divine scriptures, thus perverting the teachings of the prophets from whom they were originally received.

Above A letter sent by the Prophet Muhammad to Chosroes II, King of Persia, inviting him to accept Islam after his defeat by the Byzantines in 629.

The Najranis acknowledged Muhammad's legitimacy as a prophet but most declined his call to Islam at that time. However, they allowed one of his companions, Abu Ubaydah ibn al-Jarrah, to accompany them to Yemen as a missionary envoy for Islam. Within a few years, the majority of Yemen, including the Christians of Najran, had converted to Islam.

THE ABYSSINIAN PRIESTS

The Christian kingdom of Abyssinia had provided asylum for a number of early Muslims, whose emigration is referred to as 'the first migration in Islam'. Relations between the Negus of Abyssinia and Muhammad were extremely cordial, to the extent that the king sent a delegation of seven priests and five monks to Madinah. They were instructed to observe Muhammad and study his revelations.

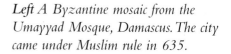

Left A Byzantine mosaic from the Umayyad Mosque, Damascus. The city came under Muslim rule in 635.

Right A mountain village mosque near Taizz. Christianity dominated Yemen until the Byzantine bishops from Najran pledged allegiance with Muhammad.

The Abyssinian clergy were visibly moved by the verses they heard and the incident was later referred to in the Quran: 'And thou wilt find the nearest in affection, to those who believe, those who say, Lo! We are Christians. That is because from amongst them are priests and monks and they are not given to arrogance.' (5:82)

In response, Muhammad sent a letter inviting the king to accept Islam. It is unclear if the Negus actually became a Muslim, but when he passed away, Muhammad announced his death and offered the congregational funeral prayer in absentia. After the 'first migration', Islam continued to flourish throughout Abyssinia.

THE JEWS OF MADINAH

Relations between the Muslims and the Jews of Madinah were at times fraught, though a large number converted to Islam. In an effort to secure peace in the city, a treaty with the remaining Jews and Christians was signed. However, although they were subject to their own religious

Right A mountain village mosque near Taizz. Christianity dominated Yemen until the Byzantine bishops from Najran pledged allegiance with Muhammad.

scriptures and exempted from many duties incumbent upon Muslims, some Jews broke their agreement. They were given two options: defend against the pagan Makkans, with whom they had allied against the Muslims, or face exile. After initially refusing to do either, they left for a region called Khaybar and launched offensives against the Muslims. The consequences of this revolt were concluded at the Battle of Ahzab ('confederates') and the later Muslim offensive at Khaybar, in which the Jewish tribes and their allies were defeated.

Once the Makkans and their allies had been defeated, Muhammad turned his attention to the establishment of peace treaties with surrounding Bedouin tribes in an effort to facilitate the spread of Islam throughout the peninsula and beyond.

Left A Bedouin Muslim prays in the Sahara. Muslims used their knowledge of ancient trading caravan routes to spread Islam throughout the peninsula and into Byzantium, Persia and Africa.

MUHAMMAD'S DEATH

IN 23 YEARS, THE PROPHET MUHAMMAD HAD TOTALLY RESHAPED
ARABIAN CIVILIZATION. AFTER HIS DEATH, THE CALL TO ISLAM WAS
CONTINUED BY HIS MANY CONVERTS, LED BY HIS FRIEND ABU BAKR.

Although Muhammad's mission was initially met with hostility and rejection from the majority of his tribal peers, his message of Islam eventually conquered them. The new religion, which had at first been seen as a challenging and disruptive force, quickly became the dominant civilization in Arabia and beyond.

Within 23 years Muhammad was able to successfully unite Arabian society into a single community of Muslims. Islam's central creed of monotheism sparked a theological revolution across Arabia. The Arabs became religious emissaries as Islam reached far beyond the desert plains of the peninsula. Muhammad stressed Islam's universality and egalitarianism, telling his followers: 'an Arab is no better than a non-Arab and a non-Arab is likewise no better than an Arab. A white man is no better than a black man, except in piety. Mankind are all Adam's children and Adam was created from dust.'

THE FAREWELL SERMON

Ten years after *hijrah*, Muhammad told his envoy to Yemen, Muadh ibn Jabal, 'O Muadh! You may not see me after this year. You may even pass by this very mosque of mine and my grave.' Muadh is said to have wept profusely at this news. As the *Hajj* approached, Muhammad

*Above Muslim pilgrims offer their
supplications as the day of prayers comes
to a climax at Arafah during the* Hajj.
*It was here that Muhammad gave
his final sermon.*

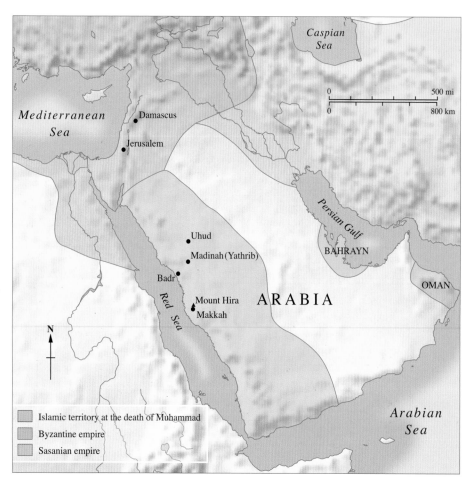

made preparations to leave for Makkah. After performing the *Hajj*, he gathered the many pilgrims on the plain of Arafah. There, he gave his final sermon, reminding them of their duty to God and that their blood and property were more inviolable than the sacredness of the *Hajj* and the city of Makkah. He then asked them all to witness that he had conveyed God's message. After they affirmed that he had, Muhammad said, 'O Allah! Bear witness'. Advising them to hold fast to the teachings of the Quran, he then concluded his sermon by receiving a divine revelation which declared: 'This day I have perfected your religion for you, completed my favour upon you, and have chosen for you Islam as your religion' (5:3).

*Left The extent of Islamic territory is
shown at the time of Muhammad's
death in 632.*

MUHAMMAD'S LAST DAYS

The pilgrims understood that the *Hajj* sermon was to be the Prophet Muhammad's final address and that their beloved leader would soon depart from this world.

Soon after the *Hajj*, Muhammad became ill, and extended his yearly seclusion during the month of Ramadhan from 10 to 20 days, informing his wife Ayesha that Jibril had, unusually, revised the Quran twice with him. As he lapsed into a fever, Muhammad requested that his family repay all debts and loans. He continued to lead congregational prayers until his very last days.

On the day of his death, he is said to have gathered his family around his bed. He kissed the foreheads of his grandsons, Hasan and Hussain, and, as the pains of death gripped him, held tightly to Ayesha. Making ablutions for prayer and raising his hands, he prayed, 'O Allah! Forgive me and have mercy upon me and join me to the most exalted companionship on high.' Then he passed away.

The Madinans were stricken with grief at the news of Muhammad's death. His closest companions gathered at his house

Above Muhammad, on his deathbed, surrounded by family and companions. He was buried where he died, in his home adjacent to his mosque.

where Abu Bakr uncovered his head and tearfully kissed his face. Medieval Arab historian Ibn Hisham says that Abu Bakr then addressed the awaiting crowd, saying, 'And now, to whoever worships Muhammad, then surely Muhammad is dead. And to whoever worships Allah, then surely Allah is the Ever-living and He never dies.'

THE FIRST CALIPH

Muhammad did not appoint a successor, leaving the choice of caliph, or viceroy, to the *ummah*, or community, who convened to select their new leader. After much deliberation, it was decided that Abu Bakr was the best candidate because he was referred to by Allah in the Quran (9:40) and was said to be the most humble in prayer.

Under Abu Bakr's leadership (632–4), Islam spread into Palestine and Syria. He also established a succession of rulers, known as 'the rightly guided caliphs', from among Muhammad's companions. All three succeeding caliphs after Abu Bakr were assassinated as a result of increasing power struggles. The murdered caliphs were respected companions and relatives of the Prophet, including Ali, his cousin and son-in-law. Matters came to a head at Karbala, Iraq, in 680CE when Ali's son Hussain was killed along with his followers and family.

THE GRAVES OF PROPHETS

The Quran promises God's prophets, saints and true believers the highest positions in paradise, and most Muslims believe that, while a physical or bodily death occurs, the soul is eternal and cannot die. Prophets are believed to be not dead, but alive in their graves, existing in a spiritual domain known as *barzakh* (meaning 'a barrier between two spaces'), where they await the Day of Judgement.

Most pilgrimages to Makkah include a trip to Madinah with the specific purpose of visiting Muhammad's mosque and grave, where pilgrims offer peace and prayers to the Prophet.

Right The entrance leads to Muhammad's grave, contained within his mosque at Madinah. The site is visited by Muslims who offer prayers and blessing to the Prophet.

HOW REVELATION CAME

MUSLIMS BELIEVE THAT THE QURAN IS THE WORD OF GOD AND THAT IT WAS REVEALED TO THE PROPHET MUHAMMAD BY ARCHANGEL JIBRIL OVER A PERIOD OF SOME 23 YEARS.

According to the traditions of Islam, it was while deep in contemplation and prayer in a mountain cave outside the city of Makkah that Muhammad received a visitation from Archangel Jibril, who delivered the first verses of the Quran to him.

From this moment, Muhammad's life was transformed forever. Receiving divine revelations meant that he had become *Rasulillah*, the Messenger of God, and the verses that Jibril instructed him to recite changed not only his life and that of his Arab tribesmen, but eventually the lives of countless millions of people the world over.

THE PROCESS OF REVELATION

Muslims believe that the archangel visited Muhammad many times – often in perfect human form – with divine revelations, and that he would first speak verses to Muhammad and then ask him to repeat them verbatim. This learning process is what is meant by the Arabic word *iqra* (literally 'read', 'recite' or 'proclaim'), and Muslims see it as a divine recognition that Muhammad was an *ummi*, or illiterate.

Right A wooden board containing Quranic verses, from northern Nigeria, on which students inscribe and memorize the text.

It is said that as the revelations continued, the nature in which they were received changed, and that sometimes they appeared as visions rather than words, which meant that Muhammad often was forced to hastily vocalize what appeared before him. But the verses from the Quran that he received responded to his anguish: 'Move not thy tongue concerning it (the Quran) to make haste therewith. It is for Us to collect it and to promulgate it: But when you have promulgated it, follow its recital faithfully. Then surely it is for Us to explain it' (75:16–19).

Muhammad described the experience by saying 'never once did I receive a revelation without thinking my soul had been torn away from me'. At other times, he said, the process was like the unbearable reverberations of a large bell, ringing agonizingly and abating only when he had comprehended the revelations fully.

MEMORIZING REVELATIONS

In 612, Muhammad began to rehearse the verses of the Quran among his Makkan tribesmen. His message contained good news for those who returned to the worship of Allah in peaceful submission and a severe warning for those who rejected his message.

As the number of his followers grew, and the process of revelation continued, these Muslims

Above Muhammad transmits revelations of the Quran to his followers as Archangel Jibril looks on in this 17th-century Turkish manuscript painting.

began to collectively commit the verses to memory. Those who were literate would scribe them on to animal skins or thigh bones. There are a number of early historical reports that refer to many Muslims who had memorized the whole Quran dying in battle.

Muhammad encouraged the memorization of the Quran among his followers to preserve the revelations, and the tradition is still practised by Muslims today.

COMPILATION OF THE QURAN

It is well established that the Quran had been transcribed in its entirety during Muhammad's lifetime, but the scriptures had been neither compiled together in one volume nor arranged in a particular order. The focus on oral transmission and memorization ensured that the Quran's chapters (surahs) had been arranged by Muhammad, however.

Above A Moroccan Muslim woman uses a wooden wipe-board to copy and memorize Quranic text. The tradition dates back to the earliest days of Islam.

As far as the written compilation of the Quran is concerned, Muhammad actively instructed scribes to write down verses as he dictated them. By the end of his life, there were numerous copies of various chapters available to the Muslim community.

When Abu Bakr became caliph, he ordered the various scripts to be collected into a single volume. This copy was later kept by Umar, the second caliph, and then by his daughter, Hafsa, until her death. The third caliph, Uthman, had several copies prepared, which he subsequently ordered to be sent throughout the Muslim world. Several debates arose as to which of these manuscripts was the most authentic before it was decided by consensus that Uthman's version (*mushaf Uthmani*) represented the most faithful account of the revelations that Muhammad was believed to have received from God.

ARABIC SCRIPTS

The written word was not widespread among the pre-Islamic Arabs, although a number of people were literate. The Arabic script of Muhammad's era was quite basic, containing only the consonant structure of a word, with much ambiguity regarding some letters. From this basic system, a number of standardized scripts were soon developed from various parts of the Arab-Muslim world – Kufic, Maghribi and *naskhi*, for example. Two early important additions to the Arabic script were made – vowel marks (*tashkil*) and diacritical marks (*ijma*) – which standardized the pronunciation and allowed the recitation of the text by non-Arabs. However, comparisons between early texts and later scripts show that these additions did not change the content.

Above A 9th-century page from the Quran in Maghribi script, complete with red vowel marks to facilitate the correct pronunciation of the written Arabic.

MEMORIZING SCRIPTURE

THE QURAN IS REVERED BY MUSLIMS WORLDWIDE: MANY HAVE
COMMITTED THE COMPLETE SCRIPTURE TO MEMORY, WHILE OTHERS
REGULARLY RECITE IT OR CONSULT THE TEXT FOR GUIDANCE.

Muslims view the Quran as a divine scripture that provides them with a complete way of life in accordance with God's will as revealed to Muhammad. During the 23-year period of revelation, the Quran was received as a living event for those who heard and believed it, forming part of their daily lives and experiences.

The Quran as a physical book only began to take shape after the final verses were revealed and Muhammad died. Before that, the revelations were committed to memory, their exact content agreed by community consensus (*ijma*).

FROM JIBRIL TO MUHAMMAD

The word 'scripture' usually refers to a written text, but this definition cannot strictly be applied to the Quran, in that its original transmission was oral. However, Muslims believe not only that the revelations were divinely imparted to Muhammad by Archangel Jibril, but also that there is an original Quranic text 'on tablets preserved' in the heavens (85:22).

The early Muslims immediately committed the newly received verses to memory and transmitted them to those who were not present. Preserving these oral transmissions of the Quran became a priority for Muhammad and his early followers, but this was not an insurmountable task in a society that had a developed oral tradition. Muhammad is recorded as saying that Jibril would revise the Quran with him annually during the month of Ramadhan.

MEMORIZING THE QURAN

Memorization was the earliest form of transmission of the Quran and remained important even after it was committed to script and then later mass-produced. It is still memorized by Muslims today.

This historical oral tradition, which can be traced back to Muhammad himself, is perhaps a unique feature of the Quran. A follower of Muhammad, Ibn Abbas, reported that Muhammad claimed 'he whose heart is devoid of a portion

Above This painting by Osman Hamdi Bey from the late 19th century portrays the religious tradition of hifz, *the memorization of the Quranic text.*

of the Quran is like a deserted house.' In the past, the tradition of memorizing the whole Quran was seen as the basis of a sound Muslim education. Today, Muslims who achieve this feat are still honoured with the title *hafiz*, which means 'protector', as someone who has memorized the whole Quran.

All Muslims need to memorize a minimum portion of the Quran in order to offer their obligatory prayers (*salah*) and as a means of remembrance and contemplation (*dhikr*) of God. During the fasting month of Ramadhan, believers will usually improve their knowledge of the Quran by reciting a section (*juz*) of the text daily, or by attending an evening prayer (*tarawih*), in which a section is recited each evening at the mosque.

ARRANGEMENT OF TEXT

The Quran is divided into 114 chapters, each containing 'signs' (*ayah*, plural *ayat*), often referred to as 'verses', of unequal length. The longest chapter has 286 *ayat*, the

Left A highly decorative handwritten Quran containing a distinctive Arabic calligraphic style framed in gold leaf – a combination of the aesthetic and the functional.

shortest has only four. Each chapter (surah) has a name or short heading, which is usually derived from an important word or event pertaining to it, and begins with the *basmalah* ('In the name of God, Most Merciful, the Most Compassionate'). Muslims believe that both the order of the *ayat* in each surah and the chronology of the latter within the Quran was determined by the Prophet Muhammad under Archangel Jibril's supervision.

The chapters fall into two main categories, Makkan and Madinan, according to the place of their revelation, and then into four further sections according to their length. Further divisions are the 30 equal sections or *ajza* (singular *juz*), often with paragraph subdivisions known as *ruh*. Two other divisions of *hizb*, four equal parts, and *manzil*, seven equal parts, allow the Quran to be recited in either four or seven days respectively. All of the above divisions and subdivisions are normally marked within the margins of the Arabic text.

AUTHENTICITY OF SCRIPTURE

The Muslim belief that the Quran remains unaltered from the time of revelation has continuously been challenged by some from outside the faith, though the overwhelming majority of scholars do not question the fact that the text still exists in its original form. It is generally agreed, however, that the Quran only exists as such in its original language and that all translations convey a general but not specific meaning.

It is widely acknowledged that while Muhammad encouraged the transcription of the Quran, he prohibited his followers from writing down his sayings (hadith) during his lifetime in order to avoid confusion between his narrations and what is seen as God's word.

Above A boy learns the sacred text in a madrasa (Islamic school) in Pakistan. All Muslims are taught to recite the Quran in Arabic from an early age.

Below Memorizing the Quran is an important part of the Muslim faith, and translations from Arabic into other languages have become widely available.

ISLAMIC CALLIGRAPHY

THE OUTSTANDING WORK PRODUCED BY MUSLIM CALLIGRAPHERS
IS ONE OF THE CROWNING ACHIEVEMENTS OF ISLAMIC CULTURE. AS
A SPECIALIST SKILL, CALLIGRAPHY WAS HELD IN VERY HIGH REGARD.

Throughout the Islamic world, calligraphers enjoyed a more exalted status than artists until the latter part of the Middle Ages. This is reflected in a tale from the *Arabian Nights*, 'The Second Dervish', in which an unfortunate prince is transformed into an ape. Undaunted, he demonstrates his regal nature by writing out a succession of verses, using six different types of script. His knowledge of calligraphy proved that he was not only a human, but also a highly cultivated one.

The development of elaborate calligraphy owed much to religion. In early societies, where literacy was scarce, the written word assumed a mysterious, almost magical aura. Calligraphers exploited this, using ever more elaborate forms of script to beautify the sacred word. This is evident in both Christian and Muslim manuscripts, but the full potential of calligraphy was explored far more thoroughly by Islamic artists, because of their restrictions on other forms of decoration.

EARLY SCRIPTS

In the earliest phase of their history, Muslims preferred to transmit their learning orally. However, the need to circulate a standardized version of the Quran created a shift in attitudes. In the 7th century, Caliph Uthman ibn-Affan sent master texts to leading Islamic centres, where they were copied by local scribes. These early manuscripts were chiefly written in Kufic, a blocklike, angular script that took its name from the Iraqi stronghold of Kufa.

Kufic had several regional variations, but it remained the preferred style of writing until around the 10th century, when it was gradually superseded by a number of more rounded, cursive scripts. These were more fluid in

Above A classic example of early Kufic script, from a 10th-century Quran produced in North Africa. The long, horizontal strokes of some characters were a feature of the Western Kufic style.

appearance, as calligraphers in this field were trained to focus on whole words, rather than individual letters. *Nashki* became the most popular of these, though it did not prevail everywhere. In the Islamic West, for example, in Spain and North Africa, calligraphers preferred to use the Maghribi script, a cursive form that managed to retain the grandeur of Kufic lettering.

DEVELOPING SCRIPTS

Islamic calligraphy underwent a profound transformation in the 10th century following the reforms of Ibn Muqla (886–940). He rationalized the system, ensuring that each character in the *nashki* alphabet was written out in a consistent, well-proportioned way. He also promoted a number of other scripts, such as *muhaqqaq*, *rayhani* and *thuluth*. Each of these served a different function, although they could often appear in the same manuscript. It was not unusual, for example, to find the text of a Quran copied out in *nashki*, but with the headings in Kufic.

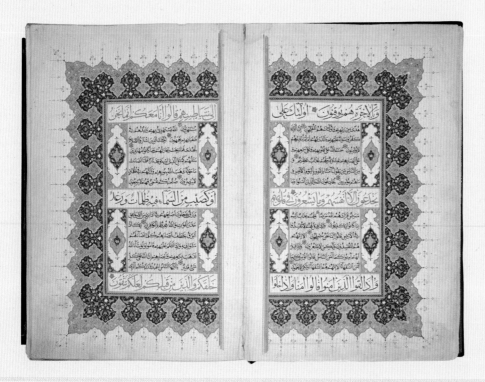

Left Calligraphers liked to combine different scripts on the same page. In this 16th-century Persian manuscript, the main text is written in nashki, *while the headings are in* thuluth.

EPIGRAPHS

None of the Arabic scripts were confined solely to manuscripts. The chief reason why Islamic calligraphy is so rich and varied is because there was considerable interaction between the different media in which it was employed.

Architectural inscriptions, known as epigraphs, date back to the 7th century, featuring on the Dome of the Rock in Jerusalem. From the outset, their content was very varied. Sometimes, they simply referred to the foundation date and the patron of a building, but more often the inscriptions consisted of blessings or verses from the Quran.

Kufic was the most widely used script, but its form was modified far more drastically than it was in manuscripts. In many cases, the shafts of the letters were interlaced – a decorative ploy that was borrowed from early coinage. Alternatively, they were enveloped in leafy scrolls and floral motifs. Occasionally, the letters themselves sprouted buds or leaves.

Legibility was not always a high priority. Often the calligraphy was set in vertical panels, even though Arabic is read horizontally, from right to left. In other instances, it was enclosed in rigid, geometric patterns, with the letters distorted, in order to fit into the design. As a result, the maze-like inscriptions became virtually indecipherable.

CALLIGRAPHY AND CRAFTS

Calligraphy was employed in virtually every art form, featuring in the designs of a diverse range of objects, from carpets and tiles to metalwork and ivory. Here, the effect could sometimes be more playful. Inscriptions on a series of medieval metal vessels, for instance, featured ribbon-like *nashki* script, topped with comical human heads or imaginary animals.

Above A seal inscribed with a Quranic verse on the Prophet's form: 'And we have not sent you [Muhammad] except as a mercy for all creation...'

Below Decorative bands of calligraphy, citing verses from the Quran, encircle the red sandstone shaft of the Qutb Minar in Delhi. The lettering itself is combined with intricate floral motifs.

LIVING THE QURAN

IN THE DAILY LIFE OF MUSLIMS, THE QURAN IS CONSIDERED A LIVING TEXT THAT COMMUNICATES TO BELIEVERS HOW TO CONDUCT THEIR AFFAIRS IN SUBMISSION TO THE WILL OF ALLAH.

Although there are a number of prophetic miracles believed to be associated with Muhammad, it is widely considered by Muslims that the greatest of these was the Quran. Over the centuries, Muslims throughout the world have been inspired to follow the teachings, prohibitions and values of the Quran, believing that to do so is to truly obey and serve God.

'THE LIVING QURAN'

When once asked to describe Muhammad's ordinary habits and daily interactions, his wife Ayesha described him as 'the living Quran'. She was alluding to Muhammad's absolute fidelity to the divine revelations, and to the fact that he lived and breathed its teachings, both publicly and privately.

Ayesha's testimony to her husband's exemplary character goes some way to explaining the Prophet's appeal, and also suggests that the moral standards set by the Quran and its teachings are achievable.

The Quran contains numerous descriptions relating to God's divine attributes, which collectively provide a theology of God's nature. Because Muslims believe that the Quran is God's word, they consider that both its text and the prophetic narrations provide them with a divine authority and direct means of religious guidance and of instruction for their daily lives.

THE *UMMAH*

As well as providing a ritual means of conducting obligatory prayers (*salah*) and an act of worship through a particular style of recitation known as *tajweed*, the Quran also gives the Muslim

Above Muslims believe that the Quran guides them toward building a peaceful and just society, in which marriage and the family are seen as the bedrock.

Left Renowned scholar, Jullundur Doab, instructs two pupils in this 19th-century depiction of Islamic education.

community, or *ummah*, a blueprint for conducting its affairs. The spiritual guidance and legal injunctions are used to draft business and marriage contracts, conduct ethical and equitable trade and commerce, engage in warfare that is just and responsible, and develop peaceful, constructive political interaction and meaningful dialogue with other communities and faiths.

The Quran, then, is seen as a book of guidance in all spheres of the community's existence. The verses relating to divine laws, collectively known as Shariah, provide the foundations of a jurisprudential system (*fiqh*) that is applied within particular contexts and circumstances.

Within developed scholarship of *fiqh* (taken from the root word *faqah*, meaning 'to understand'), there are two primary concepts: *taqlid*, the established comprehensive judgements by classical legal jurists, and *ijtihad*, the asserted effort of providing new legal judgements for new situations. This engagement with canonical law from the primary text is a unique feature of the Islamic legal system.

A BOOK OF GUIDANCE
The Quran claims to be God's final revelation to humankind and seeks to establish Islam as the completed form of the beliefs and teachings of previous divine scriptures. As such, it presents an all-encompassing way of life that is regulated by prescribed religious ordinances. Muslims believe that these laws (Shariah) are God-given and so generally obey them voluntarily. Where Muslims are a majority, living by the Quran can produce a peaceful and harmonious society.

Right The Amir (Mayoral Official) of al-Ula, Saudi Arabia, presides over his civic responsibilities for his community, ever mindful of his religious obligations.

(The impact of the Quran's teachings on Muhammad's society transformed the social and religious practices that previously divided polytheist Arabia.) However, in societies with significant non-Muslim minorities, the imposition of religious laws can prove impractical and problematic.

Understanding the Quran is important to the correct application of divine laws and injunctions. Interpretation and commentary on the text is known as *tafsir* and it is primarily concerned with the knowledge of the text as revealed to Muhammad and his early *ummah*. Without *tafsir*, it would be difficult to extract a correct understanding from the Quran.

HUMAN INQUIRY
Religion and science have always existed in Islamic civilization as complementary ways to understand the same phenomena. Muslims believe that when God created all things, he made natural laws (*fitrah*) incumbent upon them. The Quran encourages objective examination of all created things as a pathway to understanding their Creator.

Above Jabir ibn Hayyan was a medieval Muslim chemist. His scientific endeavours are believed to have been inspired by the Quran's teachings.

Although the Quran does not claim to be a book of science, it contains many seemingly scientific verses. These verses have inspired Muslim scientists to further human knowledge and learning as a means of affirming the greatness of God.

SEEKING KNOWLEDGE

'READ IN THE NAME OF THY LORD': THE FIRST WORDS BELIEVED TO HAVE BEEN REVEALED TO MUHAMMAD CHARACTERIZED HIS PROPHETIC MISSION TO EDUCATE AND CIVILIZE HIS SOCIETY.

Islam transformed a predominantly illiterate society into a leading civilization virtually within a single generation. The Quran provided a means of uniting diverse peoples into a single faith community, while developing their intellectual capacity through rulings that encouraged objective scientific and philosophical inquiry in the pursuit of a better understanding of Allah as al-Alim, 'the Source of all Knowledge'.

Muhammad was quite typical of his people in being an *ummi* (illiterate). The first revealed verses of the Quran are emphatic in their instruction to read and write – and thereby to seek knowledge: 'Read in the name of thy Lord who created, Created man from a clot! Read and your Lord is most Generous, Who teaches man by means of the pen, teaches Man what he does not know' (96:1–5).

Left This 14th-century astrolabe helped Muslims to explore the universe in pursuit of knowledge of the natural world, as inspired by the Quran.

SCIENCE AND LEARNING

Upon receiving this revelation, Muhammad immediately set about educating his followers to read and write. After the Battle of Badr, he decreed that any literate pagan captive who taught ten Muslims to read and write would gain freedom.

The Arabs had always used the stars to navigate their way across the deserts nocturnally. After their Islamization, they developed their knowledge of astronomy to map out the direction and times of prayers, and measure distances for travel, inventing instruments such as astrolabes, celestial globes, quadrants and sextants.

In order to obey the Quranic command to travel and experience the world that God had created, Muslims developed specific sciences that would aid exploration, and measure, analyze and quantify data and specimens. This led them to excel in the fields of science and technology.

CIVILIZATION AND CULTURE

Across the expanding Muslim world of the medieval era, from Delhi to Timbuktu and from Baghdad to Granada, Islamic culture and

Above Medieval Muslim astronomers, geographers and cartographers map out the heavens and earth, guided by the teachings of the Quran regarding natural phenomena.

learning began to advance. In Spain, the paved public footpaths of Córdoba and Seville were illuminated by street lamps. The cities incorporated public baths for the first time, and, even as early as the 9th century, underground sewers and city dumpswere built to the benefit of all.

Baghdad and Cairo became the intellectual and academic centres of the Muslim world with the creation of the first universities and scientific centres, which specialized in astronomy and chemistry, philosophy and the arts.

The thirst for knowledge and the advancement in sciences and technology was not a result of market economy materialism, but rather was a living testament to the Quran's rhetorical question, 'Are those who have knowledge equal to those who do not have knowledge' (39:9)? It was also an obedient response to the Prophet

Muhammad's declaration that 'the seeking of knowledge is an obligation on every Muslim.'

Throughout the ages, Muslims have always understood the pursuit of knowledge and learning to be an act of worship that fulfils divine instructions and benefits human civilization and culture through scientific inquiry and critical thought. In no way do Muslims consider that learning results in a loss of faith or an alienation from the Islamic view of the universe.

Right The Great Mosque at Córdoba, Spain. By the 10th century, the Islamic world had become a bastion of civilization and scientific learning that stretched from Iraq right across to Spain.

PHILOSOPHY AND ART

As Muslims applied themselves to some of the more spiritual and philosophical aspects of the Quran, a number of theological disciplines emerged, including Sufism, which is often understood as Islamic mysticism. Sufism focuses on the esoteric meanings of the Quran and developed into a sophisticated branch of Islamic learning and practice. Another discipline to appear at this time was *kalam*, which is concerned with understanding the Quran through discussion of the attributes of God and theological posits on issues such as free will, sin and the nature of the Quran.

In art, the Arabesque developed an abstract and symmetrical form based on the circle and the dot, which represents God at the centre of creation. The circle and its intersecting geometric lines denote God's infinite creation as the patterns are repeated endlessly.

Left Religious devotion, geometry, acoustic sciences and skilled craftsmanship combine to produce a glorious mosque and centre of learning at the Masjid-e-Shah in Isfahan, Iran.

THE WAY OF THE PROPHET

THE QURAN TEACHES THAT THE PROPHET MUHAMMAD WAS SENT BY GOD FOR THE BENEFIT OF HUMANKIND. MUSLIMS THEREFORE BELIEVE THAT HIS LIFE EXAMPLE IS THE BEST MODEL TO EMULATE.

Above Reciting the Quran during Ramadhan is considered an emulation of Muhammad's ritual practice.

The Islamic declaration of faith, the *shahadah* – 'There is no God but God and Muhammad is His Messenger' – is a covenant comprised of two distinct parts. The first, 'There is no God but God', is seen by Muslims as both a negation of all false gods and an affirmation of the one true God. The second part, 'Muhammad is the messenger of God', states the Islamic belief that Muhammad is God's Prophet and that, as such, he must be obeyed and followed. Muslims believe that to obey the Prophet is to obey God, and loyalty to Muhammad's teachings and practices is therefore considered as a manifestation of belief in God.

HADITH AND SUNNAH

Islam teaches that the Prophet Muhammad is the gateway to God and that the pathway is formed of his hadith and sunnah. 'Hadith' literally means 'speech', or 'saying', and refers to anything that Muhammad is thought to have said, that is the thousands of transmitted and recorded sayings of the Prophet as remembered and passed down by his early followers.

The Arabs' oral tradition and custom of memorizing genealogies, stories and poems proved invaluable in the preservation of Muhammad's hadith. A couple of generations after his death, the prophetic sayings were compiled into various hadith collections by a small number of important Islamic scholars, who also included the chain of transmitters. A transmitter is an individual who faithfully memorized a particular hadith and its chain of narrators leading to the Prophet. In Islam, the hadith collections are second only to the Quran in importance.

The word 'sunnah' refers to the life example of the Prophet. Sunnah includes Muhammad's hadith and the particular way in which he lived – the way he ate, dressed, interacted with people and performed his religious duties. Islam teaches that

Left The mihrab of the Prophet's mosque in Madinah, from where he led his congregation in prayer.

Right A pilgrim has a moment of reflection at the shrine of Ali ibn Abu Talib in Mazar-e Sharif, Afghanistan.

the sunnah represents the perfect life example for Muslims to follow. The accounts of Muhammad's sunnah can be found in hadith but are more commonly recorded in the biographical accounts of his life known as the *Sirah*.

EMULATING THE PROPHET

Muslims believe that Muhammad's character provides the perfect example for them to emulate in their everyday lives. The imitation of the Prophet's practices is seen as an effective way of correcting personal character traits, and in doing so, Muslims believe that they will attain God's reward.

Following the sunnah is also seen as a measure of an individual's love of the Prophet, and Muslims are particular in their appearance and conduct in an effort to faithfully imitate him. The sunnah provides a means of developing a deep spiritual bond with the Prophet.

Without Muhammad the religion of Islam could not have been realized, and Muslims believe that it is only by following his example – one seen as demonstrating love and mercy – that they are able

to practise all aspects of their religious teachings. For many Muslims, love of the Prophet surpasses the love of all other humans to the point that they may become emotional at the mention of his name, to which they will often supplicate *'sallahu alayhi wa sallam'*, meaning 'the prayers and peace of God be upon him'.

THE HADITH OF MUHAMMAD'S LAST SERMON

One of the most famous prophetic hadiths is that said to relate Muhammad's final sermon at the plains of Arafah, which he gave to his followers after his farewell pilgrimage in 632. According to this hadith, Muhammad informed his followers, 'O people listen to what I say to you for I do not know whether I will meet with you after this year in this place again...' He reminded the congregation of their duties, urging them to treat each other with kindness, then concluded by announcing to his followers, '...I have left with you that which if you hold fast to will save you from all error, a clear indication, the Book of God and the word of his prophet. O people hear my words and understand.'

Left Muhammad delivers a sermon from his Minbar, or pulpit, at the Madinah mosque in this 17th-century manuscript painting.

PRESERVING THE PROPHET'S SAYINGS

IN ISLAM, THE PROPHET'S SAYINGS ARE A SOURCE OF AUTHORITY SECOND ONLY TO THE QURAN. AUTHENTICATING WHAT MUHAMMAD ACTUALLY SAID WAS THEREFORE A PRIORITY FOR EARLY MUSLIMS.

When Muslims began to commit their religious teachings to the written word, safeguarding the authenticity and integrity of the original narrations was paramount to preserving their religion. In the process of its written compilation, the Quran was subjected to continuous scrutiny by successive caliphs and their councils. Similarly, the narrations of Muhammad needed to be collated and verified for their authenticity. Prophetic sayings are important to understanding the Quran, religious practices and legal injunctions. Preserving the correct accounts was therefore important for the development of Islamic scholarship.

BIOGRAPHIES OF THE PROPHET

The early biographies of the Prophet Muhammad are documents that capture both the critical events and developments of his mission. The works are known collectively as the *Sirah*, and the earliest is that of Muhammad ibn Ishaq ibn Yasr (d.767), who produced the book *Siratu Rasulillah (Life of the Messenger of Allah)*. These first accounts also reflect the collective memory of the Muslim community relating to the spread of Islam during Muhammad's lifetime.

Through their particular literary style, these accounts also document the love and veneration that

Right A trainee Muslim scholar learns hadith in the traditional way, at the feet of his shaykh, *or teacher, in the Islamic* madrasa *in Shiraz, Iran.*

Muhammad's first community had for him. According to ibn Ishaq, Abu Bakr's comment upon the Prophet's death was designed to affirm Muhammad's human status as compared with the eternal nature of God, who had revealed his guidance to humankind through his messenger. Abu Bakr reminded his fellow believers of God's word: 'Muhammad is but a messenger; messengers have passed away before him, will it be that when he dies or is killed, you will turn back on your heels?' (3:144) Thus Muhammad's companions were careful to avoid him becoming an object of worship in his death by focusing on the continuation of his divine mission.

However, the biography written by ibn Ishaq, while it provides details of the major events of Muhammad's life, is not more than

Above A 13th-century copy of the Quran preserves in handwritten Arabic script the original oral revelations that Muhammad is believed to have received some 600 years earlier.

a general portrait of him sketched from the shared memory of his contemporaries. Collecting the Prophet's actual hadith necessitated a more rigorous approach.

RECORDING HADITH

Two specific terms became associated with the process of writing down the Prophet's hadith: *matn*, which refers to the actual content of a hadith, and isnad, which relates to the chain of transmitters linking the Prophet to a particular hadith.

The collection of hadith gathered great momentum in the first two centuries of Islam. This was largely because the memorized accounts had been either lost with the deaths of previous generations or taken from the community at Madinah by migrating Muslims. Frequently, a hadith would find its way back to Madinah, carried by Muslims settling there who had learnt it at their place of origin from an early emigrant.

Often, early compilers would travel huge distances in order to record a single narration. For example, one scholar set out from

Below Islamic scholars in Qom, Iran, discuss religion and memorize the Quran in the precincts of the Grand Mosque, a tradition that has endured for over a millenium.

Madinah to Damascus to seek out Abu al-Darda, a companion of Muhammad who was a transmitter of a particular hadith. The journey took a month, and necessitated some degree of discomfort, which demonstrates the extraordinary dedication of these scholars to the pursuit of religious knowledge.

THE SCIENCE OF HADITH

The collected hadiths were selected for their considered authenticity after a critical analysis of the chronological accuracy, linguistic content, geographical parameters and the character of individual transmitters connected to them.

Scrutinizing each of the links in the chain of a hadith became a biographical science called *ilm ar-rijal* (literally 'knowledge of men'). Scholars researched the reliability of character of the transmitters and also tried to establish whether linked individuals had met or if they had any political or sectarian motives. Once hadiths had satisfied the above criteria, they were classified into accepted categories of 'agreed' (or 'sound'), 'good', 'weak' or 'fabricated'.

COLLECTING HADITH

Scholars who dedicated their lives to locating and codifying hadith became known as *al-Muhaddithun*. Imam al-Bukhari (d.870) was the greatest of the hadith scholars and is attributed with collecting some six million hadith before accepting only 7,275 for his nine-volume work. Five other major classical volumes of hadith are still widely used throughout the Muslim world: Muslim, Tirmidhi, Ibn Majah, Abu Dawood and An-Nisai.

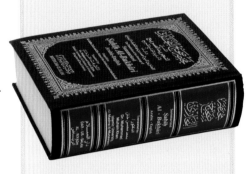

Above One of the most famous hadith collections, the nine-volume Sahih al-Bukhari *contains more than 7,000 narrations.*

STORIES FROM THE PROPHET'S LIFE

MUHAMMAD'S INTERACTIONS WITH PEOPLE, ANIMALS AND THE ENVIRONMENT ARE SEEN BY MUSLIMS AS A TESTIMONY TO HIS COMPASSION AND EVIDENCE OF HIS EXEMPLARY BEHAVIOUR.

Hadiths and biographies of the Prophet Muhammad contain a wealth of detail about his life – not only about how he worshipped, but also how he dressed, what he preferred to eat, and so forth. There are also many interesting stories and anecdotes that provide an insight into his society. Muslims throughout the world see a humanity and compassion in these stories of the Prophet that they try to emulate in their own lives.

According to Islamic tradition, Muhammad was not only a consummate leader and statesman, but also someone full of kindness, empathy and warmth. Indeed, the stories tell that on occasions he would laugh so much that his molars were visible. It is said that he was approached constantly by people in his community asking him to explain the new religion to them, and that on many occasions he did so with great humour.

TWO OLD WOMEN

One story tells that an old woman once asked Muhammad if she would enter paradise. He teased her by replying no, there would be no old women in paradise. The poor old woman cried, only to be comforted by Muhammad's smile as he explained that she would enter paradise, but in a young form – no one would remain old there.

On a different occasion, Umm Ayman, another old woman, is said to have come to Muhammad and asked for a camel. He told her that he would give her only the offspring of a she-camel. She was rather disappointed, and worried that a small camel would not carry her weight, until she realized he was teasing her, for of course all camels are the offspring of a she-camel.

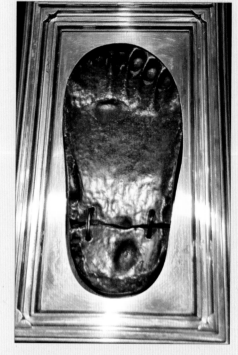

Above The Prophet Muhammad's footprint has been preserved. Images of the Prophet are frowned upon; however, sacred relics from his life are revered.

THE COMPANIONS AND THE BIRDS

Both the Quran and hadith are very clear on the need to treat animals with kindness and love, and stories about the Prophet's life tell that he always acted toward animals with care and sensitivity.

It is told that one day, while Muhammad was travelling with his companions, they stopped to rest. While he went away from them for a short time, his friends spotted a sparrow flying with her two fledglings above their heads. The tiny birds were not steady flyers, and as they flew lower, his companions thought it would be fun to try to catch them as they were so beautiful.

Although the men were very gentle, the fledglings struggled in fear in their hands, while the mother bird flew around in great distress. When

Right Muhammad, seen here in green surrounded by a halo of light, hears the complaint of a doe. His treatment of animals is the subject of many anecdotes from hadiths.

Muhammad returned, he asked 'Who has terrorized this bird by taking her young ones?' He explained to his companions that, while they meant no harm, they had in fact distressed the mother. He then released the birds, who flew away to their mother.

THE OLD NEIGHBOUR

The rights of neighbours have been so emphasized in Islam that Muhammad even commented on one occasion that Archangel Jibril impressed their rights so much on him that he thought he would have to include them in his will! This statement emphasizes the importance Islam places on keeping good relations with neighbours so that disputes can be minimized and the home can indeed be a haven.

Muhammad's patience is said to have been severly tested on many occasions. A story tells that he had an old neighbour who was hostile to his message of Islam and threw rubbish at him whenever he passed her house. He never retaliated, nor did he enter into an argument with her. This went on for a considerable length of time. One day, however, the woman was not there. Although

Above *This casket is said to contain the Prophet's tooth. Such relics allow people to connect with Muhammad, and are a reminder of a messenger who once lived and walked among people.*

he was understandably pleased not to have rubbish thrown at him, Muhammad was concerned when on the following day she was still absent. He asked another neighbour about her and was told she was ill.

Muhammad decided to visit her, but she feared that he had come for retaliation when she was weak. In fact, he had gone simply to see if

Above *Socializing is an important facet of Muslim life. According to stories of the life of the Prophet, he was renowned for generously spending his time with people.*

she was alright and to fulfil his duty to visit the sick. His kindness won the old woman's heart, and she subsequently entered the faith.

APPLYING HADITH

A STUDY OF QURANIC TEXT AND PROPHETIC HADITH ESTABLISHED THE AUTHORITY OF A CORE OF RELIGIOUS SCHOLARS, WHO CODIFIED HADITH AND DEVELOPED THE PRINCIPLES OF ISLAMIC LAW.

By the third century after the death of Muhammad, Islamic scholarship had gravitated around a small group of specialist teachers who had devoted themselves to hadith study. These teachers also developed a system of learning, complete with a graduation. Students would study manuscripts with their master scholars, or *ulama*, either by dictation or from the original text.

CONTROVERSY

As devoted scholars of hadith worked methodically to authenticate the millions of hadiths attributed to Muhammad, other less scrupulous Muslims were engaged in their distortion and fabrication.

There were two main sources of erroneous and forged narrations. The first came from the *qussass*, or professional storytellers, who earned a living as public entertainers, relating the ancient oral narratives of the Arabs. Their tales incorporated ancient mythology, biblical legends, Quranic stories and prophetic traditions, which they fused into elaborated, entertaining plots. While the *qussass* were popular cultural communicators, the errors contained in their religious tales were often translated to the masses as fact. The result was a popular but incorrect version of many hadiths.

The second source of faulty hadiths were certain political and sectarian figures, who, for whatever reason, needed to support their claims of religious orthodoxy. In the temporary absence of a widely agreed authentic body of hadith literature, these people were able to fabricate prophetic narrations to provide justification for their various heterodox positions.

CODIFICATION

Once hadiths had been verified as genuine, it became necessary to begin codifying them into specific categories according to their

Above The imam delivers the Friday sermon to his congregation in the Grand Mosque in Almaty, Kazakhstan, praising the virtues of the Quran and hadith.

reliability and subject matter. The thematic arranging of hadith aided religious rulings relating to ritual practices and the application of Islamic law. Scholars then employed the hadith literature to explain principles of jurisprudential law known as *fiqh*.

One of the first works of this type was *al-Muwatta* (literally 'The Beaten Path') by Imam Malik (717–801). This book was followed by a number of equally important works that formed the basis of the major jurisprudential schools. Students from each of these law schools would present their own newly completed manuscripts, copied from the works of their teachers, for correction. Sometimes manuscripts would be reproduced through correspondence; others were simply copied without any supervised oral readings. Most

Left The famous university of al-Azhar, Cairo, was established in the 10th century to develop scholarship in the study of Islamic law, the Quran and hadith.

commonly, however, the scholar would provide a certificate (*ijazah*) to his student, granting him permission to transmit what he had learned.

Classical jurists, such as Imam Malik, were careful to stress that their individual opinions and rulings should not be accepted uncritically and that wherever a more appropriate ruling was available it should be preferred. Over time, the rulings of the four leading scholars, Malik, Abu Hanifah, Ash-Shafii and Ibn Hanbal, came to dominate Sunni thought, while the rulings of Imam Jafar al-Sadiq formed the leading legal school among the Shiah.

HADITH AND LAW

Islamic jurisprudence, *fiqh*, is derived from prescribed canonical laws contained in the Quran that relate to criminal and civil rulings (*muamalat*) and personal and religious commands (*ibadat*). The Quran deals with both these types of issues in broad and general terms. For example, it instructs Muslims to make ritual ablution and establish prayers, but it does not give the details of how, where and when.

The Prophet's hadith and sunnah provide precise information on these and all other matters relating to Quranic teachings. The hadith is therefore extremely important in helping Muslim scholars understand the practical application of divine laws and instructions. Had early Islamic scholars neglected to collate, authenticate and codify the hadith, the much-needed minutiae of religious law and practice would have been lost to subsequent generations of Muslims.

Right The minaret of the Oqba Mosque at Kairouan, Tunisia, which dates back to the 9th century. Its university is a bastion of Islamic learning and civilization.

HADITH COLLECTIONS

The five major collected volumes of hadith, and the special science concerned with their transmission, validation and authentication, became a distinguishing feature of Muslim civilization. The hadith collections also facilitated a unique and vast body of religious legal literature that remains available to Islamic scholars and lay Muslims.

As Muslims continue to migrate and settle into new domains, the Prophet's hadith and sunnah continue to be extremely significant

Above Students study hadith literature in the traditional manner – at the feet of their shaykh, *or teacher – in this 13th-century manuscript painting.*

in developing and establishing a functioning community, complete with its traditional values and beliefs. The wide availability of the volumes of codified hadith literature allows contemporary Islamic scholars to address new situations in accordance with the primary religious teachings of Islam.

LAWS AND SCHOLARS

THE BODY OF AUTHENTICATED PROPHETIC HADITH PROVIDES THE MUSLIM *UMMAH* WITH A UNIQUE SOURCE FOR ISLAMIC SCHOLARSHIP IN THE FIELDS OF THEOLOGY AND RELIGIOUS LEGAL RULINGS.

Islamic scholarship has developed over 1,500 years through the study of the Quran and sunnah. As Islam spread beyond Arabia, the need to understand and apply its teachings in new geographical and cultural contexts grew. Muslim theologians, philosophers and legal scholars engaged in intense debates, formulating diverse theological and legal stances based on their varied interpretations of text.

ISLAMIC LAW

The laws of the Quran are called the Shariah. The method by which these rules of Shariah are applied to specific or new situations became a

Below Muslim students from Oman study the Quran, the contents and ordinances of which guide Muslims through every aspect of their daily lives.

science known as *fiqh*. *Fiqh* has four methodological principles, known collectively as *usul*: the Quran, sunnah, reasoning by analogy (*qiyas*) and consensus of opinion (*ijma*).

Fiqh scholars are known as *fuqaha* (singular *faqih*), and issues relating to legal questions are dealt with by a specialist jurist called a *mufti*, whose considered opinion is a *fatwa*. A judge dispensing with criminal and civil disputes is a *qadi* or 'grand judge'.

THE IMPORTANCE OF LEGAL SCHOOLS

Shariah is a dynamic and elaborate system that has evolved from Muhammad's time to the present. It is of major importance to the Muslim *ummah*, for whom its rules and teachings form the guiding principles and values of daily life. Although there is no notion of

Above An ancient Quranic manuscript handwritten in Kufic script. The Quran provides the foundations of Islamic jurisprudential law, or fiqh, through Shariah, or canonical, law.

absolute religious authority in Islam, there is a general consensus of scholars (*ijma*) concerning the fundamental beliefs and practices. The dominant theological position within the *ummah* is referred to as *Sunni* – those who adhere to the major teachings of the Prophet and the majority opinions of the *ulama* or religious scholars.

MAJOR ISLAMIC SCHOLARS AND SCHOLARS

During the periods of the ruling Muslim dynasties of the Umayyads and the Abbasids, *fiqh* scholarship evolved into major recognized legal schools called *madhhabs*, founded on the teachings of individual scholars. Originally there were many schools, but eventually five main ones emerged. In order of their founding, these were Hanafi, Maliki, Shafii, Hanbali and Jaafari.

The founders of these legal schools were all exceptional scholars and they share similar biographies. All spent their early lives mastering hadith literature, which they later taught. Notably, they all also resisted oppressive Umayyad and Abbasid Muslim rulers, for which most of them received public humiliation, imprisonment and even death. For example, the founder of the Hanafi School, Abu Hanifah (702–67), was born in Kufa, Iraq, and became a leading scholar in the Umayyad court, where he was offered, but declined, the position of *qadi*. Despite imprisonment, he refused another royal appointment under the Abbasid caliph al-Mansur (754–75) and thus remained in prison, where he died. Despite the fact that during their lifetimes these scholars were considered by a succession of Muslim rulers to be heterodox or heretical, their scholarship has continued to influence Muslim thought right up to the present day.

Today, the Hanafi School predominates in Turkey, Eastern Europe, Iraq, Central Asia and South Asia; the Shafii School is the main school in Yemen, Egypt, Somalia and East Asia; Muslims in North Africa and Sudan largely

Right *Female law students study in a university library in Egypt. Islam has a history of women scholars specializing in religious law and jurisprudence.*

follow the Maliki School; while the Hanbali school is predominant in Saudi Arabia. The main Shiah legal school, the Jaafari School, dominates Iran, Lebanon and southern Iraq.

INTERPRETATIONS

Significantly, the written script of the Quran was the first book in the Arabic language and it is the foundational text of all the various original branches of early Islamic sciences. In order to grasp the Quran's context, and thus interpret the text correctly, it is essential to understand the chronology of the Quranic revelations – the when, where, why and to whom they were given. Likewise, it is important to have an awareness of the Quran's specific language and diction, and its particular rhetorical style has been the subject of numerous detailed studies.

Above *Ornately decorated copies of the Quran, some of which contain interpretations of the text, are displayed in an Islamic bookshop.*

These explanatory works, which are known as *tafsir*, have three major approaches. *Tafsir bil-ra'i* gives an explanation by comprehension and logic based largely on an exegete scholar's considered interpretation of the text. *Tafsir bil-riwayah* expounds what has previously been transmitted through either other correlating verses from the Quran, specific hadiths relating to the text, or the generally agreed consensus of meaning by exegete scholars. *Tafsir bil-isharah* deals with the esoteric interpretations of the text. No individual has absolute authority on the Quran's exact meaning, but these commentaries offer a deeper knowledge of its contents.

CHAPTER 2

THE HISTORY OF ISLAM

In 706–15, Caliph al-Walid I, ruler of the vast and still-growing Umayyad Islamic empire, built the Grand Mosque of Damascus in the historic Syrian city that his forerunner Muawiyah I had chosen as his capital. Al-Walid was the sixth ruler in the Umayyad caliphate (line of successors to the Prophet Muhammad). By the time of his rule, less than 90 years after the death of the Prophet Muhammad (in 632), the faith of Islam had already won wide territories for Allah by military conquest.

Subsequent Umayyad caliphs continued this expansion of territories, creating a powerful Islamic empire. They are revered by Arab nationalists, who see their rule as a 'golden age', but reviled by Shiah Muslims because they came to power through violence and at the expense of the descendants of Ali ibn Abu Talib, cousin and son-in-law of Muhammad. Many Sunni Muslims also see the Umayyad as worldly kings rather than true caliphs (religious leaders and successors to the Prophet).

Opposite At the Great Mosque in Damascus, remains of beautiful mosaics installed by Byzantine craftsmen can be seen on the façade of the transept facing the courtyard.

Above Under Sultan Suleyman I (reigned 1520–66), the Topkapi Palace in Istanbul was a great centre for calligraphy and other arts, attracting artists from all over the empire.

SUCCESSORS TO THE PROPHET

THE FIRST FOUR CALIPHS – OR SUCCESSORS TO THE PROPHET MUHAMMAD – ESTABLISHED ISLAM AS A MAJOR RELIGIOUS AND POLITICAL FORCE IN THE MIDDLE EAST AND NORTH AFRICA.

The Prophet did not name a successor before his death in 632. His followers chose Abu Bakr to be political and religious leader of the faith. Abu Bakr was named caliphate Rasulillah ('Successor to God's Prophet, Messenger of Allah'), and his rule as caliph lasted just over two years (8 June 632 until 23 August 634).

A merchant from Makkah who, like Muhammad himself, was a member of the Quraysh tribe, Abu Bakr had been a long-term companion of the Prophet, whom he had known since boyhood. He was the fourth convert to Islam, and the first outside Muhammad's own family. According to later tradition,

he purchased the freedom of eight slaves who converted to the new faith in its early days.

His principal achievement was consolidating the nascent Muslim state by establishing control over the whole of Arabia. In central Arabia, his forces put down several rebel uprisings in the Ridda wars (from Arabic for 'Wars of Apostasy', and so called because a number of rebel leaders declared themselves prophets to rival Muhammad).

The most powerful rebel prophet was Musaylimah, but he and his tribe, the Banu Hanifah, were defeated at the Battle of Yamama on the plain of Aqraba (now in Saudi Arabia) in December 632. Moreover, under Abu Bakr's leadership, Bedouin tribesmen won the first of many astounding victories for the new faith against the Persian Sasanian empire and the Byzantine empire in what is now Iraq and Syria.

THE SECOND CALIPH

In August 634, Abu Bakr fell seriously ill. Before he died, he appointed Umar ibn al-Khattab to succeed him as caliph. Umar was another Makkah-born merchant and a long-term follower of Muhammad,

Above Muhammad is pictured with the first three men to serve as caliphate Rasulillah ('Successor to God's Prophet') – Abu Bakr, Umar and Uthman.

and another member of the tribe of Quraysh. He proved a tremendously effective leader: directing operations from Madinah, in his ten-year rule (634–44) he oversaw major Islamic military expansion as his armies continued the assault against the Byzantine and Sasanian empires.

Umar's Arab armies attacked the Byzantines in Syria and captured Damascus in 635. Further south, they took control of Jerusalem from the Byzantines in 638. They also moved against the Byzantines in North Africa and took Alexandria. They seized Ctesiphon, the Persian capital, in 637, forcing the Sasanian king Yazdegerd III to flee, and vanquished the Persian army at the Battle of Nahavand in 642; in 651, Yazdegerd was killed at Merv, and the Sasanian dynasty was at an end.

To consolidate their gains, Umar's followers built garrison towns such as Kufa and Basra in Egypt. Umar was the first caliph to call himself *amir al-mumineen* ('Commander of the Faithful').

Left The Prophet's daughter Fatimah and her husband Ali ibn Abu Talib, the fourth caliph, witness Muhammad's death in 632 in Madinah.

Above The Imam Ali mosque in Najaf, Iraq, contains the tomb of Ali ibn Abu Talib and is a major pilgrimage site for Shiah Muslims.

Below Ctesiphon (now in Iraq) had been a major city for 700 years when it was captured by Arab troops in 637 in the time of Caliph Umar.

UTHMAN SUCCEEDED BY ALI

In 644, Umar was stabbed in the mosque in Madinah by a Persian slave named Pirouz Nahavandi (or Abu-luluah); he died two days later. A council of elders chose Uthman ibn-Affan, – another former merchant from Makkah and another of Muhammad's original converts – as his successor, and third caliph. Some Muslims were unhappy at the choice, and dissent burst into the open after Uthman was murdered in 656.

Ali ibn Abu Talib, Muhammad's cousin and son-in-law, assumed the position of caliph and moved the capital of the Islamic community from Medina to Kufa (now in Iraq), where he had substantial support. He encountered opposition, causing the first great schism in the *ummah*.

First, he crushed a faction led by Ayesha, one of Muhammad's widows, together with Talhah and al-Zubayr, two *sahabi* ('companions of the Prophet', Muslims who were alive in the Prophet's lifetime). He defeated them decisively at the Battle of the Camel at Basra, Iraq. He also met opposition from a leading member of the Ummayad clan named Muawiyah, who refused to accept his authority.

SHIAH AND SUNNI VIEWS

Shiah Muslims regard Ali ibn Abu Talib as the first legitimate leader of the Islamic religious community by virtue of his blood relationship with the Prophet and his status as Muhammad's first convert to Islam. Entirely rejecting the authority of the first three caliphs, Shiah Muslims regard Ali as the first in a line of infallible religious leaders called imams.

Sunni Muslims, however, identify Abu Bakr and his three followers as the equally rightful successors to the Prophet in ruling the *ummah*. The Sunni celebrate Islam's first four caliphs as the *Rashidun* (the 'rightly guided caliphs'). This term and idea originated during the Abbasid caliphate (750–1258).

CIVIL WAR

THE CIVIL WAR SPARKED BY THE CLASH BETWEEN ALI AND MUAWIYAH
CONTINUED INTO THE NEXT GENERATION AND LED TO THE INFAMOUS
MURDER OF ALI'S SON HUSSAIN BY MUAWIYAH'S SON YAZID IN 680.

Not long after assuming power as caliph, Ali ibn Abu Talib dismissed the regional governors appointed by his predecessors. Muawiyah, Governor of Syria, refused to obey, and proved a formidable opponent. A leading member of the Umayyad clan who had been named Governor of Syria in 640 by Umar, Muawiyah had a significant independent power base and had won major military victories, including the conquests of Cyprus in 649 and Rhodes in 654.

In response to this show of defiance, Ali led his army into Syria and fought Muawiyah in the three-day Battle of Siffin in July 657; the battle was inconclusive and the two men agreed to a six-month armistice followed by arbitration of the dispute. However, when the time came, neither man backed down and the standoff continued – with Ali as caliph and Muawiyah still defying him and acting as Governor of Syria.

Some Muslims hatched a plot to end what they saw as a damaging conflict: on the 19th day of Ramadan in 661, both Ali and Muawiyah were stabbed with poisoned swords while at prayers. Muawiyah recovered, but Ali died from his wounds two days later.

MUAWIYAH GAINS POWER

Ali's supporters named his son Hassan caliph, and Muawiyah marched against them with a vast army. The two armies fought a few inconclusive skirmishes near Sabat and subsequently, after negotiations, Hassan agreed to withdraw his claim to the caliphate. Muawiyah was at last the undisputed caliph. Under the terms of the agreement, Muawiyah was to be caliph for his lifetime. According to Sunni accounts,

Above Ali is shown fighting the forces of Ayesha, a widow of the Prophet, at the Battle of the Camels in this 17th-century Persian wall painting.

Muawiyah agreed that on his death, a leadership consultation (*shura*) should be held to determine the next caliph, but according to Shiah accounts, Muawiyah agreed that the caliphate would pass to Hassan's brother Hussain ibn Ali.

Below Outnumbered perhaps 500 to one, Hussain and his followers took on impossible odds at the Battle of Karbala.

Right The Imam Hussain Shrine at Karbala, close to the battlefield, contains the tombs of both Hussain and his half-brother Abbas.

Muawiyah ruled as caliph with no further challenges until his death in 680. He governed from Damascus, which he developed as a city and where he established a liberal court. His rule was notable for its tolerance towards Christians, who came to occupy many prominent government positions, and for its introduction of Byzantine-style bureaucracies, especially a postal service and chancellery. When he died, however, the terms of his agreement with Ali were ignored in his desire to found a dynasty: the caliphate was passed to his son Yazid.

EVENTS AT KARBALA

Hussain ibn Ali, brother of Hassan and grandson of Muhammad, claimed the caliphate. He marched from Makkah to Kufa in Iraq, the base of his father Ali's support. At Karbala on 10 October 680, he was intercepted by a 40,000-strong army sent by Yazid and commanded by Umar ibn Said. Hussain was vastly outnumbered, with only 72 men in his travelling party. The only survivor was Hussain's son Ali ibn Hussain, who was too sick to fight and was taken prisoner, carried off to Damascus and kept as a prisoner of Caliph Yazid. However, many years later he was freed, and in time he became the fourth Shiah imam.

The Battle of Karbala was a key cause of the centuries-long split between Sunni and Shiah Muslims. Shiahs, descendants of the supporters of Ali (their name comes from that of their party in the 7th century, the *shiat Ali*, 'the party of Ali'), do not

Right Around 1 million Shiah Muslims travel to Karbala each year to take part in the ceremony of Ashura that commemorates Hussain's death there.

admit the legitimacy of any of the other early caliphs nor of the Umayyad descendants of Muawiyah. Sunnis (so called because they claim to follow Muhammad's sunnah, or 'example') celebrate Abu Bakr, Umar, Uthman, Muawiyah and the Umayyads in addition to Ali as the rightful successors of Muhammad.

A SECOND CIVIL WAR

Yazid ruled, as second caliph of the fledgling Umayyad dynasty, for three years, until his sudden death in 683. He had to fight an uprising in the Hijaz region led by Abdullah ibn al-Zubayr, a member of the *sahabi* ('Companions of the Prophet'). This war is known, together with the struggle between Yazid and Hussain, as the Second Fitnah, or Islamic Civil War. Yazid captured Madinah and besieged Makkah. In the course of the fighting, the *Kaabah* was damaged, making Yazid and the Umayyad dynasty more unpopular still. Yazid's death in 683 did not bring an end to the war, which continued through the reign of the next three caliphs.

THE POWER OF THE UMAYYADS

THE FIRST GREAT CALIPHATE DYNASTY, THE UMAYYADS, RULED THE ISLAMIC WORLD FOR 90 YEARS, FROM 660 TO 750, AND CREATED A GLITTERING CAPITAL IN THE HISTORIC SYRIAN CITY OF DAMASCUS.

The Umayyad caliphate was founded by Muawiyah I, the provincial governor who had challenged the authority of the fourth caliph, Ali ibn Abu Talib. The Umayyads took their name from Muawiyah's great-grandfather, Umayya ibn Abd Shams, and from the Banu Umayyad clan named after him. The Umayyad clan were members of the same Quaraysh tribes as the Prophet Muhammad and shared an ancestor with him – Abd Manaf ibn Qusai.

THE EARLY YEARS

Muawiyah ruled for 19 years (661–80) and established a powerful court in Damascus, Syria, but the next three caliphs of the line – Yazid, Muawiyah II and Marwan – ruled for just five years between them. The fifth Umayyad caliph, Abd al-Malik, however, imposed his authority and established the dynasty on a firm footing.

Early in his reign, Abd al-Malik defeated a rebellion in Kufa led by al-Mukhtar, who had wanted to establish another of Ali's sons, Muhammad ibn al-Hanafiyyah, as caliph. By 691, he had reimposed Umayyad authority in Iraq, and in 692, he recaptured Makkah, so ending the long-running uprising in the Hijaz; the prominent rebel, Abdullah ibn al-Zubayr, was killed in the attack.

UMAYYAD GOVERNMENT

Abd al-Malik built on the achievements of dynastic founder Muawiyah by improving and centralizing the administration of the caliphate. He introduced a new Muslim coinage with non-figurative decoration and established Arabic as the caliphate's official language.

The Arab armies and the rulers that came in their wake differed from many of their predecessors as conquerors in that they did not

Above The impressive remains near Jericho in the West Bank were once part of the Umayyads' Kirbat al-Mafjar Palace, built there in c.743–4.

force people to convert to their faith. Christians, Zoroastrians and Jews were free to continue to follow their own religion so long as they paid a head tax to their new rulers. However, many conquered peoples chose to convert to Islam. Conversion was simple: the only requirement was that the new believer acknowledge formally that there is no God other than Allah and that Muhammad is his Prophet. The principal benefits were freedom from slavery – for Islam

Below The peaks of the Eastern Lebanon Mountain range rise behind the ruins of the Umayyad trading city of Anjar, which was probably built in 705–15.

guaranteed that no Muslims could be slaves – and the right to pay the lower tax that was generally levied on believers.

This financial concession, and the willingness of conquered people to convert, in fact posed a problem for the expanding empire, since the spread of conversions necessarily reduced the amount of head tax raised; there were reports of provincial governors discouraging conversions in order to protect revenue. According to traditional accounts, this problem was addressed by the Umayyad caliph Umar ibn Abd al-Aziz (717–20), a ruler revered by later generations for his wisdom, tolerance and the ascetic life he led as a ruler.

UMAYYAD DEGENERACY?

Muawiyah established – and many of his descendants maintained – a cosmopolitan court in Damascus. They appointed Syrian Christians to important administrative positions and they patronized non-Islamic artists, such as the poet al-Akhtal (640–710), who was a Christian. According to some accounts, life at court was degenerate. Not only did senior Umayyads flout Islamic law by permitting the drinking of wine, but it is claimed that one Umayyad prince even enjoyed swimming in wine. However, as tales of this kind

were circulated by the opponents of the Umayyads, there must be some doubt as to their truthfulness.

CITIES AND PALACES

The Umayyads developed the city of Damascus. Under Byzantine rule, it had been a fortress town, but the Umayyads transformed it, albeit briefly, into a great imperial city. They also built cities in the desert to facilitate the by-then flourishing international trade that made Damascus and the empire rich. One was Anjar, around 50km (31 miles) from Beirut in Lebanon, which was built by Abd al-Malik or al-Walid at the intersection of the trade routes to Damascus, Homs and Baalbek (in southern Lebanon).

Umayyad caliphs also built fine desert castles and palaces, many of which appear to date from

Above The plain exterior of the 8th-century Umayyad desert castle of Qasr Amra in Jordan conceals remarkable surviving murals depicting hunting scenes.

the brief reign of Caliph al-Walid II (743–4). Qasr Amra, in eastern Jordan, was used as a hunting lodge; its walls are covered in hunting scenes, images of fruit and naked women. Khirbat al-Mafjar, at Jericho in Palestine (c.725–50), contains a palace and bathhouse, an audience hall and a mosque. Mshatta Palace, around 30km (19 miles) south of the modern city of Amman, Jordan, was also probably built under al-Walid II; its very impressive stone façade can now be seen in the Pergamon Museum in Berlin.

Below The façade of the Umayyad Mshatta Palace, given by Ottoman sultan Abd al-Hamid II to Emperor Wilhelm II of Germany, is now in Berlin.

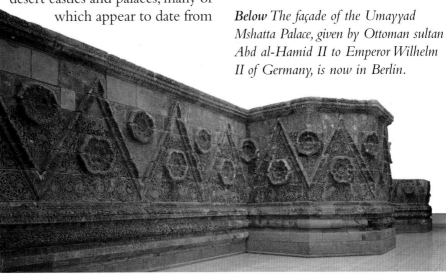

JERUSALEM: HOLY CITY TO THREE FAITHS

THE ANCIENT CITY OF JERUSALEM CONTAINS SITES SACRED TO JEWS, CHRISTIANS AND MUSLIMS, AND ITS POSSESSION HAS BEEN HOTLY CONTESTED BY ADHERENTS OF THE THREE FAITHS FOR CENTURIES.

The Jews revere Jerusalem as the centre of creation, the place where they believe that God made the world and the first man, Adam. For them, it is also the city of the biblical King David, who established the united kingdom of Israel and Judah, and the place where his successor, Solomon, built the first great temple.

To Christians, the city is sacred because it was the place where Jesus Christ, whom they believe to be the son of God, was crucified, buried, then rose from the dead.

Muslims honour the city, which is known in Arabic as al-Quds, principally as the place to which the Prophet Muhammad took his Night Journey and from where he made his ascension to heaven. In addition, Jerusalem is honoured in Islam because of its association in Judaism with earlier prophets, whom Muslims revere as Muhammad's forerunners and fellow prophets. Jerusalem, to Muslims, is the third most sacred city on earth after Makkah and Madinah.

FOUNDATION STONE

In the area of the city in which Solomon's Temple once stood is a large rock, which is known as the

Right Beautiful Iznik tiles were added to the Dome of the Rock's outer walls in a decorative programme under Ottoman sultan Suleyman the Magnificent (reigned 1520–66).

Foundation Stone. According to Jewish tradition, this is the place not only where God created the world, but also where Abraham prepared to sacrifice his son Isaac, where Jacob dreamt of a ladder ascending to heaven, and where the Ark of the Covenant resided within the Holy of Holies in Solomon's Temple.

Muslims honour the stone because of its associations with earlier prophets, although they believe that Abraham's sacrifice was of his other son, Ismail (forefather of the Arabs), and that it took place elsewhere, in the desert of Mina (east of Makkah, in Saudi Arabia). They also believe that the stone was the place from which the Prophet made his ascension to heaven – according to tradition, the rock even tried to rise with him but was held down by Archangel Jibril, and a mark on the stone is the hoof print of his supernatural steed, al-Buraq.

Above The Dome's octagonal plan is clearly shown in this 18th-century Arab manuscript illustration. The upper image is of the al-Aqsa Mosque.

THE DOME OF THE ROCK

In 687–92, fifth Umayyad caliph Abd al-Malik built the Dome of the Rock over the Foundation Stone. According to 10th-century traveller and geographer al-Maqdisi, the caliph wanted a lavish building to match the splendour of the Church of the Holy Sepulchre and to create a unique structure for Muslims that would be 'a wonder to the world'. He built the Dome as a pilgrimage shrine.

The shrine was constructed on a magnificent scale. The octagonal dome is 20m (65ft) tall and the same across, and stands above an arrangement of 12 columns and four piers within an octagonal walkway of 16 columns and eight piers and octagonal outer

Above Within the Dome of the Rock, an inscription celebrates Jesus as prophet and servant of Allah but attacks the Christian doctrine that he is God's son.

walls. Each of the eight outer sections of the wall is approximately 11m (36ft) high and 18m (59ft) wide. It is lavishly decorated within and without with mosaic, marble, tiles, carpets and faience. The dome, originally made of lead, was re-covered using a gold-coloured aluminium and bronze alloy as part of renovations in 1964 and again in 1993. The Dome of the Rock is the world's oldest surviving Islamic sacred monument.

'THE DISTANT MOSQUE'

The faithful do not pray in the Dome of the Rock but in the al-Aqsa mosque at the southern end of the Temple precinct. According to tradition, the original al-Aqsa mosque was raised by the second *Rashidi* caliph, Umar ibn al-Khattab, after the capture of Jerusalem in 638, and incorporated part of the *chanuyot*, or storehouse, of the ancient Jewish Temple of Jerusalem. It was rebuilt then in the time of the fifth Umayyad caliph, Abd al-Malik, and completed by his son al-Walid I (reigned 709–15). It was probably first called the al-Aqsa mosque at this time. The name means 'the distant mosque' and refers to a passage of the Quran that describes the Prophet's Night Journey: 'Glory be to Him Who carried His servant by night from the Sacred Mosque to the Distant Mosque, the environs of which We have blessed, that We might show him some of Our Signs. Surely, He alone is the All-Hearing, the All-Seeing' (17:2).

Above The Holy Sepulchre (reputedly the tomb in which Jesus was buried) is a free-standing structure within the church to which it gives its name.

GREATER THAN ROME

By 732, A CENTURY AFTER THE DEATH OF MUHAMMAD, THE AREA UNDER THE RULE OF THE UMAYYAD CALIPHATE WAS GREATER THAN THAT COVERED BY THE ENTIRE ROMAN EMPIRE AT ITS HEIGHT.

By the beginning of the Umayyad caliphate in 661, the *Rashidun* caliphs had already taken Syria, Armenia, Egypt and most of the lands belonging to the Persian Sasanian empire. Under the Umayyads, the caliphate then expanded further east and north-east towards India and China, and far to the west and north-west across North Africa and into the Iberian Peninsula.

By 750, when the Umayyad caliphs were ousted by the Abbasids, they had created a vast empire that stretched from north-west India in the east to the Pyrenees in the north-west, and incorporated much of Central Asia, the Middle East, North Africa and what is now Portugal and Spain.

Below The army of the Goths flees before the Arab–Berber cavalry at Guadelete, in this detail from a 19th-century painting by Martinez Cubells.

EXPANSION EASTWARDS

The crushing of the Sasanian army in 642 at the Battle of Nahavand near Hamadan in Iran – a triumph celebrated by Muslims as 'the victory of victories' – delivered most of Persia into Arab hands. Afterwards, the Arabs moved on eastwards, taking Herat in 652 and Kabul in 664.

They also pressed north and north-east beyond the Persian plateau into Khorasan (an ancient region comprising parts of modern Afghanistan, Tajikstan, Uzbekistan, Turkmenistan and Iran) and Transoxiana (another ancient region in central Asia). By the early 8th century, most of this area was under Muslim control, and Arab armies pressed on still further, right to the borders of China.

After the capture of Kabul, the Indian subcontinent beckoned. The Arab armies launched attacks into the southern Punjab (in modern

Above The fortified desert palace of Qasr al-Hayr al-Sharqi in Syria was built in 728–9 in the reign of Caliph Hisham (reigned 723–743).

Pakistan) from 664 onwards. A great expedition led by Muhammad ibn-Qasim in 711 established Umayyad rule in Sindh by 712.

In one major military endeavour, however, the Umayyad armies failed. In a series of attacks in 674–8 under Caliph Muawiyah I, and again in 717–18 under Caliph Suleyman ibn Abd al-Malik, the Umayyad military machine tried and failed to capture the Byzantine capital, Constantinople.

Right A world map drawn in the 12th century by Spanish Arab geographer Abu Abdallah al-Idrisi. As is common in Islamic maps, the south is at the top.

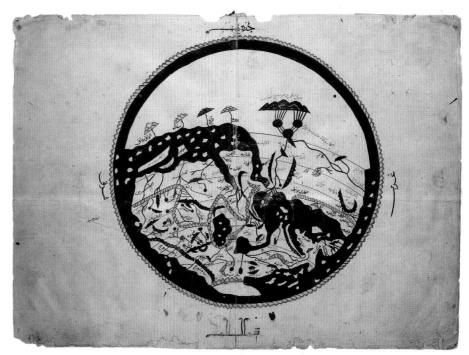

EXPANSION WESTWARDS

Alexandria in Egypt had been taken in 643. The Arabs then pressed westwards across North Africa, taking Tripoli in 647, but met fierce resistance from the Berber peoples of the Atlas Mountains. In 670, they subdued the Berbers in building the fortress city of Kairouan (around 160km (100 miles) south of Tunis in modern Tunisia).

Once conquered, the Berbers mostly converted and joined in the expansion. Arab–Berber armies swept through the Maghreb region of north-northwest Africa, reaching Tangier (now in northern Morocco) by the early 8th century. In northern Africa, they established a Muslim territory, known to historians as Ifriqiya, which encompassed coastal regions of what is now eastern Algeria, Tunisia and western Libya. They then looked further: across the narrow Straits of Gibraltar lay the former Roman province of Hispania, ruled by the internally divided kingdom of the Visigoths.

An Arab–Berber army invaded southern Spain in 711. Berber general Tariq ibn Ziyad inspired the invaders to defeat a much larger force commanded by King Roderick of the Visigoths at the Battle of Guadalete on 19 July 711. Roderick fled, or was killed, and his kingdom was quickly taken. The invaders captured the city of Seville and swept northwards. A second army, commanded by Musa bin Nusair, Governor of Ifriqiya, arrived in 712, and the combined Umayyad forces conquered almost the entire peninsula in five years. Only in the far north did the Visigoths survive.

Umayyad forces made a number of excursions further north into southern France, but these ended in 732 at the Battle of Tours when they were defeated by Christian troops. Thereafter the Umayyads withdrew into the Iberian Peninsula, where they established the territory of al-Andalus, initially as a province of the Umayyad caliphate.

THE BATTLE OF TOURS

On 10 October 732 near Tours in France, an Islamic army of some 80,000, commanded by Abd al-Rahman al-Ghafiqi, Governor General of al-Andalus, was defeated by a Frankish–Burgundian army commanded by Charles Martel in a battle known to Muslim chroniclers as the 'Battle of the Court of Martyrs'.

Traditionally, European historians have seen this battle as a key moment in the history of the continent, when the seemingly unstoppable global progress of Islam was turned back. Certainly, after this crushing defeat, Muslims abandoned attempts at northward expansion and settled in the Iberian Peninsula, where they maintained a presence until 1492.

Right The Battle of Tours is imagined as a single combat between commanders Charles Martel and Abd al-Rahman al-Ghafiqi in this 19th-century bronze sculpture by Théodore Gechter.

TRIUMPH OF THE KILLER

IN 750, THE CALIPHATE WAS SEIZED BY THE ABBASIDS, DESCENDANTS OF MUHAMMAD'S UNCLE AL-ABBAS. THE RUTHLESS FIRST CALIPH, ABU AL-ABBAS, WAS NICKNAMED *AS-SAFFAH* ('THE KILLER').

The Umayyads faced recurrent opposition to their rule from Shiah Muslims, who would not allow the murder of Ali ibn Abu Talib in 661 and the slaughter of Hussain ibn Ali and family at Karbala in 680 to be forgotten.

The Abbasids, cousins of and long-term rivals to the Umayyads, began to agitate for a change in leadership. The Shiah Abassids were members of the Hashim clan, descended from the Prophet's great-grandfather Hashim through Muhammad's uncle al-Abbas. Their rebellion against the Umayyads is known as the Hashimiyyah.

THE HASHIMIYYAH

In 747, Abu Muslim became leader of the Hashimiyyah in eastern Iran. A native of the region and a convert to Islam who had become a fervently committed Shiah Muslim, Abu Muslim won the support of a group of fellow converts and non-Muslim subjects of the Umayyads to name the prominent Abassid Abu al-Abbas as a rival ruler to the Umayyad caliph Marwan II. The rebels fought under the sign of a black flag. In 749, a Hashimiyyah army captured Kufa and proclaimed Abu al-Abbas caliph there.

Marwan II attempted to put the revolt down, but on 25 January 750, an Abbasid army commanded by Abu Muslim defeated the Umayyads in the Battle of the Zab (fought on the banks of the Great Zab River, now in Iraq). Marwan escaped with his life. The Abbasids took Damascus in April 750, and in August the same year, Marwan was killed at Busir in

Egypt. The struggle between the Abbasids and Umayyads is often referred to as 'the Third Islamic Civil War'.

Some Shiah clerics promoted this war as the great final conflict between good and evil prophesied for the last days of creation. They said that Abu al-Abbas was the Mahdi, or 'Redeemer', whose appearance will, according to Islamic tradition, usher in the Day of Resurrection (*yawm al-qiyamah*). Belief in the Mahdi is strong among Shiah Muslims, but generally less important to Sunni Muslims.

'THE KILLER' TAKES POWER

Abu al-Abbas established himself as caliph by ruthlessly eliminating all opposition. He invited all the leading Umayyads to a dinner at which they were all clubbed to death – all save only one. Abd al-

Above Abu al-Abbas was brutal with the Umayyads, but otherwise mild in victory. He allowed Jews, Christians and Persians in his service.

Rahman, a grandson of Caliph Hisham, escaped and fled to al-Andalus, where he forcibly removed the provincial governor of Córdoba and set himself up as Umayyad caliph, in opposition to Abu al-Abbas in Baghdad.

In Iraq, every enemy, every potential threat, was put to the sword. In their indignation, the Abbasids even despoiled all the tombs of the Umayyad caliphs in Syria, sparing only that of Umar ibn Abd al-Aziz (717–20), whose golden reputation as a wise ruler had won him the enduring respect of later generations, both Sunni and Shiah.

After establishing his family in power, Abu al-Abbas ruled for just three years, until 754. His reign is notable for the setting up of the first paper mills in the Islamic empire at Samarkand (an ancient city, now in Uzbekistan). The Arabs had learned the secret of paper making from prisoners taken in the Islamic victory at the Battle of Talas (751) against an army of the Chinese Tang dynasty.

Above This silver dirham was issued by the Abbasid caliph al-Mahdi (reigned 775–85), and minted at Bukhara (now in Uzbekistan).

On the death of Abu al-Abbas from smallpox in 754, the Islamic world was plunged into civil war once more: Abu al-Abbas had named his brother al-Mansur as his successor, but the latter had to fight to win power. With the support of the great general Abu Muslim, al-Mansur eventually won control of the empire; however, once established in power, he proved himself every bit as ruthless as his brother 'The Killer', ordering the execution of Abu Muslim, the man to whom the Abbasids owed their position.

UMAYYAD DOWNFALL

The Umayyads may have failed because they were so successful in secular terms. The empire expanded so extraordinarily fast, and millions of newly subject peoples converted to Islam. However, these mass conversions caused problems: the Umayyads tended to favour Arab Muslims (and particularly those of the old Arab families) over converts, and in time, the non-Arab Muslims – known as *mawali* ('clients') – grew unhappy at their treatment. This *mawali* unrest was exploited very effectively by the rebel Hashimiyyah movement that swept the Abassids to power.

Above On arriving in Spain, Abd al-Rahman, the sole survivor of Abu al-Abbas' coup, was greeted with great honour as an Umayyad prince.

Below Shiah women perform their devotions at a mosque in Baghdad, the city built by the second Abbasid caliph, al-Mansur.

THE GOLDEN AGE OF THE ABBASIDS

FROM A NEW CAPITAL AT BAGHDAD, THE ABBASIDS PRESIDED OVER A FLOWERING OF ARTISTIC, SCIENTIFIC AND COMMERCIAL LIFE THAT ESTABLISHED THE EARLY YEARS OF THEIR RULE AS A 'GOLDEN AGE'.

In 762, the second Abbasid caliph, al-Mansur, built a new imperial capital called Madinat as-Salam ('City of Peace') at the village of Baghdad, beside the river Tigris in Iraq. The first Abbasid power base was at Harran (now in Turkey), but al-Mansur moved to Iraq partly to be closer to the Persian *mawali* supporters who had helped the new dynasty to power.

THE NEW CAPITAL

Al-Mansur laid out the city in the form of a circle 2.7km (1.75 miles) in diameter, with three concentric walls – and it became known as 'the

Below Al-Mutawakkil (reigned 847–61) greatly expanded the new capital at Samarra and built a splendid palace and parks beside the river Tigris there.

Round City'. At the centre stood a mosque and palace complex: four roads led outwards to the cardinal points of the compass, dividing the area within the city walls into four equal quarters, which consisted of administrative buildings and residential quarters for the caliph's guards and other members of his administration.

The city expanded outside the walls: in the area around the south gate, later known as al-Karkh, merchants built housing and bazaars. At the north-east gate, a bridge of boats led across the Tigris to the river's east bank, where the palace of the heir to the caliphate, al-Mahdi, was built.

The Abbasid capital quickly eclipsed Damascus as the trade capital of the Islamic empire. Its

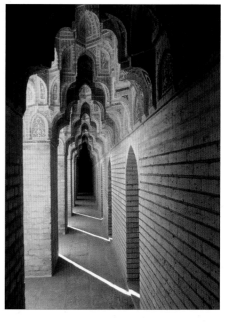

Above The Mustansiriya madrasa, built from 1227–34 during the reign of the Abbasid caliph al-Mustansir, was a centre for the four schools of Sunni law.

streets were packed with craftsmen and buyers, and merchant ships from India, China and East Africa unloaded and loaded on the city's wharves. Baghdad became a city of international standing, at the height of its prosperity and fame in the late 8th and early 9th century.

Above The minaret of the Great Mosque of Samarra, built by al-Mutawakkil in c.848–52, is 52m (170ft) tall. A spiral ramp leads to the top.

PERSIAN INFLUENCE

Under the Abbasids, the Islamic world took on Persian influence; the round design of Baghdad was based on that of cities such as Ardasher-Khwarrah, or Firuzabad, in the Persian Sasanian empire. The caliphs welcomed non-Arab Muslims to their court, and many Persians rose to powerful positions in the imperial administration.

A new position of vizier, or chief administrator, was introduced, and the caliphs became more isolated from the day-to-day exercise of power, living instead in a palace amid great luxury and elaborate court ceremony, much of it derived from Sasanian models. Nevertheless, the language of the empire, spoken by caliph, courtiers and people alike, remained Arabic.

The 'golden age' of the Abbasids saw a great flowering of learning. Caliph al-Mamun founded the Bayt al-Hikmah ('House of Wisdom') as a library and centre for translation of ancient Greek, Roman, Indian and Persian works of science and philosophy, agriculture, geography, medicine, zoology and chemistry.

Yet for all their wealth and success, the Abbasids were never secure, and they faced persistent opposition. Having come to power with the support of Shiah Muslims, they had embraced Sunni Islam. Shiah Muslims living in Baghdad regularly scrawled slogans against the caliphate on the city walls, and riots in the so-called 'City of Peace' were not uncommon.

MOVE TO SAMARRA

In 836, riots engineered by the Abbasid regime's Armenian and Turkish slave soldiers persuaded Caliph al-Mutasim to move his capital to Samarra, 125km (78 miles) along the river Tigris in central Iraq. He and his successors built a beautiful palace there as well as the Great Mosque of Samarra (852); at its height the city stretched 32km (20 miles) along the banks of the

A THOUSAND AND ONE NIGHTS

The fifth Abbasid caliph, Harun al-Rashid, and his vizier Jafar al-Barmaki feature as characters in several tales of *A Thousand and One Nights* (in Arabic *Alf laylah wa laylah*). Its main source seems to have been a translation into Arabic of a Persian story collection, but all kinds of elements were added, including Islamic religious stories from the time of the Abbasids. The oldest surviving manuscript of the work is a fragment found in Syria and written in Arabic in the 800s.

Above The Thousand and One Nights inspired many later works of art, including the ballet Scheherazade *by Nikolai Rimsky-Korsakov in 1888.*

Tigris. Samarra remained the Abbasid capital until 892, when Caliph al-Mutamid moved the empire's chief city back to Baghdad.

The Abbasid caliphate lasted from 750 until 1258, but for much of this period the caliphs had little real power. Beginning in the mid-900s, they became increasingly marginalized by the explosive rise of Turkish military power. They retained merely nominal authority under the rule of the Buyid and Seljuk Turks.

ARCHITECTURE OF MOSQUES

THE MOSQUE (*MASJID*, 'PLACE OF PROSTRATION', IN ARABIC) IS AT THE HEART OF EVERY ISLAMIC COMMUNITY. IN ITS ARCHITECTURE, MUSLIMS GIVE EXPRESSION TO PROFOUND ELEMENTS OF THEIR FAITH.

Among key features of mosque architecture are the *musallah,* or prayer hall, the *qubbah*, or dome, above it, and the minaret or tower, from which Muslims are traditionally called to prayer.

The earliest developed form of the mosque was a square enclosure with a flat-roofed prayer hall and an open courtyard. The first mosques, founded by Muhammad – the Quba Mosque, outside Madinah, and the Mosque of the Prophet in Madinah itself – were probably originally of this type. Such simple mosques were easy to construct and, in a warm climate, large numbers of believers could worship in the open courtyard. They did not originally have domes or minarets. The *adhan*, or call to prayer, could be made from the flat rooftop – or perhaps by a man running through the streets.

QUBBAH

Domes were adapted from Persian palace architecture and from the basilicas of Orthodox Christianity. They gave a mosque grandeur and an imposing presence, while also providing good acoustics in the prayer hall within. Among the first domed Islamic religious buildings was the pilgrimage shrine of the Dome of the Rock in Jerusalem.

Domes were used widely in the typical Iranian form of the mosque, in which one or more domed halls, or *iwans*, were arranged around a central courtyard used as the prayer area. The *iwans* were open at one end and opened directly on to the yard. The Ottomans built very grand domed mosques, which sometimes had a large central dome over the prayer hall and several subsidiary domes around it.

Above The dome of the Suleymaniye Mosque (1550–7) in Istanbul is typical of mosque interiors: beautifully decorated without using representational images.

MINARETS

The first minarets were built by the Umayyad caliph Muawiyah I in Damascus in 673. In 703, Umar ibn Abdul-Aziz built four minarets on the Prophet's Mosque in Madinah, each 9m (30ft) tall. Minarets served to mark out the mosque, as they could be seen for miles around, and by their size were designed to inspire and impress. They also had a functional role as a raised position from which the *muezzin* could make the call to prayer.

Some of the early minarets were also used as watchtowers. In other places, for example the Qutb Minar in Delhi, they doubled as victory columns, marking military conquest. Another practical use – of great significance, given that these mosques were built in countries with hot climates – was as a cooling

Left Mosques often featured monumental gateways. This is the gateway to the Great Mosque of Córdoba, built in 784–6 by Abd al-Rahman.

tower: air flowing into the *musallah* beneath the dome would be drawn by natural convection up the minaret tower, thereby reducing temperatures in the prayer hall.

These days, the call to prayer is made in the prayer hall with a microphone and speakers, and the minaret has a purely symbolic function. Yet as a statement of the glory of Islam and of the aspirations and faith of believers, modern minarets are often built to extraordinary heights. The world's tallest is at the Hassan II Mosque in Casablanca, Morocco, which stands 210m (689ft) high.

MINARET STYLES

A great variety of minaret styles developed over the centuries, with regional variations. In Samarra, Iraq, the Great Mosque built by

Below The Blue Mosque (1609–16), also called the Sultan Ahmed Mosque, in Istanbul has one large, several subsidiary domes and six slim minarets.

Abbasid caliph al-Mutawakkil in 849–52, had a square-based conical minaret, 52m (170ft) high, with a wide spiral staircase winding around the exterior of the tower. According to tradition, Caliph al-Mutawakkil used to ride up the staircase to the top on a donkey. The conical minaret with a spiral exterior staircase became the typical form in Iraq.

In Turkey, minarets were usually slim and circular, and were often built in larger numbers – up to six, depending on the size of the mosque. A fine example are the six minarets of the Sultan Ahmed Mosque, also known as the Blue Mosque, one of the finest of all the beautiful mosques of Istanbul, which was built by the Ottoman sultan Ahmed I (reigned 1603–17). Another alternative was to build twin minarets flanking an entrance gateway, as in the magnificent Mosque of al-Hakim in Cairo (*c*.1003).

DECORATION

Mosques often feature beautiful decoration, both interior and exterior. As Islam does not permit

Above This decorated mihrab or prayer niche is in the 16th-century Mosque of Prince Lotfollah, built in Isfahan, Iran, by Shah Abbas I.

representational images, artists developed decorational forms based on floral patterns and various geometrical shapes. The repeating geometric arabesques that are often found on the walls of mosques symbolize the infinite creation of Allah.

MATHEMATICS, MEDICINE AND ASTRONOMY

DURING THE ABBASID CALIPHATE, SCHOLARS TRANSLATED PERSIAN, GREEK AND INDIAN TEXTS TO CREATE A REMARKABLE BODY OF WORK, MOST NOTABLY IN MEDICINE, MATHEMATICS AND ASTROLOGY.

For a period, Abbasid Baghdad was the intellectual capital of the world. The vast Islamic empire brought under one ruler the descendants of several ancient civilizations of the Middle East, Asia and southern Europe for the first time since the age of Macedonian empire-builder Alexander the Great in the 4th century BCE. Frontiers were opened and Abbasids' former enemies were drawn to al-Mansur's 'City of Peace', where Greeks, Persians, Indians, Chinese, Berbers and Egyptians exchanged and compared ideas.

One of the essential features of the Abbasid 'golden age' was its tolerance. The Abbasid caliph and his administration generally promoted according to merit, and allowed Jews, Buddhists, Hindus and Christians to serve them.

THE HOUSE OF WISDOM

In 830, Caliph al-Mamun (reigned 813–33) founded the Bayt al-Hikmah ('House of Wisdom') as a library and translation centre, modelling the institution on the Imperial Library of the Sasanian Persian emperors. Authors whose works were translated include the ancient Greeks Pythagoras (c.580–c.500BCE), Hippocrates (c.460–c.377BCE), Plato (c.427–c.347BCE), Aristotle (384–322BCE) and Galen (129–c.216CE), and the Indians Sushruta (c.6th century BCE), Brahmagupta (598–c.665CE) and Aryabhata (476–c.550CE).

Now Arabic – the language in which Allah is believed by Muslims to have made his divine revelations to the Prophet Muhammad – replaced Greek as the international language of ideas.

Above Muhammad ibn Musa al-Khwarizmi's work in the House of Wisdom makes him one of the greatest figures in the history of mathematics.

MATHEMATICS

In 830, with the Byzantine emperor's permission, Caliph al-Mamun sent a delegation of scholars to Constantinople to seek classical texts for translation. Among these scholars was al-Hajjaj ibn Yusuf ibn Matar, who brought back and translated a copy of the ancient Greek mathematician Euclid's 13-volume masterpiece *Elements* (c.300BCE). Al-Hajjaj's successors translated from Latin a commentary on Euclid's geometry by the ancient Roman mathematician Hero of Alexandria (c.10–70CE) and several works by another ancient Greek mathematician, Archimedes (c.290–c.212BCE).

Perhaps the most important Islamic mathematician of the period was Muhammad ibn Musa al-Khwarizmi (c.780–c.850CE), who

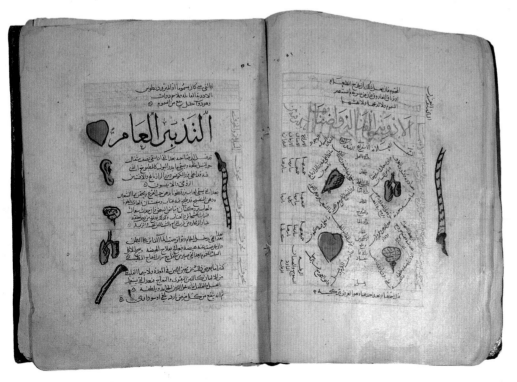

Left These pages of the al-Qanun fil-Tibb (Canon of Medicine) of Ibn Sina, or Avicenna, discuss illnesses that affect the heart, stomach, skull and lungs.

Right Ibn Sina teaches medical colleagues to make remedies for smallpox in this illustration from a 17th-century Ottoman manuscript painting.

worked in the House of Wisdom under al-Mamun. Beginning in the 4th century BCE, ancient Indians had developed the figures 1, 2, 3, 4, 5, 6, 7, 8, 9 and 0 and their use in the place-value system that allows us to write any number using only these ten figures. Al-Khwarizmi learned the system through Arabic translations and explained what he called the 'Indian numbers' in his book *On Adding and Subtracting in Indian Mathematics*; this work was translated into Latin, and from it, the system he had outlined passed into European mathematics as 'Arabic numerals'.

MEDICINE

Scholars in Baghdad also made a significant contribution to later knowledge of medicine. Hunain ibn Ishaq (809–73) was a noted translator of key Greek medical works, including those of Galen and Hippocrates, and also wrote no fewer than 29 medical books of his own, including a series on ophthalmology, which were the first of the Arabic medical books to include anatomical artwork.

Two other important Islamic medical figures were the men known in the West as Rhazes and Avicenna. The first, Abu Bakr Muhammad ibn Zakariyy Razi, wrote more than 50 medical books and practised as a physician in the Iranian town of Rayy. The second, the physician and philosopher Abu Ali al-Husayn ibn Abd Allah ibn Sina (c.908–1037) wrote *The Book of Healing* and *The Canon of Medicine*.

ASTRONOMY

Encouraged by the Quran – 'And He it is Who hath set for you the stars that ye may guide your course

by them amid the darkness of the land and the sea' (6:97) – scholars in Baghdad focused on astrology and astronomy. Under Caliph al-Mamun and the direction of Sahl ibn-Harun, the House of Wisdom concentrated, in particular, on astrology and mathematics; under Caliph al-Mutadid (reigned 892–902), another gifted translator named Thabit ibn Qurra (836–901) was appointed court astrologer. Many astronomical observatories were built throughout the empire and several navigational stars have Islamic names.

ARAB ORIGINS OF SCIENTIFIC TERMS

Several key mathematical and scientific words have their origins in Arab terms, or derive from the names of Muslim authors. The name for the mathematical discipline of algebra, for example, derives from the word *al-jabr* in the title of one of Baghdad mathematician al-Khwarizmi's books, written in c.825, *al-Kitab al-mukhtasar fi hisab al-jabr wa-l-muqabala* (*Overview of Calculating by Completion and Simplification*). According to one theory, 'chemistry' also has an Islamic origin, deriving from the Old Persian word *kimia* ('gold').

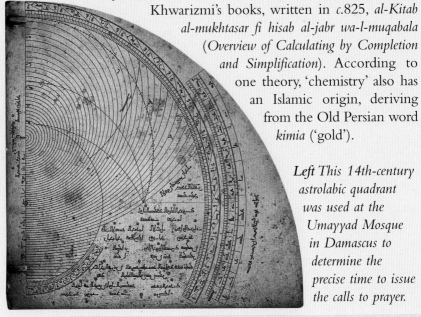

Left This 14th-century astrolabic quadrant was used at the Umayyad Mosque in Damascus to determine the precise time to issue the calls to prayer.

THE SHIAH EMPIRE OF THE FATIMIDS

FROM 909 TO 1171, THE SHIAH FATIMID CALIPHATE WAS A RIVAL POWER TO THE ABBASIDS OF BAGHDAD IN NORTHERN AFRICA AND PARTS OF THE MIDDLE EAST. IT FOUNDED CAIRO AS ITS CAPTIAL.

Above Begun by al-Aziz in 990, the al-Hakim Mosque in Cairo was finished in 1003 by al-Hakim and named after him.

The Fatimids were militant Shiah Muslims who rejected the authority of the Sunni Muslim Abbasid caliphate. They were members of the mystical Ismaili sect of Shiah Islam and their rulers were Shiah imams (religious leaders). The Fatimid imams are recognized by most Muslims as holders of the office of caliph, and as a result, the period of Fatimid rule represents the only period (aside from the caliphate of Ali ibn Abu Talib) in which the caliphate and the Shiah imamate coincided.

THE FOUNDING OF THE FATIMID DYNASTY

The Fatimid dynasty was founded by Ubayd Allah al-Mahdi Billah, who claimed descent from the Prophet through Muhammad's daughter Fatimah and her husband Ali ibn Abu Talib, the first Shiah imam. Starting in Tunis in 909, al-Mahdi extended his power to cover all of the central Maghreb region (Tunisia, Libya, Algeria and Morocco), and ruled from a newly built capital at Mahdia on the Tunisian coast.

Egypt was at this time ruled by the Ikhshidid dynasty, under overall authority of the Abbasid caliph in Baghdad. The Fatimids invaded and conquered the Ikhshidids, took their capital, Fustat, and founded a new royal city in Qahirah (Cairo) in 969. Cairo became a royal enclave for the Fatimid caliph, while the administrative government of his territory was carried out from nearby Fustat.

FORCEFUL EXPANSION

At the height of the Fatmids' power in the late 10th and early 11th century, their empire included the whole of northern Africa, the Hejaz and Yemen, the island of Sicily and the Mediterranean coast as far north as Syria (including Palestine and Lebanon and Syria itself).

The Fatimid imams, by virtue of their descent from the Prophet, declared themselves infallible and incapable of wrongdoing, and they denounced the Abbasid caliphs as usurpers. Their aim was not simply to establish a regional power base independent of Baghdad but to supersede Abbasid power altogether to become leaders of a universal Islamic religious state. They sent missionaries throughout the Islamic world, attempting to make converts, and were a constant ideological as well as a political threat to the Sunni Abbasid caliphate.

FATIMID CAIRO

The Fatimids named their new royal enclave Qahirah after the planet Mars (then called *al-Najim al-Qahir*, 'the destroyer', or *Qahirat*

Left The beautiful al-Azhar Mosque in Cairo dates right back to the city's foundation. It was named after Fatimah az-Zahra, daughter of Muhammad.

al-Adaa, 'Vanquisher of foes'.) The enclave was built in 1069–73 by workers under the command of General Jawhar al-Siqilli during the reign of the Fatimid imam al-Muizz. General Jawhar himself laid the foundation stone for the splendid Mosque of Qahirah (later called al-Azhar Mosque) in 970. In 988, a *madrasa* (religious college) was established in its vicinity; this would become the prestigious al-Azhar University of Cairo.

TRADE AND GOVERNMENT

The Fatimid empire thrived on trade, particularly after an earthquake in the port of Siraf on the Persian Gulf drove traders to divert shipping into the Red Sea, close to Cairo. The empire traded in the Indian Ocean as well as the Mediterranean and established diplomatic and commercial links as far afield as the Chinese Song dynasty.

Although the Fatimids were staunch Shiah Muslims, they generally promoted to the imperial

Below Prominent Fatimids were buried in fine mausoleums in the cemetery at Aswan in southern Egypt from the 10th century onwards.

administration according to ability rather than religious orthodoxy, and Sunni Muslims, Jews and Christians all achieved high office. One major exception to this rule, however, was the eccentric and radically religious Caliph al-Hakim bi-Amrillah, (996–1021), who was violently anti-Christian and responsible for the destruction of the Church of the Holy Sepulchre in Jerusalem.

FATIMID DOWNFALL

During the last decades of the 11th century in Syria, Lebanon and Palestine, the Fatimids suffered a number of losses at the hands of the

Above These thick, sea-washed walls are remains of the 10th-century defensive fortifications at the original Fatimid capital of Mahdia on the Tunisian coast.

Buyid and Seljuk Turks and the European Christian crusaders, including that of Jerusalem to the army of the First Crusade in 1099. Their empire fell away and the Fatimids were reduced to their territory in Egypt.

During the 12th century, Fatimid power continued to wane, and they were finally defeated by Shirkuh, general of the Syrian Zangid leader Nur ad-Din, in 1169.

THE ISMAILIS

The second largest branch of Shiah Islam after the 'Twelvers', the Ismailis take their name from that of Ismail ibn Jafar (*c.*721–55), whom they recognize as the divinely chosen spiritual successor to his father, the sixth Shiah imam, Jafar al-Sadiq (702–65). (The Twelvers regard Musa al-Kazim, Ismail's younger brother, as the seventh imam.) The Ismailis follow a more mystical approach in their religion than do the more conservative Twelvers.

BUYIDS AND SELJUKS

IN THE 10TH CENTURY, THE ABBASID CALIPHS WERE OVERPOWERED BY PREVIOUSLY SUBJECT PEOPLES, AS FIRST THE IRANIAN BUYIDS AND THEN THE SELJUK TURKS TOOK CONTROL IN BAGHDAD.

The collapse of Abbasid power began with a waning of central authority. A key development was the decision of Caliph al-Mutasim (reigned 833–42) to form an imperial bodyguard from non-Muslim Slavs, Turks and Berbers, who had been taken as prisoners of war. These bodyguards, called *ghilman*, were answerable only to the caliph. The soldiers converted to Islam, but they proved a hugely disruptive force as soon as they realized the power that lay in their hands: in the 860s, they revolted a number of times and even killed four caliphs.

The Abbasids' difficulties arose, in part, from the structures of their imperial government. With a vast empire to rule, the caliphs and their viziers, or administrators, allowed regional governors a large degree of independence, and over time, these men became increasingly autonomous and even created their own dynastic power bases.

A profusion of more or less independent dynasties – they paid only nominal respect to Baghdad – began to establish themselves. They included the Samarids of Khorasan and Transoxiana, the Hamdanids of Syria, and the Taharids, Alids and Saffarids of Iran. In North Africa, the Idrisids in the Maghreb and the Tulunids and Ikhshidids of Egypt were already effectively independent of Abbasid control by the time that the Fatimids arose in open opposition to Baghdad after 909.

BUYIDS TAKE CONTROL

The Buyids – Shiah tribesmen from western Iran – built up their power in western Iran and Iraq in the years after c.930 and then effectively took

Above Both Buyids and Seljuks imposed military authority on the lands of the caliphate but left the Abbasid caliphs in religious authority.

power in Baghdad in December 945 under Ali, son of Buya, who declared himself *amir ul-umara* ('Great Commander'). He demanded from the Abbasid caliph al-Mustakfi (reigned 944–6) that the Buyids be allowed to rule their several territories in western Iran and Iraq as independent states. Under the nominal control of the Abbasid caliph, and with the honorific name of Imad ad-Dawlah, Ali shared power with his younger brothers Hasan and Ahmad.

The Buyid state was strongly Shiah Muslim and also had a pronounced Iranian character. Its rulers revived the Sasanian (ancient Persian) royal title of Shahanshah ('King of kings'). They were patrons of the arts, supporting both the pre-eminent Arabic poet of the day, al-Mutanabbi, and the great Persian poet Firdawsi, author of the Iranian national epic *Shahnameh* (*Book of Kings*). Their rule is known for its very fine metalwork marked with Sasanian motifs, and its pottery, some of it decorated with scenes from stories found in Firdawsi's superb epic. The Buyids encouraged

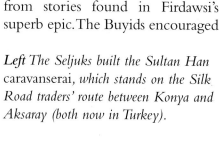

Left The Seljuks built the Sultan Han caravanserai, *which stands on the Silk Road traders' route between Konya and Aksaray (both now in Turkey).*

ومختلفتين أحدهما شابهة الزرفة والأخرى يميل إلى السواد ولحاظهما أنظر إلى فوق والأخرى إلى أسفل وكانت أسنانه دقيقة حادة الرؤوس وكان وجهه كوجه الأسد وكان شجاعاً جريئاً على الحروب منتصراً نصره الله

أبو لكتاب الألكمة الملك الحكيم ملك جيل الدنيا

Left A Seljuk sultan issues decrees from his throne in an illustration from a 13th-century manuscript. The Seljuks were Sunni Muslims.

Byzantine empire at the Battle of Manzikert in 1071; the third Seljuk sultan, Malik Shah I, built on Alp Arslan's success, winning further victories over the Byzantines and defeating the Fatimids in Syria, where he established client principalities in Damascus, Aleppo and Edessa. Meanwhile, in Anatolia, his cousin, Suleyman bin Kutalmish, captured Nicaea (modern Iznik) and Nicomedia (modern Izmit) from the Byzantines in 1075 and established an independent Seljuk state in the area, called the Sultanate of Rum, with a capital at Nicaea.

The Seljuks are celebrated for restoring unity to the Islamic world under the nominal rule of a Sunni caliph. They left a great legacy to the Islamic world, building a large number of *madrasas*, or religious colleges, throughout the empire. They were also responsible for making major improvements to the Great Mosque at Isfahan, Iran, in 1086–8, adding two great brick domed chambers. Persian influence in literature, pottery and other arts continued through the Seljuks' era.

people to observe Shiah festivals and to make pilgrimages to Shiah holy places, such as Karbala and Najaf.

ERUPTION OF THE SELJUKS

In the 11th century, the Buyids were swept away by the Seljuk Turks. The Seljuks were descendants of originally Oghuz tribes from Turkestan, who had migrated southwards and settled in the Persian province of Khorasan and eventually converted to Sunni Islam. They are named after an early tribal leader, Seljuk, who led these migrations. In 1055, one of Seljuk's grandsons, Toghrul Beg,

took power in Baghdad, where he was given the title 'Sultan of the East and the West' by Caliph al-Qaim (reigned 1031–75), himself no more than a figurehead.

Toghrul took control of the imperial armies in battles against the Byzantine empire and the Fatimids of Egypt. His nephew and successor as sultan, Alp Arslan ('Brave Lion'), inflicted a crushing defeat on the armies of the

Right Alaeddin Kekyubad I (reigned 1220–37) rebuilt many towns and fortresses, including the Red Tower at Alanya on the Mediterranean coast.

Wars of the Cross

In 1096-9, European armies fighting under the cross of Christ invaded the Middle East, establishing Christian states there. Muslim powers fought back in the 12th century.

On 27 November 1095, at Clermont in France, Pope Urban II, leader of the Roman Catholic Church, issued a stirring call to arms to the knights (the landed warrior class) of Europe. Urban spoke out in response to a plea from Alexius Comnenus I, ruler of the Christian Byzantine empire of Constantinople, for help in fighting the Sunni Muslim Seljuk Turks. The Seljuks had established the Sultanate of Rum in central Anatolia and were threatening the Byzantine empire.

In his sermon at Clermont, Urban called on the knights of Europe to travel to the aid of their beleagured Christian brethren in Byzantine lands who were suffering terribly at the hands of 'Turks and Arabs'. According to some accounts of the speech, he also called on the knights to liberate Jerusalem, the scene of Christ's crucifixion, personifying the city and telling his listeners, 'from you, she asks for help!'

THE PEOPLE'S CRUSADE

Alexius Comnenus had envisaged an army of mercenaries; Urban directed his call at the princes, great lords and leading knights of Europe. Both were surprised: a great popular movement arose, known to historians as the People's Crusade. A 25,000-strong army, with a core of experienced soldiers supplemented by vast numbers of ill-equipped hangers-on, set out overland in April 1096 and reached Constantinople by 1 August. They crossed the Bosphorus into Anatolia but were crushed by the Seljuk Turks led by teenage Sultan Kilij Arslan I.

The few bedraggled survivors of the People's Crusade were joined by five great princely armies, led by

Above *The crusader knights offered military service to Christ. They each took a vow to reach Jerusalem and pray in the Church of the Holy Sepulchre.*

Count Raymond of Toulouse, Duke Robert of Normandy, Godfrey of Bouillon, Bohemond of Taranto and Hugh of Vermandois, younger brother of King Philip I of France. The united force captured Nicaea, the capital of the Sultanate of Rum in May-June 1097.

Kilij Arslan had not expected a serious assault and had departed to fight a local war; now he hurried back. But in the Battle of Dorylaeum, on 1 July 1097, he and his men were shocked by the power of the western knights' mounted charge and impressed by the strength of their chain-mail armour. They called the knights 'Franj' (for Franks, men of France, since a large part of the army was from France) and 'men of iron', in

Left *Godfrey of Bouillon, one of the leaders of the First Crusade, leads heavily armed and armoured crusaders in battle against Muslim warriors.*

honour of their armour. Ibn al-Qalanisi, chronicler of Damascus, wrote: 'The Franj sliced the Turkish army to pieces. They slaughtered, pillaged and seized many prisoners.'

The Christian army took Antioch in Syria from the Seljuks in June 1098, then defeated a vast relief army under Kerbogha, ruler of Mosul in the Seljuk empire. The following year, they marched on, and captured Jerusalem itself from the Shiah Muslim Fatimids of Egypt on 15–16 July 1099, slaughtering its inhabitants – Muslim and Jew alike. Arab chronicler Ibn al-Athir wrote 'The Franj spent a week slaughtering Muslims…the Jews had come together in their synagogue and the Franj roasted them alive. They also attacked the monuments of saints and the tomb of Abraham himself, may peace be upon him.' The crusaders consolidated the victory when they defeated a 50,000-strong Fatimid relief army led by the vizier (administrator) al-Afdal Shahanshah at the Battle of Ascalon on 12 August 1099.

During the crusade and in its aftermath, the westerners created four Christian territories in the Middle East: the Kingdom of Jerusalem; the County of Edessa, which was based on the ancient city of that name (now Urfa in Turkey); the Principality of Antioch; and the County of Tripoli, which was centred on that coastal city (now in Lebanon). Together these lands were known as Outremer, from the French for 'the Land overseas', so called because they lay on the far shore of the Mediterranean.

Above Capturing Antioch after a long siege in June 1098, the crusaders ran wild. Citizens fled for their lives, some leaping from the battlements in terror.

CRUSADES AND CRUSADERS

The troops who fought in 1096–9 did not call themselves crusaders: they believed they were making a journey, or *peregrinatio* (pilgrimage). Because their clothing was marked with the sign of the cross (*crux*) they became known as *crucesignati* (meaning people marked

Right In this image from an English psalm book of c.1265, Christ is depicted presiding over a map that shows Jerusalem as the centre of the world.

with the cross); they were also sometimes called the *milites Christi* (knights of Christ). The word 'crusade' was not used until the 12th–13th century.

The campaign of 1096–9 was later known as the First Crusade, because it turned out to be the first of a long series of Christian wars against Islam. Traditionally, writers numbered nine main crusades, fought in the Middle East and North Africa between 1096 and 1272, but modern historians argue that the crusades continued for many hundreds of years and were still being fought in wars against the mighty Ottoman empire in the 17th century.

MUSLIMS RESURGENT

The Artuqid Turkish ruler Ilghazi led the Muslim fightback early in the 12th century. He won a crushing victory over a Christian army in 1119 in a clash in the Principality of Antioch known to western chroniclers as the Battle of the Field of Blood. Then, in 1144, Imad ed-Din Zangi, ruler of Mosul and Aleppo, captured Edessa from its Christian rulers. A new crusade was called in 1145 and launched in 1147, but this Second Crusade was a disaster that ended in 1149 in a failed siege of Damascus.

Zengi's son Nur ed-Din took control of Damascus in 1154 and reunited Syria. A pious Sunni Muslim, Nur ad-Din was revered for just rule and commitment to his faith; he built many mosques, *caravanserais* (inns for Muslim travellers) and *madrasas*. He made a series of attempts to conquer the Shiah Muslim Fatimid regime in Egypt, which resulted, eventually, in the emergence of Salah al-Din Yusuf ibn Ayyub (later called Saladin), the nephew of Nur ad-Din's foremost general, as the vizier (administrator) of Egypt in 1169.

RIGHTEOUSNESS OF FAITH: SALADIN

SALADIN, FOUNDER OF THE SUNNI MUSLIM AYYUBID EMPIRE, PROVED A FORMIDABLE FOE TO CHRISTIAN SETTLERS IN THE HOLY LAND, FROM WHOM HE RECAPTURED JERUSALEM IN 1187.

Muslims honour Saladin for his learning, refinement and brilliance as a general – for establishing the great Ayyubid empire, uniting Muslim forces, humbling the crusader armies and recapturing the holy city of Jerusalem. But even those hounded by his armies afforded him a far-from-grudging respect, celebrating him for his military strength, proud bearing and magnanimity in victory. Indeed, in an extraordinary contradiction for 12th-century Christians, who generally believed that being a Christian lord was a key component of chivalry, they praised him as a 'chivalrous infidel'.

LEARNED AND INTELLIGENT

Salah al-Din Yusuf ibn Ayyub, more commonly known as Saladin, meaning 'Righteousness of Faith', was born in Tikrit, Iraq, to a Kurdish family. The Ayubbid dynasty he founded takes its name from that of his father, Najm ad-Din Ayyub.

He was educated in Damascus at the court of Nur ad-Din, where he studied Arabic grammar, rhetoric and Islamic theology. From early in life, Saladin was known as a refined and brilliantly intelligent man, entertaining in conversation, well versed in the traditions of Arab tribes, an expert in the genealogies of the best Arab horses, and a peerless polo player.

He also had a brilliant military upbringing, serving alongside his uncle Shirkuh, Nur ad-Din's leading general, with whom he three times invaded Egypt in the 1160s. On the third campaign in Egypt, Saladin helped his uncle oust the Fatimid vizier Shawar, establishing Shirkuh as vizier and then succeeding him in the position on his death just three months later.

RISE TO POWER

As vizier of Egypt, Saladin was nominally subject to Nur ad-Din, but his scarcely concealed desire was to take power himself and unite Syria and Egypt in a new empire,

Above *Saladin's fame in Christendom meant that he was the subject of European works of art, such as this 16th-century Italian portrait.*

and he became increasingly estranged from his overlord. Nur ad-Din and Saladin were both Sunni Muslims and one initial point of his conflict was Saladin's refusal to oust the Shiah Fatimid caliph in Cairo, al-Adid. Saladin waited until al-Adid died in September 1171, then ended the Fatimid caliphate and declared the authority of al-Mustadi, the Sunni Abbasid caliph in Baghdad.

Below *Saladin and Richard 'Coeur de Lion' were exemplars of chivalry. This (imagined) jousting clash between them is from the English Luttrell Psalter.*

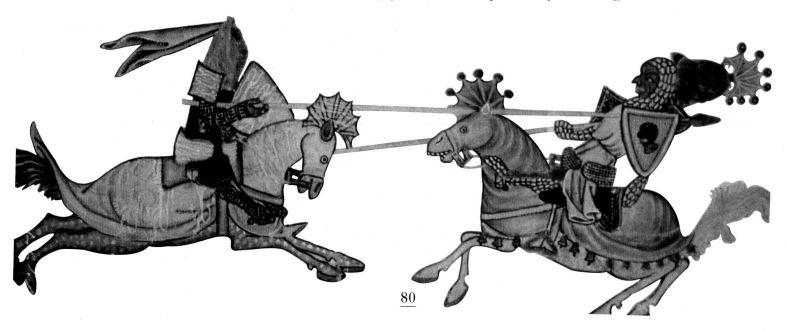

Matters came to a head on Nur ad-Din's death, from fever, in 1174. Saladin marched to Damascus, where he was welcomed by the people. He bolstered his position by marrying Nur ad-Din's widow and publicly setting himself up as leader of a *jihad*, or a 'just war', against the Christian kingdoms of the Middle East. He established his authority in Syria, northern Iraq, the Hejaz and Yemen and led several campaigns against the Christians, culminating in the Battle of the Horns of Hattin in 1187. Here, he captured the most sacred relic of the Christians – reputedly a piece of the cross on which Jesus Christ was crucified – and destroyed the military strength of the kingdom of Jerusalem.

ENCOUNTERS WITH COEUR DE LION

After capturing Jerusalem in 1187, Saladin encountered the Christian armies of the Third Crusade (1189–92) led by Richard I *Coeur de Lion* ('the Lion-hearted') of England and King Philip II of France. In Richard, Saladin met his match, and the encounter of these two great generals was widely celebrated in European chivalric literature, ensuring Saladin undying fame in the West as well as the East.

Although he twice marched towards Jerusalem, Richard did not attempt to retake it, and the Third Crusade ended in a negotiated settlement at the treaty of Jaffa, under which the Christians were guaranteed access to Jerusalem as pilgrims and could keep certain chiefly coastal territories, including the ports of Acre and Jaffa.

Saladin died at Damascus on 4 March 1193, shortly after the end of the crusade, and was buried in a mausoleum beside the Umayyad Mosque in Damascus. A member of Saladin's entourage, Baha ud-Din ibn Shaddad, wrote a biography, in which he praised his master's

character and his unswerving commitment to *jihad*. According to Baha ud-Din, Saladin did not spend a single coin on anything other than *jihad* and pious work and was a fascinating and learned man, who would not hear ill spoken of other Muslims and was always caring for the elderly and for orphans.

Above Saladin lost twice to Richard 'the Lion-hearted' in 1191, at Acre and Arsuf, and at Jaffa in September 1192 agreed a peace treaty.

Below Saladin's tomb in Damascus. Kaiser Wilhelm II of Germany donated a marble sarcophagus, but Saladin's body lies in the wooden one at the rear.

THE BATTLE OF BAGHDAD

THE NOMINAL RULE OF THE ABBASID CALIPHATE IN BAGHDAD ENDED IN 1258, WHEN AN INVADING MONGOL ARMY DESTROYED THE CITY, BUT THE ABBASIDS SURVIVED IN EGYPT UNTIL THE 16TH CENTURY.

The Battle of Baghdad, which took place in January and February 1258 between the city's defenders and a vast besieging Mongol army, was a devastating event for the Muslims of the Middle East. The attack culminated in a week-long orgy of pillaging and looting, from which the beautiful city of Baghdad took centuries to recover. The Mongol army moved on, and with the support of local Christian powers, conquered Aleppo and Damascus in 1260. In just two years, the two

great centres of Islamic power in the Middle East, Baghdad and Damascus, were lost. The principal surviving centre of Muslim rule in the East was Mamluk Egypt.

BACKGROUND TO THE CONFLICT

By the mid-13th century, the Abbasid caliphate in Baghdad had regained a measure of power, although the caliphs were still essentially dependent for their position on the Turkish and Mamluk military power. In 1258,

Above When the Mongols took Baghdad, the last Abbasid caliph, al-Mustasim, was captured and forced to watch the destruction of his city.

Below A 14th-century manuscript painting shows the Mongol army making preparations prior to attacking Baghdad.

the caliph was al-Mustasim Billah (reigned 1242–58). His opponent, Hulagu Khan, who was a grandson of Genghis Khan, had been despatched by his brother Mongke, the Great Kahn, to lead the military destruction of Islamic states in Iran, Iraq and Syria.

Commanded by Hulagu and Chinese general Guo Kan, a vast Mongol army, which reputedly contained a tenth of the fighting force of the entire Mongol empire, approached Baghdad in November 1257 and initially offered a peaceful takeover. Although he had made no preparations for the assault, al-Mustasim was defiant. Evidently unable to appreciate the gravity of the situation, or else deliberately deluding himself, he had reputedly accepted the advice of his vizier that the Mongols would be easily driven away by the simple tactic of ordering the women of Baghdad to throw stones at them.

THE FALL OF BAGHDAD
The Mongol army laid siege to the city on 29 January, and on 10 February, al-Mustasim surrendered. The Mongols swept into the city, pillaging, raping and looting, and hundreds of thousands of people were killed as they tried to flee.

Mosques, libraries, hospitals and palaces were burned down. The invaders did not spare even the Grand Library, repository of much of the wisdom of the ancient world: one account reports that the river Tigris was turned black with the ink from the manuscripts hurled into its waters.

The Mongol army moved on from Baghdad to attack and capture Damascus from its last Ayyubid ruler, An-Nasir Yusuf, in alliance with Christian armies from the Principality of Antioch and Cilician Armenia.

THE RISE OF THE MAMLUKS IN EGYPT
Following Saladin's death in 1193, the Ayyubid empire he had created survived for around 50 years, with Ayyubid lords in power in Syria and Egypt. In 1250, however, the Ayyubid sultan of Egypt, Turanshah, was murdered. His Mamluk slave general, Izz al-Din Aybak, took power and founded the Mamluk sultanate, which ruled Egypt (and later Syria) until 1517.

The Mamluk army won a series of astounding victories, defeating the previously invincible Mongols at the Battle of Ain Jalut in 1260 and afterwards driving the Christians from the Holy Land. To

Above Mamluk general Baybar was ruthless in conflict: it is said he beheaded Christian knights who had surrendered in the belief that they would be spared.

legitimate their rule, Mamluk sultans re-established the Abbasid caliphate, now in Cairo rather than Baghdad. The first caliph under this dispensation was al-Mustansir (reigned 1226–42). With strictly nominal authority, Abbasid caliphs succeeded one another in Cairo until 1517, when, after Ottoman sultan Selim I defeated the Mamluks, the final Abbasid caliph al-Mutawakkil III was taken to Constantinople. On al-Mutawakkil's death, by prior agreement, the title of caliph passed to Selim I.

END OF OUTREMER
After the loss of Jerusalem to Saladin in 1187, the capital of the Christian kingdom of Jerusalem was moved to Acre. In the late 13th century, the crusader states lost a series of their territorial possessions – including Arsuf, Caesarea, Antioch and Tripoli – to the armies of the Egyptian Mamluk sultans. The Christians made a last stand in Acre in 1291, but, despite heroic defensive efforts by the military orders of the Knights Templar and Knights Hospitaller, the city was captured by the Mamluk sultan Khalil on 18 May 1291. Within a few weeks, the final remaining crusader towns of Beirut, Haifa, Tyre and Tortosa were surrendered to the Mamluks. The Christian kingdoms of Outremer were at an end.

Left Astride the city's crumbling walls, French knight Guillaume de Clermont leads the final stand of the kingdom of Jerusalem as Acre falls to the Mamluks.

LIGHT IN THE DARKNESS

THE SCHOLARS OF ISLAMIC BAGHDAD AND CAIRO KEPT THE FLAME
OF SCHOLARSHIP ALIGHT AT A TIME KNOWN AS THE 'CHRISTIAN DARK
AGES', WHEN LEARNING WAS NOT GREATLY VALUED IN EUROPE.

When European cultural life enjoyed a Renaissance, or 'rebirth', in the 14th century, much of its knowledge of classical Greek, Roman and other ancient learning came from translations into Latin of Islamic authors who had written in Arabic at the Abbasid House of Wisdom in Baghdad and at other Islamic establishments of learning.

THE TRANSMISSION OF KNOWLEDGE

The principal works of Islamic mathematician Muhammad ibn Musa al-Khwarizmi (c.780–c.850) were translated into Latin, and introduced Europe to the concept of what came to be known as the Arabic numerals, the concept of zero and the positional value system. Another highly influential mathematical work was the *Book of Measuring Plane and Spherical Figures*, which was translated into Latin by the Lombardian scholar Gerard of Cremona (c.1114–87). Gerard also translated into Latin

Ibn Sina's *Canon of Medicine* and the key writings of Aristotle from Arabic translations made in the 9th century by gifted Mesopotamian linguist Thabit ibn Qurra (known in Latin as Thebit), who worked at the House of Wisdom. The *Canon* of Ibn Sina became a key medical textbook in western universities and was still in use in some places in the mid-17th century.

The translator Hunain ibn Ishaq's work on ophthalmology was likewise translated into Latin and became a key reference book in universities both in Europe and in the East for many hundreds of years. Arab philospher al-Farabi (c.878–c.950) wrote a book called *The Catalogue of Sciences*, in which he noted the following key areas of study, listed in order of importance: languages, logic, mathematics, physics, metaphysics, politics, law and theology. Later translated into Latin, the work became a major influence on the curricula of study that was followed in many early European universities.

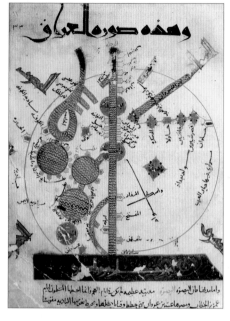

Above Baghdad, great centre of learning, is marked on this page from the 11th-century Book of Routes and Provinces *by Abu Ishaq Ibrahim al-Istakhri.*

AL-ANDALUS

Classical philosophy and learning was also preserved and passed to Western European scholars through the work of Islamic thinkers and authors in al-Andalus, the Muslim territories of the Iberian Peninsula. A key figure was Abu'l-Walid Muhammad ibn Ahmad ibn Rushd (1126–98), known in the West as Averroes. Another great Muslim polymath, he wrote on philosophy, theology, law, medicine, astrology, geography and physics. Among his works were a medical encyclopedia and commentaries on the *Canon* of Ibn Sina and the works of Aristotle and Plato, for which his sources were the Arabic translations made in the 10th century in Iraq.

SCHOLARLY PRACTICES

A number of key scholarly methods were pioneered at the House of Wisdom, many of which are still in

Left East meets West in this painting by Julius Köckert as Harun al-Rashid receives envoys from Charlemagne, King of the Franks, in Baghdad.

reasonings of pagan thinkers from the ancient world. But Islam had a strong commitment to learning from the beginning. Muslims are enjoined to seek knowledge by the Prophet himself: according to hadith literature, Muhammad said 'Seeking knowledge is obligatory for every Muslim' and 'go after learning, even to China'.

Muslim chronicles recount how philosopher Aristotle (384–22BCE) appeared to the Abbasid caliph al-Mamun, founder of the House of Wisdom, in a dream. The Aristotle of the dream was a figure of profound beauty, and when al-Mamun asked him the cause of his beauty, Aristotle replied that it derived from 'the beauty of the laws of reason'. Aristotle also assured al-Mamun that there was no clash between the human reason he exercised and praised and the revelation of God's law to the Prophet Muhammad.

Above *One of the great Islamic scholars of Spain, Averroes wrote commentaries on the works of Aristotle and Plato for Almohad caliph Abu Yaqub Yusuf.*

use today, for example a library catalogue system in which works are categorized by genre or other characteristics. Scholars at the House of Wisdom were also the first to collate various manuscripts of a work in order to make a definitive edition, to add annotations to the margins of works, to write glossaries and to draw up dictionaries of key technical words.

REASON AND REVELATION

The Islamic scholars who saved so much classical learning for future generations had a deep intellectual curiosity and profound commitment to the study of philosophy, mathematics and logic, medicine, mechanics and physics.

At first sight, it might seem curious that adherents of a faith founded on Allah's revelation of truth to the Prophet Muhammad should be interested in the

Right *Ancient Greek philosopher Aristotle was honoured by many Islamic thinkers. He wrote on theatre and politics, on logic, ethics and physics.*

AL-ANDALUS

ISLAMIC RULERS GOVERNED PART OF THE IBERIAN PENINSULA FOR ALMOST 800 YEARS. MUSLIM LANDS, WHICH INCLUDED THE CITIES OF CÓRDOBA, SEVILLE AND GRANADA, WERE KNOWN AS AL-ANDALUS.

The Arab–Berber invasion of the Iberian Peninsula, begun in April 711, was one more in a series of stunning military successes for the armies of Islam. Under first Tariq ibn Ziyad and then Musa bin Nusair, the Islamic troops captured almost the entire peninsula in only five years. The land was initially a province of the Umayyad caliphate under overall rule of Caliph al-Walid I (reigned 705–15) in Damascus. From 717, this province made its capital at Córdoba.

In these early years, the Christian Visigoths, previous rulers of much of the Iberian Peninsula, were driven to the far north, but there they maintained a foothold that proved to be the base for a centuries-long fight back, known to Christian historians as the *Reconquista* ('Reconquest').

EMIRATE OF CÓRDOBA

In Iraq, the Hashimiyyah revolt led to the establishment of the Abassid caliphate by Abu al-Abbas in 750, and Abd al-Rahman, sole surviving member of the Umayyad royal family, fled to what is now southern Spain. In 756, he defeated the ruler of Al-Andalus, Yusuf al-Fihri, in battle, and set himself up as Amir of Córdoba, an independent Umayyad ruler in opposition to the Abbasids in Baghdad.

Abd al-Rahman ruled in Córdoba until *c.*788. He put down a number of revolts, including a major uprising backed by Abbasid caliph al-Mansur (reigned 754–75) and led by al-Ala ibn Mugith, who was the governor of the province of Ifriqiya (Africa). Besieged in Carmona, Abd al-Rahman led a daring breakout, defeating the Abbasid troops. He then sent the heads of al-Ala and his generals, pickled in salt, in a bag all the way to Makkah, where al-Mansur was making the *Hajj*.

Left The Reconquista *was gathering pace by the 9th century. However, the heroic victory of Christian King Ramiro at the Battle of Clavijo (844), shown here, is in fact legendary.*

Above The Arab–Berber army under Tariq ibn Ziyad captures Córdoba in 711. The city would remain in Muslim hands until 1236.*

CALIPHATE OF CÓRDOBA

Abd al-Rahman III (reigned 912–61) was the most powerful of the Umayyad rulers in Spain. In 929, he defied the Abassids and the rising power of the Fatimids in Egypt by declaring himself Caliph of Córdoba, claiming authority over the entire Islamic world. He won several victories against the Christian kings of northern Spain and was hailed as *al-Nasir* ('Defender of the Faith').

During the reign of Abd al-Rahman III and his son al-Hakam II, Al-Andalus was at the height of its glory, but decline set in within 50 years of his death in 961. The caliphate did not recover from civil war among rival claimants to power in 1010, although it limped on until 1031, when it was broken up into smaller *taifa* ('successor') kingdoms.

ALMORAVIDS AND ALMOHADS

These *taifa* states proved vulnerable to the advance of the Christian kingdoms of northern Iberia and

then were swept away by the Almoravids, a Berber power from North Africa. The Almoravid ruler Yusuf ibn Tashfin declared himself as *Amir al-Muslimin* ('Commander of the Muslims') in opposition to the caliph in Baghdad, who was revered as *Amir al-Mumineen* ('Commander of the Faithful').

Power switched hands again in the second half of the 12th century, when Abu Ya'qub Yusuf, leader of another Berber confederation, called the Almohads, took control of Muslim Iberia and established his capital at Seville. Abu Ya'qub Yusuf was known as al-Mansur ('the Victorious') following his great victory over King Alfonso VIII of Castile in the Battle of Alarcos on 19 July 1195. However, his successor, Muhammad III al-Nasir, suffered a devastating defeat in the Battle of Las Navas de Tolosa on 16 July 1212 at the hands of a Christian army. Following this defeat, the power of the Almohads unravelled swiftly, and King Ferdinand III of

Above Islamic rule in Spain ends as Sultan Boabdil surrenders Granada to crusaders led by Ferdinand and Isabella.

Below Ferdinand and Isabella are depicted leading their troops into Granada in 1492 in a wooden panel from an altarpiece of c.1522.

Castile recaptured the great Islamic cities of Córdoba in 1236 and of Seville in 1248.

Thereafter, the sole surviving Islamic territory in Iberia was the Muslim kingdom of Granada in the far south, which was ruled from 1232 by the Nasrid dynasty, or Banu Nazari, as a client state of the local Christian kingdoms.

LAST STAND IN GRANADA

The days of Islamic rule in al-Andalus were numbered, yet remarkably – principally because of infighting among the Christian kingdoms – the end did not come until 1492. Besieged in Granada by a Christian army that was equipped with the latest weaponry and bolstered by crusading troops from many parts of Europe, Nasrid sultan Boabdil surrendered. After making a triumphant entry into Granada, the fervently Catholic King Ferdinand and Queen Isabella set about rebuilding the main mosque as a church.

THE ISLAMIC RENAISSANCE IN SPAIN

THE YEARS OF ISLAMIC RULE IN SPAIN, NOTABLY UNDER THE CALIPHATE OF CÓRDOBA (929–1031), WERE A GLORIOUS AGE OF LEARNING, ARTISTIC ACHIEVEMENT AND RELIGIOUS TOLERATION.

Abd al-Rahman III, the man who proclaimed himself caliph in Córdoba in 929, was a great patron of architecture and reputedly spent one-third of the income from his vast territories on building works. Beginning in 936–40, he built the palace-city of Madinat al-Zahra outside Córdoba. Although little remains of the city today – it was sacked in 1010 during the civil war that brought the caliphate to its knees – it was once vast and magnificent, described in accounts by contemporary travellers as a series of palaces filled with extraordinary treasures.

GLORIES OF CÓRDOBA
Caliph Abd al-Rahman III greatly developed Córdoba itself. Scholars estimate that in the 10th century, the city had a population of up to 500,000 people. He built a new minaret for the superb mosque in Córdoba, begun in 784 by dynastic founder Abd al-Rahman I. This magnificent sacred building, which was originally called the Aljama Mosque in honour of Abd al-Rahman I's wife but is now known as the Mezquita of Córdoba, was built on the site of a 6th-century Christian church. The mosque was further extended by Abd al-Rahman III's son, al-Hakam II, and work on it continued until 987. After Córdoba was captured by King Ferdinand III of Castile in 1236, the building was reconsecrated as a church, and today it is a Christian cathedral, although its celebrated arches, beautiful blue-tiled dome and magnificent *mihrab* can still be seen.

The second caliph in Córdoba, al-Hakam II, made peace with the northern Christian kingdoms

Above Abd al-Rahman III: according to legend, he named his palace city outside Córdoba after his foremost concubine and raised her statue over the main gateway.

and concentrated his efforts and wealth on the improvement of the caliphate's infrastructure and the advancement of learning. Under his rule, irrigation works advanced agriculture, while in cities, the building of markets and widening of streets promoted commerce.

In Córdoba, al-Hakam II created a vast library containing 400,000 books and established a committee of learned men, including both Arab Muslims and Mozarab Christians, to translate works from Latin and Greek into Arabic. (Mozarab Christians were the descendants of Iberian Christians who had lived on under Muslim rule and, while keeping to their own faith, had adopted Arabic customs and language.)

Left The illuminated Mezquita, begun in 784 by Abd al-Rahman I, looks down on the Guadalquivir, the longest river in Andalucía, which connects Córdoba to the Gulf of Cadiz.

Left The beautiful octagonal dome in the Mezquita rises above the mihrab and maqsura enclosure and was built by al-Hakam II.

conquered the city. However, because it was so well established as an international centre of learning under Islam, it remained a meeting place for scholars, where both Arabs and Jews were welcome and Christian scholars, such as Gerard of Cremona (*c.*1114–87), could come to meet them.

RELIGIOUS TOLERATION

This great cultural flowering of Al-Andalus was made possible – as had been the golden age under the Abbasid caliphs in Baghdad – by a remarkable degree of religious toleration. Despite the fact that for almost the entire history of Al-Andalus, the territory's Islamic rulers were engaged in a stop-start war against Christians seeking to win control of the Iberian Peninsula, within Al-Andalus itself, Muslims, Jews and Mozarab Christians were able to live in peace, and together played a major role in the cultural flowering of Islamic Spain.

CENTRES OF LEARNING

The great cities of Al-Andalus, such as Toledo and Córdoba, were the intellectual capitals of Western Europe. Students came from as far away as England and northern France to learn from the Arab, Jewish and Christian scholars who gathered there.

The great Jewish poet, physician, astrologer and scholar, Abraham ben Meir ibn Ezra (1093–1167), was born in Tudela under Muslim rule and lived for many years in Córdoba. Jewish philosopher and physician Moshe ben Maimon, better known by his Greek name Moses Maimonides and generally recognized as the greatest Jewish

philosopher of the Middle Ages, was also a product of this culture, and was born in Córdoba in 1135.

Córdoba was celebrated for its copyists, producers of religious manuscripts, and artisans, who made leatherwork, jewellery, brocades and woven silks that were among the best in the world and were traded both in Western Europe and across the markets of the East.

Toledo was a great centre for scholars, home both to a large community of Mozarab Christians and a sizeable Jewish colony. Conquered for Islam by Tariq ibn Ziyad in 711, it was part of Al-Andalus until 1085, when Christian King Alfonso VI of Leon

Right Jewish philosopher Moses Maimonides rose to prominence in Córdoba, then lived in Morocco and in Egypt, where he was doctor to Saladin.

THE GARDENS OF ALHAMBRA

THE MOORISH GARDENS OF ALHAMBRA EPITOMIZE THE BEAUTY AND SPLENDOUR OF MEDIEVAL SPANISH ISLAM AND ARE AN ATTEMPT TO IMITATE THE GARDENS OF PARADISE DESCRIBED IN THE QURAN.

The Muslim Moors of North Africa were ruled by the dynastic Umayyads when, led by their Berber general, Tariq ibn Ziyad, they invaded Spain in 711. Muslim expansion across the Iberian Peninsula was swift, and a sophisticated culture grew up in the region, which produced a very distinctive architectural style known as the Hispano-Mauresque.

THE FORTIFIED PALACE OF ALHAMBRA

Typical of this style, Alhambra is a fortified palace that extends over some 10.5ha (26 acres). Originally constructed separately from its medina, Granada (from the Arabic, *Gharnata*), it is connected by four large wooden gateways. The stunningly ornate palatial dwellings are decorated throughout with the Arabic calligraphic motif, *wa la ghalib-a-illa Allah* ('and there is no victor but God').

Alhambra (the word means 'red palace') was first built in about 860CE, but major reconstruction and development was undertaken by the Nasrid amir Muhammad bin al-Ahmar in the 13th century. Modifications to the palace and gardens were continued until the ruling Moors of the region, led by Boabdil (Abu Abdullah), conceded defeat by handing the keys to the palace and the city to the Catholic monarchs Ferdinand and Isabella on 2 January 1492.

Surrounded by the towering peaks of the Sierra Nevada, Granada is perhaps the most beautiful of Spain's cities. Its unique topography provides a breathtaking backdrop for the green and fertile plain, around 700m (2,300ft) above sea level, called the *vega*, in which the city is set. Even today, water is still carried from the mountain range along the plains and into the city and

Above In the Generalife Gardens, a sophisticated hydraulic system of canals and fountains constantly supplies water to an abundance of vegetation.

the palace gardens by ancient Moorish-built aqueducts through earthen pipes. The sight and sound of moving water is a particular feature that constantly recurs throughout both the palace and gardens of Alhambra. It is said that the Moors' love of water stemmed from their roots in the arid desert lands of North Africa and that all life stems from water. Hence, wherever they settled in Spain, water was their first necessity.

THE GENERALIFE GARDENS

Adjacent to the walled Alhambra are the splendid Generalife gardens (Arabic, *jannat al-rafiah*, meaning, 'garden of lofty paradise'), which were designed to imitate the Quran's description of the celestial gardens, complete with flowing waters and fruit, flowers and vegetation of every kind. The complex is watered by a sophisticated hydraulic system, directed through a central canal,

Left This view of the Moorish palace of Alhambra is taken from Albaicin, and shows the snow-capped Sierra Nevada Mountains in the background.

acequia, resulting in a series of elegant fountains that adorn the many ornate patios.

Alhambra and Generalife were eventually linked by Jardines Nuevos del Generalife ('the new gardens'), which were completed in about 1930 and include an ornate maze garden.

ALHAMBRA HIGHLIGHTS

The Court of the Lions, which dates from the 14th century, was built originally as a series of private residences connected via a rectangular patio bounded by columns and familiar horseshoe arches. At its centre is a fountain powered by an ingenious ancient hydraulic system that ensures the water feed is kept at a constant level. The dodecagonal bowl is perched on the backs of 12 stone lions, from whose mouths flow jets of water that feed four intersecting channels in the courtyard. The flowing water symbolizes life, and each of the lions represents a sign of the zodiac. Together they allude to both the divine symmetry of the universe and eternal life, as reflected in the carved Arabic couplet by Ibn Zamrak (1333–94), vizier and poet of Alhambra, that decorates the fountain's rim.

Overshadowing the Court of the Myrtles is the highest of Alhambra's many towers, the Torre do Comares, which traditionally housed the Moorish throne. Set on the north side of the courtyard, the tower is accessed by the magnificent *muqarnas* arch, a highly and purely decorative carved Arabesque stucco facia. On the southern side of the patio is a splendid two-storey building that houses an arched balcony overlooking the courtyard. Below, myrtle hedges flank a rectangle pool that is fed by a fountain and bordered by a marble pathway.

Above Each stone lion in the impressive Court of the Lions is meant to represent a sign of the zodiac, while the free-flowing water symbolizes eternal life.

Below The Court of the Myrtles is a stunning symmetrical pooled entrance, flanked by myrtle bushes and marble pathways, to the Torre de Comares.

ISLAM IN ASIA

AFTER MUSLIM AFGHANS ESTABLISHED THE DELHI SULTANATE IN THE LATE 1100S, ISLAM BECAME A MAJOR FORCE BOTH IN THE INDIAN SUBCONTINENT AND BEYOND IN MALAYA, SUMATRA AND JAVA.

In 711, Arab troops under Syrian general Muhammad ibn-Qasim conquered Sindh (in the south-east of modern Pakistan), and many locals converted to Islam. However, there were no further invasions until Muslim Afghan ruler Mahmud of Ghazni launched a series of raids from eastern Afghanistan in the 11th century. Mahmud achieved control over much of north-west India and what is now Pakistan, but he came principally to loot the wealth of temples, and his rule was only periodically enforced.

The first permanent Muslim presence in India was achieved by the troops of another Afghan ruler, Muhammad of Ghor, when they captured Delhi in 1193. Muhammad's general, Qutb-ud-din Aybak, declared himself Sultan of Delhi (reigned 1206–10) and founded the Mamluk dynasty, first of the Delhi sultanate. By c.1235, the Mamluks had taken control of the whole of northern India.

TUGHLUQ POWER

The Delhi sultanate ruled India until 1526. In the 14th century, its sultans achieved power over almost the entire subcontinent under the Tughluq dynasty. Only the native Pandava kings (in the far south) and Rajputs (in the north-west) held them at bay.

However the sultanate's power was smashed in a devastating raid on Delhi unleashed in 1398 by

Right The tomb of the second ruler of the Mughal dynasty, Humayan, in Delhi has Persian-style gardens and was built in 1562–70.

Timur (or Tamerlane), Mongol ruler of Samarkand. Thereafter, the sultanate could not recover its former status, although it survived until 1526, when Ibrahim Lodhi was defeated in battle by Afghan ruler Babur at Panipat, north of Delhi. Babur went on to conquer large parts of India and to found the Mughal dynasty, which created a vast Islamic empire in the region.

MUGHAL GLORIES

The Mughal state founded by Babur suffered early setbacks but was doubled in size and established as an empire by Akbar the Great in 1556–1605. By 1600, his empire covered most of north India as far south as the river Narmada. The empire continued to grow under his sons Jahangir and Shah Jahan, and achieved its greatest extent, covering the entire Indian subcontinent save the southern tip, in c.1700 under Aurangzeb.

Above This scene from the superb Hamzanama, created at the court of Akbar the Great in c.1562–77, shows an escape from prison.

Akbar the Great presided over a magnificent court with a vibrant cultural life. He created a vast library, with books in English, Greek, Persian and Hindi as well as Arabic and including Hindu scriptures and the Bible. He also oversaw the creation of an illustrated manuscript of the *Hamzanama*, an originally Persian romance, telling the adventures of a fictional uncle of

Left Mughal emperor Shah Jahan wrote that the sight of the beautiful Taj Mahal, which he built in memory of his wife in 1631–54, provoked 'sorrowful sighs'.

dynasty (618-907). China's first mosque was built in Guangzhou at this time. A modest number of Arab and Persian merchants settled in China and became dominant in the import/export trade. Then, under the Mongol Yuan dynasty (1274–1368), Muslims settled in China in large numbers, where they served as administrators for the Mongol rulers.

Islam was also a major force elsewhere in Asia. The Sultanate of Malacca in southern Malaysia was an important Islamic regional power at its height in the 15th century, while the Sultanate of Demak on the north coast of Java in Indonesia was founded in the late 15th century. The Masjid Agung Demak, or Great Demak Mosque, in Demak, on Java, was built at this time. The Sultanate of Aceh was another important Islamic regional power, with its base in Sumatra, Indonesia, in the 16th and 17th centuries. Its capital was Kutaraja (modern Banda Aceh).

the Prophet Muhammad, Amir Hamza. With 1,400 canvas miniature illustrations, this manuscript is one of the masterpieces of Islamic art.

Akbar rebuilt the celebrated red fort of Agra and constructed nearby the city of Fatehpur Sikri as his capital. His grandson, Shah Jahan, built the most celebrated of all Mughal monuments, the Taj Mahal in Agra (1632–54), to house the tomb of his favoured wife, Mumtaz Mahal. He also built the magnificent Jama Masjid, one of India's most famous mosques, in Delhi in 1656.

Ultimately, the Mughal empire declined in the face of a rival Hindu confederation, the Maratha empire, and the growing power of

the British East India Company in the region. Nevertheless, it survived in various forms until 1857, when the last emperor, Bahadur Shah II (reigned 1838–57), was exiled to Rangoon in Burma by the British.

BEYOND INDIA

Islam was introduced to China in 651, within 20 years of the death of the Prophet Muhammad, when the latter's maternal uncle Saad ibn Abi Waqqas was sent as an envoy to Gaozong, an emperor of the Tang

Right The Kampung Kling Mosque in Malacca, Malaysia, was built in 1748, using the traditional square design of the earliest mosques.

BEYOND THE SAHARA

ISLAM WAS ESTABLISHED IN NORTHERN AFRICA IN THE EARLY DAYS OF THE FAITH, AND SPREAD SOUTHWARD ALONG TRADE ROUTES. MAJOR AFRICAN ISLAMIC EMPIRES INCLUDED THE MALI AND SONGHAI.

Arab Muslims had invaded Egypt in 639 during the reign of Caliph Umar (634–44), capturing Alexandria in 643 and establishing Sunni Islam there. The faith had spread along the north of the continent as far as Morocco by 711, when general Tariq ibn Ziyad carried it across the Straits of Gibraltar into the Iberian Peninsula. Right from these early days, Arab trade caravans bore the Islamic faith along with their goods as they made their way across the Sahara into sub-Saharan Africa. At around the same time, Arab merchants sailed down Africa's east coast and established Islamic trading ports there.

GHANA EMPIRE

In western Sudan, between the upper Senegal and Niger rivers, an empire called the Ghana, or Wagadou ('Land of Herding'), grew very rich on trade in gold, ivory and slaves from the 8th century onward. The empire was ruled by a Muslim elite and was at its height in c.1050. It is said to have comprised two linked cities, one inhabited by Muslims, containing at least 12 mosques and the royal palace, and a second around 10km (6 miles) away for the pagan natives.

The capital was sacked by the Muslim Almoravids of Morocco in 1076. Then, in the 13th century, the lands of the Ghana empire were

Above *The 14th-century Djinguereber Mosque in Timbuktu, Mali, is made entirely from mud, straw and wood. It has space for 2,000 people to pray.*

Below *The Great Mosque of Djenné in Mali is the world's largest mud-brick building. The mosque was built in 1907 on foundations dating from the 1200s.*

subsumed by a new power, the kingdom of Mali, established by a Muslim ruler named Sundiata Keita in *c*.1240.

MALI EMPIRE

Beginning from a small state on the upper Niger River, Sundiata Keita conquered many neighbouring kingdoms and created a sizeable state that acquired enormous wealth from controlling trade throughout West Africa and even beyond, to Asia and Europe.

Sundiata Keita's great-nephew Mansu Musa (reigned 1312–37) conquered the cities of Timbuktu and Gao and established Mali as a great empire. A celebrated account survives of the *Hajj* pilgrimage to Makkah that Mansu Musa made in 1324: when passing through Cairo he gave so many gifts of gold that it created inflation across Egypt.

Mansu Musa brought the Arabian architect and poet Abu Es Haq Es Saheli back from Makkah and, under his influence, built religious schools and a university in Timbuktu. In 1327, Es Saheli built the Djinguereber Mosque in Timbuktu. Along with the mosques of Sankoré and Sidi Yahya, it formed part of the university, which itself played a major role in the spread of Islam in Africa.

SONGHAI EMPIRE

The Mali empire thrived until the mid-15th century, when it was eclipsed by another West African Muslim state, the kingdom of the Songhai. Under Ali the Great (reigned 1465–92) and Askia Muhammad I (reigned 1492–1528), the Songhai created a trading empire to rival that of the Mali. Its leaders were just as devout as their predecessors and fostered the growth of learning in Timbuktu. Under Askia Muhammad's rule, scholars made translations of ancient Greek philosophers Plato

Above The Sankoré Mosque in Timbuktu was built in the 15th century. Its courtyard is said to have been built to match the dimensions of the Kaabah.

and Aristotle, Abd al-Rahman al-Sadi compiled the great African history *Tarikh al-Sudan* ('Chronicles of Africa') and the great legal scholar Ahmed Baba was at work.

The Songhai empire survived until 1591, when it was crushed by a Moroccan invasion, and afterward, minor kingdoms attempted without success to fill the gap left by the Mali and Songhai.

In West-central Africa, the Muslim Kanem–Borno empire to the north and west of Lake Chad was at its height in the 16th century. Under Mai Idris Alooma (reigned 1571–1603), the imperial army used firearms purchased from the Ottoman Turks to take control of trade with Egypt and Libya. The empire faded after *c*.1650, but survived in name until 1846, when it was eclipsed by another regional power, the Adai empire.

EAST AFRICAN CITY-STATES

In East Africa, Muslim Arab traders settled along the coast from *c*.900 and created city-states such as Mogadishu (today the capital of Somalia), Mombasa and Malindi

(both now in Kenya), and Kilwa Kisiwani (an island port off the coast of modern Tanzania). Islam spread inland from these port cities, and in East Africa became better established among the people than in West Africa, where the faith remained largely the preserve of the governing elite for many years.

Above The atmospheric prayer hall of the Great Mosque on the island of Kilwa Kisiwani is still standing. The mosque was founded in the 900s and rebuilt in the 11th and 12th centuries.

Land of the Shahs

From 1502 until 1722, the Shiah Muslim Safavids ruled a great Islamic empire in Persia. With its magnificent capital at Isfahan, it was at its height under Shah Abbas I in the 1620s.

The rise of the Safavids was a major development in the history of Islam: theirs was the first large and enduring Shiah Muslim state since the Fatimids. They established the Shiah branch of the faith as the dominant form of Islam in the Caucasus and much of western Asia, especially Iran.

The Safavids were descended from Turkish adherents of the mystical branch of Sunni Islam named Sufism who had converted to Shiah Islam in the 15th century. They came to believe that they were called to spread Shiah Islam through military conquest.

THE 'HIDDEN IMAM'

At the start of the 16th century, a young Safavid leader, Ismail, claimed to be a representative of the 'Hidden Imam', the 12th Shiah imam Muhammad al-Mahdi. According to Shiah tradition, after the 11th Shiah imam, Hassan al-Askari, was killed in 874, his successor was hidden by Allah through a process called *ghaybah* (occultation) in order to

Above The greatest of Safavid rulers, Abbas I, restored the dynasty's power, winning a string of military victories.

Below The beautiful Imam Mosque in Isfahan, central Iran, was built by Abbas I in 1611–29. The minarets flanking the main gateway are 42m (137ft) high.

save his life. Shiah Muslims claim that he remains miraculously alive and will one day return to guide the faithful. In this guise, Ismail gained a

ISFAHAN
In central Iran, Abbas I built a new capital alongside the ancient city of the Sasanians. At its peak, Isfahan was one of the wonders of the world: it had no fewer than 163 mosques, more than 250 public baths and around 1,800 shops. The city was also rich in beautiful parks, large squares, libraries and religious schools. The mosques included the stunning Shah Mosque, begun in 1611, with its elegant calligraphic inscriptions and mosaic tiling; it is often described as one of the world's greatest examples of mosque architecture.

devoted following, despite the fact that he was only 12 years old, and led troops to capture the kingdom of Shirvan (now part of Azerbaijan) and the city of Tabriz. He declared himself Shah of Azerbaijan, and proclaimed the Shiah faith to be the official religion in his lands.

Ismail then announced that he was the Hidden Imam himself, returned to rule and to lead the faithful. Within ten years, Ismail had taken control of all of Iran, and captured Baghdad and Mosul in Iraq. In the north-east, he defeated and drove back the Uzbeks.

OTTOMANS HIT BACK

The Safavids now posed a threat to the might of the Ottoman empire: Ismail's Shiah missionaries converted many Turkmen tribes in Ottoman territories in Anatolia and Iraq. Ottoman sultan Selim I marched into Iran and defeated Ismail in the Battle of Chaldiran in 1514. Though wounded and nearly captured, Ismail survived, but his position was seriously weakened, for he lost his aura of invincibility.

The Safavid empire was crucially undermined during the reigns of the next three shahs, Tahmasp I

Above In the elegant Ali Ghapu palace on Nagsh-i Jahan Square, Isfahan, Abbas I received ambassadors and dignitaries from around the world.

(1524–76), Ismail II (1576–77) and Muhammad Khudabanda (1578–88), which saw civil war and internal power struggles as well as repeated attacks by the Ottomans and the Uzbeks, but the dynasty rose to the height of its power and glory under Abbas I (1587–1629).

CONQUESTS OF ABBAS I

The Safavids had lost Baghdad and much of Iraq to the Ottomans, and Abbas recognized that his army needed updating. He negotiated a peace treaty with the Ottomans, and, with the help of two Englishmen, Anthony and Robert Shirley, set about reorganizing the military on the European model of a standing army fully equipped with artillery and muskets.

The new force recaptured Herat and Mashhad from the Uzbeks, and then Baghdad, the eastern part of Iraq and the provinces in the Caucasus from the Ottomans. He regained control of the port of Hormuz on the Persian Gulf from

Above A superb edition of Iran's national epic, the 11th-century Shahnahmeh by Firdawsi, was made for Shah Tahmasp I.

the English and developed lucrative trading links with the Dutch and English East India companies.

Following the death of Abbas I in 1629, the Safavid empire endured for around 100 years, but this was generally a period of slow decline, enlivened only by the reign of Abbas II (1642–66). The Safavid dynasty ended in 1760, when Karim Khan Zand founded the Zand dynasty.

RISE OF THE OTTOMANS

FROM MODEST BEGINNINGS IN THE 14TH CENTURY, TURKISH TRIBES IN ANATOLIA CREATED THE GREATEST ISLAMIC EMPIRE IN HISTORY, THE OTTOMAN EMPIRE, WHICH LASTED FOR MORE THAN 600 YEARS.

The Ottoman dynastic founder, Osman, was a descendant of the nomadic Kayi tribe, originally from Turkestan in central Asia, who settled in Anatolia in the 12th century and established a base in Söğüt, north-western Anatolia (now in Turkey) in the late 13th century. According to one legend, Osman's father, Ertugrul, was leading a force of around 400 horsemen across the region when he chanced upon a battle: he joined in support of the losing side and turned the conflict in their favour, and as a reward the Seljuk sultan he had helped gave him land on which to settle.

Osman (reigned 1258–1324) expanded the territory, and under his son Orhan (reigned 1324–60), the Ottomans became a major regional power. Among other cities, Orhan captured Bursa (in 1326), which he made into a great centre for Islam. He also helped John Kantakouzenos take the Byzantine imperial throne from his rival John V Palaeologus and was rewarded with the hand of the emperor's daughter, Theodora, in marriage and the right to raid with impunity in Thrace (a historical region of south-eastern Europe).

THE FIRST SULTAN

Orhan's son Murad I (reigned 1359–89) expanded Ottoman power in Thrace. He was the first Ottoman ruler to adopt the title sultan, in 1383. He founded a number of enduring Ottoman institutions, including the elite military corps of the Janissaries, and the offices of *beylerbeyi* (military commander-in-chief) and grand vizier (principal government minister).

Within the rapidly expanding empire, the Ottomans allowed local rulers to remain in nominal control so long as they paid annual tribute and provided troops for the imperial army. Many Christian rulers in south-east Europe, and even the Byzantine emperor John V, became client rulers under Ottoman overlordship.

Above Osman's name means 'breaker of bones' and Ottoman writers saw in this a prophecy of the military strength of the empire he founded.

THE THUNDERBOLT

Murad's son Bayezid I (reigned 1389–1402) was known as *Yildirim* ('Thunderbolt') because of the speed of his military campaigns. He imposed Ottoman authority in Anatolia, then occupied Bulgaria, and, though the Europeans launched a crusade against him, he defeated them in the Battle of Nicopolis in 1396. Bayezid maintained a siege of Constantinople for no less than seven years (1391–98), but he met his match in the Mongol leader Timur (or Tamerlane), who invaded Anatolia and defeated the Ottomans at the Battle of Ankara in 1402. Bayezid died in captivity the following year.

Timur did not press home his advantage: his interest lay in conquering India, so he restored power in Anatolia to Turkmen princes and allowed control of the Ottoman empire to pass to Bayezid's sons.

Left The Great Mosque in Bursa was built by Sultan Bayezid I to celebrate victory over European crusaders at Nicopolis in 1396.

Above In preparation for his attack on Constantinople, Mehmed II built a great fortress, Rumeli Hisar, to control shipping in the Bosphorus.

In 1421, Bayezid's grandson, Murad II, re-established Ottoman power over Turkmen principalities of Anatolia, forcing the Byzantine emperor to become his vassal once again. He besieged Constantinople in 1422–3, and withdrew only on payment of vast tribute.

CONQUEST

Murad's son Mehmed II laid siege to Constantinople with a vast army backed up by a fleet of 280 ships. After several weeks, in May 1453, the city fell in a matter of hours.

The conquest of Constantinople was a momentous day in the history of Islam: one of the most famous cities in the world, founded as a Greek trading colony, then re-established by Constantine as a new capital for the Roman empire and a centre of the Christian faith, was now the capital of an Islamic empire. The rapid Ottoman expansion that delivered this prize had been made possible by military might but was also powerfully driven by trade, which accrued wealth as well as necessary goods, and by religion, in particular by the activities of Sufi *tariqahs* (fraternities). The Ottomans renamed the city Istanbul and converted the Hagia Sophia and other churches into mosques.

THE CRESCENT MOON

The crescent moon and single star is an international symbol of the Islamic faith, and appears on the flags of several Muslim countries including Pakistan and Turkey. According to legend, its origin lies in a dream of Ottoman founder Osman I, in which he saw a crescent moon arching from one side of the world to the other. The Ottomans later saw in this a prophecy of their greatness.

In fact, the crescent moon and star was an ancient religious symbol in central Asia, also associated with the Greek goddess Diana. It became the symbol of the Greek colony of Byzantium, which was later transformed into the great city of Constantinople. When the Ottomans conquered Constantinople in 1453, they adopted the symbol as their own.

Left Ottoman triumph in Constantinople is depicted as the slaughter of haloed Christians in this 16th-century fresco from a Romanian monastery.

SULEYMAN THE MAGNIFICENT

THE OTTOMAN EMPIRE WAS AT ITS HEIGHT DURING THE REIGN OF SULTAN SULEYMAN 'THE MAGNIFICENT' (1520–66), WHO RULED OVER VAST TERRITORIES AND 115 MILLION PEOPLE.

The conquest of Constantinople in 1453 by Sultan Mehmed II (reigned 1451–81) was the foundation for a period of continuous Ottoman territorial expansion that brought the empire to the peak of its power and influence. Mehmed's numerous victories won him the byname of 'the Conqueror'. He captured Serbia, Bosnia, Albania and most of the territories around the Black Sea, and re-established Ottoman control in Anatolia.

His successor Bayezid II (1481–1512) consolidated these gains, with victories over Poland, Hungary and Venice. Selim I led campaigns against the Safavids of Iran and the Mamluks of Egypt, and by the end of his reign in 1520 all the territories of the old Islamic

Above Suleyman the Magnificent receives Prince Sigismund of Transylvania at his glittering court in Istanbul in this 16th-century manuscript illustration.

caliphate – aside from Iran and Mesopotamia – were now in Ottoman hands.

Suleyman I (reigned 1520–66) went even further, capturing the territory of modern Hungary from the Hapsburgs and even besieging Vienna in 1529. In the East, he won several victories over the Safavids and captured Baghdad in 1535. He extended Ottoman power all the way through Mesopotamia to the Persian Gulf, while in North Africa, he annexed Tripoli. His navy, which was commanded by the widely feared Barbarossa, dominated the eastern Mediterranean.

'THE MAGNIFICENT'
Suleyman was regarded by his contemporaries – both Christian and Muslim – as the world's

Left At the time it was built, in 1550–7, the Suleymaniye Mosque's dome was, at 53m (174ft) high, the tallest dome in the Ottoman empire.

pre-eminent ruler. Abroad, he was known as 'the Magnificent' because of the vastness of his domain and the splendour of his court. In his era, the Ottoman empire matched the Byzantine or east Roman empire in its pomp, and the extent of its territories almost exactly matched that of the eastern Roman empire under Emperor Justinian I the Great 1,000 years earlier.

Suleyman called himself 'ruler of the lands of Caesar and of Alexander the Great' and 'master of the world'. But although he promoted his own greatness, he remained devout and subject to Allah. His inscriptions also declared him to be a 'slave of Allah' and 'deputy of Allah on earth, obeying the commands of the Quran and enforcing them around the world'.

'THE LAWGIVER'

By his own people, Suleyman was called *Kanuni* ('the Lawgiver'). He revised and developed the *Kanun Nameh*, a code of imperial law first collected and promulgated by Mehmed II 'the Conqueror'. The Kanun code of law was independent of the Shariah law derived from the Quran. By tradition, Shariah law

Above Barbarossa ('Red Beard') was the scourge of western fleets in the Mediterranean for 40-odd years, first as a pirate, then as an Ottoman admiral.

Above The splendid Topkapi Palace in Istanbul was home to an imperial entourage of 4,000 people at its peak.

was applied in all Islamic states; the Ottoman Kanun law derived from the Turkish tradition, under which the law of the emperor was sacred. The code issued by Suleyman principally covered criminal law, taxation and landholding.

A number of his laws safeguarded the rights of Jews and of the *rayas* ('protected'), Christians living in their own communities within the empire. In the Ottoman empire, religious groups were permitted to set up their own communities called millets, in which they kept their own religious and other customs under their own leaders and the Sultan's protection.

In an inscription in the Suleymaniye Mosque, Suleyman was lauded as *Nashiru Kawanin al-Sultaniyye* ('Spreader of Sultanic laws'). He is traditionally viewed as the successor to the biblical King Solomon, who is praised in the Quran as the embodiment of justice. Muslims revere him as the perfect Islamic ruler.

POET AND PATRON

Suleyman was a highly cultured man. Writing under the pen name Muhibbi, he was an excellent poet, his work celebrated by Muslims as some of the finest in Islamic history. He was also a skilled goldsmith. Above all, he was a discerning and immensely generous patron of the arts. From the Topkapi Palace in Istanbul, he funded and presided over artistic societies named *Ehl-i Hiref* ('Groups of the Talented') that were a magnet for the empire's finest artists, artisans and craftsmen. During his reign, Istanbul became the artistic centre of the Islamic world, where craftsmen developed distinctively Ottoman styles.

Suleyman also embarked upon a vast building programme in Istanbul and the cities of the empire, raising bridges, palaces and mosques in great numbers. He was patron to Mimar Sinan, perhaps the greatest architect in Islam, whom he commissioned to build his first masterpiece, the beautiful Sehzade Mosque (1543–8) to honour his favourite son, Mehmed. Sinan also built the majestic Suleymaniye Mosque in Istanbul (1550–7).

FROM WORLD POWER TO 'SICK MAN OF EUROPE'

FOLLOWING THE DEATH OF SULEYMAN I IN 1566, THE OTTOMAN EMPIRE BEGAN A LONG, VERY SLOW DECLINE THAT MADE IT, IN THE WORDS OF TSAR NICHOLAS I OF RUSSIA, THE 'SICK MAN OF EUROPE'.

For more than 100 years following Suleyman's death and the accession of Sultan Selim II in 1566, the Ottomans continued to increase their empire. However, the roots of the ultimate Ottoman decline have been traced by historians to this period.

The imperial economy was badly hit when the Dutch and British developed a sea route to Asia to replace the overland one through Ottoman lands. The economy was further damaged by inflation, partly caused by the influx of Spanish silver from 'New World' colonies in South America. A succession of weak sultans allowed decay of the previously strong administrative and military structures. The Ottoman navy was defeated by a Holy League formed by Pope Pius V and lost control of the Mediterranean. Then, during the course of the 17th

Above Under Sultan Mahmud II, the Ottoman empire began to break up as Greece won independence and Algeria was taken by the French.

century, ever more powerful nation states emerged in Europe and made alliances to curb Ottoman power.

STAGNATION AND REORDERING

Matters worsened in the 18th and early 19th centuries. The empire stagnated; many successive sultans were unsuccessful in their attempts to introduce reforms; the Ottomans failed to keep up with European developments in science, technology and military tactics. Central power waned drastically, and many areas of the empire, such as Algeria and Egypt, became effectively independent.

During the Tanzimet period (so-called from the Arabic word for 'reordering') from 1839 until 1876, Sultans Abdulmecid I and Abdulaziz

Left In the revolution of 1908–9, Young Turks fought and defeated soldiers loyal to the sultan in the streets of Istanbul.

made reforms that included the introduction of factories, an education system and a modernized army. In 1856, Abdulmecid issued the *Hatt-i Humayun* ('Imperial Reform Announcement'), which guaranteed equality for all Ottoman subjects, regardless of religious faith. Yet Ottoman power and prestige continued to fade.

LOSS OF TERRITORIES

Throughout the 19th and early 20th centuries, the Ottoman empire shrank. Nationalism was on the rise, and many former imperial territories won independence: Greece in 1829, then Montenegro, Romania and Serbia in 1878. In North Africa, Egypt was occupied by the British in 1882, while Algeria and Tunisia were colonized by the French in 1830 and 1881 respectively. During the Balkan Wars (1912–13), the empire lost all its Balkan territories except Thrace and the city of Edirne.

CONSTITUTIONAL REFORM

In 1876, Western-educated reformers named the Young Ottomans led a military coup to try to establish a constitutional monarchy. This resulted in the empire's first constitution, the *Kanun-I Esasi* ('Basic Law'), issued by Sultan Abdulhamid II in 1876. But just two years later, the sultan suspended the parliament and once again assumed absolute rule. In 1908, the revolution of the Young Turks (a coalition of reformers including secularists and nationalists) forced Abdulhamid II to restore the parliament he had suspended and reinstate the 1876 constitution.

SECULAR REPUBLIC

Following defeat in World War I, the empire was partitioned under the Treaty of Sèvres (signed in August 1920), Istanbul was occupied by

Above Mehmed Vahideddin VI was the 36th and last of the Ottoman sultans. Deposed in 1922, he died in exile in 1926 in Sanremo, Italy.

British and French troops, and a Turkish national movement mobilized to fight the Turkish War of Independence (1919–23). Mustafa Kemal led the nationalist army to victory. The Ottoman sultanate was abolished on 1 November 1922 and the last reigning sultan, Mehmed VI (reigned 1918–22) left Istanbul on 17 November. The Republic of Turkey was declared on 29 October 1923, with Mustafa Kemal as its president.

Mustafa Kemal introduced a series of secular reforms. In 1924, he abolished the Islamic caliphate and Shariah law and closed Islamic religious schools. The following year, he outlawed the wearing of

Right The memory of revolutionary leader Mustafa Kemal, the 'Father of the Turks', is celebrated in this equestrian statue in Ankara.

the fez, on the grounds that it was a symbol of the Ottoman regime, and took moves to dissuade women from wearing the veil and to encourage all to wear Western clothing. In 1926, he introduced new legal codes, under which polygamy was abolished, and religious weddings were replaced with a compulsory civil service. In 1928, he introduced a new Turkish alphabet (based on the Latin one) to replace Arabic script, and declared the state to be secular, removing the constitutional clause under which Islam was named as the official state religion. In 1933, a new law required the call to prayer and the reading of the Quran to be in Turkish rather than in Arabic.

In 1934, another law required all Turks to take Western-style surnames and the Turkish Grand National Assembly awarded Mustafa Kemal the surname Ataturk – 'Father of the Turks'.

REPUBLICS AND KINGDOMS

THE PRINCIPAL SELF-DECLARED ISLAMIC STATES ESTABLISHED IN THE 20TH CENTURY – INCLUDING PAKISTAN, SAUDI ARABIA, SUDAN, IRAN AND MOROCCO – CHOSE DIFFERENT MODELS OF GOVERNMENT.

Some Islamic states were founded as monarchies. The kingdom of Saudi Arabia (al-Mamlakah al Arabiyah as Saudiyyah), for example, is an absolute monarchy, established as a unified kingdom in 1932. The kingdom of Morocco (al-Mamlakah al Maghribiyah), which gained independence from France in 1956, is a constitutional monarchy, with a hereditary crown and a two-house parliament under a constitution agreed in 1972 and amended in 1992 and 1996.

Other states declared themselves 'Islamic republics', but this title can mean very different things. The Islamic Republic of Pakistan (Jamhuryat Islami Pakistan) was the first country to use the title, in its constitution of 1956. In this case, 'Islamic republic' was primarily a statement of religious and cultural identity: the constitution was a largely secular one, and Pakistan had no state religion until a revised

constitution, naming Islam as the state religion, was adopted in 1973. Iran was a monarchy until the Iranian revolution of 1979, which resulted in it being declared the Islamic Republic of Iran (Jomhuri-ye Eslami-ye Iran). The form of government in Iran is termed a 'theocratic republic': its official religion is Shiah Islam and the chief of state or supreme leader is a Shiah imam. Its legal system is based on Shariah law.

A CALIPHATE?

Some Muslims today call for the abolition of Islamic monarchies on the grounds that they are too authoritarian. Some believe that the very notion of a republic – whether secular or Islamic – is necessarily contrary to the proper form of government as established by the Quran and Islamic tradition of the sunnah. Government, according to this theory, should be by a caliph as religious leader and successor of the Prophet, basing governance on Shariah law and Islamic religious tradition. Some call for the re-establishment of an international caliphate uniting disparate Islamic countries under religious rule. Sunni Muslims hold that when a state is ruled according to Shariah law, then this is, in fact, caliphate government in practice, whether or not the leader uses the title 'caliph'.

HISTORICAL PERSPECTIVE

The great Islamic empires were ruled by caliphs: the first four, or Rashidun, caliphs, the Umayyads, the Abbasids, and the Ottomans. The

Above The 12th-century Hassan Tower stands amid the ruins of an unfinished mosque in Rabat, the capital of the kingdom of Morocco.

Ottomans initially took the title *bey* (a Turkish tribal name for a ruler), then sultan and only began to use the title caliph from the reign of Selim I (reigned 1512–20) onward. When Selim defeated the Mamluk Sultanate in Egypt in 1517, the final Abbasid caliph, al-Mutawakkil III, was carried off to Istanbul; al-Mutawakkil was permitted to rule

Above Zulfikar Ali Bhutto was President of Pakistan in 1973 when a new constitution declared Islam to be the state religion of the country.

Above The Republic of Sudan, in north-eastern Africa, has been mostly ruled by military Islamic governments since its independence from Britain in 1956.

RELIGION AND SECULARISM IN TURKEY

The country created from the heartland of the great Ottoman empire, the Republic of Turkey (*Turkiye Cumhuriyeti*) has a secular constitution. There is no state religion, although Islam is a dominant force. Ninety-nine per cent of the Turkish population is Muslim, 75 per cent of these being Sunni Muslims, and around 20 per cent Alevi Muslims. (Alevis have links both to Shiah Islam and to Sufism.)

Individuals in Turkey have freedom of religion guaranteed in the constitution. Religious communities are not permitted to establish faith schools or form religious parties and no political party can claim that it represents a particular form of religion.

until his death, whereupon the title of caliph was attached to the Ottoman sultanate. Following the removal of the last Ottoman sultan Mehmed VI Vahideddin (reigned 1918–22) and the declaration of the Republic of Turkey, the first President of the Turkish Republic Mustafa Kemal abolished the caliphate as an institution in 1924.

SELF-PROCLAIMED CALIPHS

In the wake of Ataturk's decree, various individuals tried to proclaim themselves caliph. Hussein bin Ali, Sharif of Makkah and self-appointed King of the Hijaz, declared himself caliph of all Muslims just two days after Ataturk's statement. However, few paid attention to his claim and he was in any case forced to abdicate later the same year by Ibn Saud, subsequently the first King of Saudi Arabia. Mehmed VI Vahideddin, the deposed Ottoman sultan, himself attempted to declare himself caliph in the Hijaz but this also came to nothing.

The kings of Morocco and Mullah Muhammad Omar, leader of the Taliban regime of Afghanistan in the 1990s, later gave themselves the title of *amir al-mumineen* ('Commander of the Faithful') that was associated with caliphs from the 7th century onward. However, none of them claimed international jurisdiction over all Muslims, choosing to limit their power to those within their borders.

Below Built in 1971, the Shahyad Tower ('Memorial of Kings') in Tehran, Iran, was renamed Azadi ('Freedom') Tower in the 1979 Iranian Revolution.

THE MUWAHIDDUN MOVEMENT

THE REFORMIST MOVEMENT IN ISLAM THAT STRESSES *TAWHID* (THE UNITY AND UNIQUENESS OF ALLAH), WAHHABISM HAS BEEN A NOTABLE FORCE IN THE MUSLIM WORLD SINCE THE 18TH CENTURY.

Followers of scholar and religious reformer Muhammad ibn Abd al-Wahhab (1703–92) were given the name Wahhabi (*Wahhabiyyah*) by their opponents. For this reason, they reject it, preferring to be known as 'unitarians' (Muwahiddun) because of their emphasis on the oneness of Allah. This is the predominant form of Islam in Saudi Arabia and Qatar.

MUWAHIDDUN BELIEF

Muwahiddun believe that Islam should be practised as it was in the first three generations after the death of the Prophet Muhammad in 632, as revealed in the Quran and the hadith, and they reject later innovations (bidha). They denounce traditions such as venerating Islamic 'saints' and visiting the tombs of former religious leaders as idolatry, and declaim against the practice of *Tawakkul* ('drawing near to Allah'), which, in the religious practice of some Sufi, other Sunni and Twelver Shiah Muslims, involves praying to Allah through intercession to a prophet, imam or scholar.

Muwahiddun theology is largely based on the teachings of medieval Sunni Islamic scholar Taqi ad-Din Ahmad ibn Taymiyyah (1263–1328), who called for a return in Islam to following its sources in the Quran and sunnah. Its jurisprudence

Above The defenders of the first Saudi state fought bravely but were overcome by an army led by Muhammad Ali Pasha, Viceroy of Egypt, in 1818.

Below At al-Diriya (today on the outskirts of Riyadh), Muhammad ibn Saud and Ibn Abd al-Wahhab became allies. The town was capital of the first Saudi state in 1744–1818.

is derived from the school of Ahmad ibn Hanbal (780–855), Persian Sunni Muslim scholar and theologian. Muwahiddun hold that a Muslim state should be governed solely according to Shariah Islamic law.

The Muwahiddun movement is identified by some as a form of the Sunni Islamic tradition of Salafiyyism, which draws on the actions and speeches of the Salaf (ancestors in the era of the Prophet Muhammad). The word *salaf* goes back at least until 1166, when Abu Sa'd Abd al-Kareem al-Samani wrote of '*al-Salaf*' as exemplars for Muslims in his book *Al-Ansab*. Some trace the phrase to the Prophet himself, who, according to hadith, said 'I am the best *salaf* for you'. For all the possible connections to Salafiyyism, however, Abd al-Wahhab himself condemned over-reliance on scholarly tradition and stressed the capacity of the individual to discern Allah's will.

BIRTH OF THE MOVEMENT

Muhammad ibn Abd al-Wahhab established his movement in his birthplace of al-Uyayna, a village

Left Ibn Saud, first ruler of the Kingdom of Saudi Arabia, spent most of his teenage years in exile in Kuwait after the rival Al-Rashid clan seized his ancestral lands.

north-west of Riyadh in Saudi Arabia, in c.1740. He led his followers in a number of public actions that expressed their puritan reforming zeal, including ordering the stoning of an adulteress and levelling the grave of Zayd ibn al-Khattab, brother of Caliph Umar (reigned 634–44) and one of the *sahabah* ('Companions of the Prophet'). This provoked the ire of local ruler Sulaiman ibn Muhammad ibn Ghurayr, who ordered Ibn Abd al-Wahhab to leave al-Uyayna.

Exiled in the nearby town of al-Diriya, Ibn Abd al-Wahhab won the support of its ruler, Muhammad ibn Saud, an event that would have enormous consequences over the following centuries. Ibn Abd al-Wahhab agreed to make Ibn Saud and his family the temporal leaders of his movement on condition that the Saud family would implement his teachings when they established themselves in power.

SAUDI CAMPAIGNS

Over the next 150 years or so, Ibn Saud and his heirs mounted a long succession of military campaigns to win power in the Arabian Peninsula. These campaigns brought the Saudi Wahhabis into violent conflict with other Muslims, driven particularly by their strong opposition to the practice of revering the tombs of early Muslim figures. In 1801–2, for instance, Wahhabis commanded by Abd al-Aziz ibn Muhammad ibn Saud attacked the Shiah cities of

Najaf and Karbala in Iraq, where they violated the tombs of Muhammad's son-in-law, Ali ibn Abu Talib, and grandson, Hussain ibn Ali, both of which were (and are) revered by Shiah Muslims.

Their military campaigns created what historians call the first Saudi state. The Ottoman empire, which derived prestige and authority in the Muslim world through its possession of the holy cities of Makkah and Madinah, sent troops under Muhammad Ali Pasha, Viceroy of Egypt, and he regained control of the region in 1818. A second Saudi state was created in 1824, but was brought down in 1891 by rival Arab clans. Finally, the long campaigns of the House of Saud culminated in the establishment of the Kingdom of Saudi Arabia by Abd al-Aziz ibn Saud, a direct descendant of Muhammad ibn Saud, in 1932. King Abd al-Aziz ibn Saud established his territory as a Muwahiddun state.

Above As King of Saudi Arabia, Abdullah ibn Abdul al-Aziz Al Saud is ruler of a Muwahiddun state and head of the House of Saud.

THE LAND OF THE TWO HOLY SANCTUARIES

SAUDI ARABIA, BIRTHPLACE OF ISLAM, WAS ESTABLISHED IN 1932 AS AN ISLAMIC KINGDOM, GOVERNED ACCORDING TO SHARIAH LAW AND IN LINE WITH THE PRINCIPLES OF THE MUWAHIDDUN MOVEMENT.

The kingdom of Saudi Arabia (al-Mamlakah al Arabiyah as Saudiyyah) derives great status in the global Muslim community because it contains the faith's two most sacred cities in Makkah and Madinah. The Holy Mosque in Makkah and the Prophet's Mosque in Madinah are the two holiest mosques for Muslims worldwide, and as a result Saudi Arabia is referred to reverentially as 'the Land of the Two Holy Sanctuaries'.

The Saudi king's official title is 'Custodian of the Two Holy Sanctuaries': this title was first adopted by King Fahd bin Abd al-Aziz Al Saud (reigned 1982–2005), and his successor, King Abdullah ibn Abd al-Aziz Al Saud, also uses it.

The country's motto is the first *kalimah*, or statement of the Islamic faith: 'There is no God but Allah and Muhammad is his messenger'. The motto is written on the Saudi flag, in white Arabic script against a green background and above a horizontal sabre, also in white.

ABSOLUTE POWER

King Abdullah is an absolute monarch, his powers not limited by the constitution. He himself serves as prime minister, and every four years appoints those on his Council of Ministers and the principal legislative body, the Consultative Council (*Majlis al-Shura*). In 2005, however, elections were held for half the members of 179 local assemblies, and further elections are to provide one-third of the members of the Consultative Council.

The Basic Law of Saudi Arabia, also known as the Basic System of Governance, was issued by royal decree by King Fahd in January 1992. It is based on Shariah law: limited secular legal codes have also been introduced, but these do not override Islamic laws.

Left Muslim pilgrims making the Hajj *reach up to touch the Black Stone and door of the* Kaabah *within the Holy Mosque in Makkah.*

Above The kalimah – *'There is no God but Allah and Muhammad is his messenger' – is the central feature of the flag of the kingdom of Saudi Arabia.*

CREATION OF THE KINGDOM

The kingdom was established by Abdullah's father, Abd al-Aziz ibn Saud in 1902. Ibn Saud first captured the city of Riyadh, ancestral base of the Saud family, from the rival al-Rashid clan in a daring night raid on 15 January 1902. Over the following two years, he took large parts of the Nejd, the interior Arabian highlands that had been the basis of earlier states governed by the Saud dynasty in the 19th century. However, his cause suffered a major setback when, following an appeal from Ibn Rashid, leader of the al-Rashid clan, Ottoman troops marched into the region and defeated the Saudis decisively in June 1904.

Ibn Saud relaunched his campaign of expansion in 1912. During World War I, he gained British financial backing and military supplies to help in an attack on Ibn Rashid, on the grounds that the al-Rashid clan were allies of the Ottomans, and in 1922, he finally conquered all Rashidi territories. Then, in 1925, Ibn Saud captured the Hijaz, the long territorial strip along the eastern bank of the Red Sea that contains Makkah and Madinah. Ibn Saud was declared King of the Hijaz in the Great Mosque at Makkah on 10 January 1926, and the following year, under the Treaty of Jeddah, the

Above The Prophet's Mosque in Madinah contains the tombs of Muhammad and of early caliphs Abu Bakr and Umar.

British recognized the independence of his realm as the kingdom of the Nejd and the Hijaz.

Finally, in 1932, Ibn Saud renamed his unified realm the kingdom of Saudi Arabia. The new country comprised the regions of the Hijaz and the Nejd plus al-Qatif and al-Hasa (two oasis regions in eastern Saudi Arabia).

OIL AND RELIGIOUS FUNDING

In March 1938, vast reserves of oil were discovered in Saudi Arabia, and following World War II – in which the new county remained neutral – development began. By 1949, oil production was under way on a large scale. Saudi Arabia became the world's largest exporter of petroleum and grew very wealthy

on the proceeds. Particularly after the sharp rise in the price of oil in the mid-1970s, the Saudi government reputedly spent lavishly around the world promoting Islam.

After Iraq invaded Kuwait in 1990, Saudi Arabia accepted the exiled Kuwaiti royal family and 400,000 Kuwaiti refugees, and then, in 1991, allowed US and Arab troops to deploy on its soil prior to

attempting the liberation of Kuwait. The fact that US troops remained on Saudi soil following the liberation of Kuwait in 1991 caused rising domestic tension until the final US troops left in 2003.

Below Scores of pilgrims take part in noon prayer (dhuhr) *outside the al-Masjid al-Haram Mosque (Holy Mosque) in Makkah during the* Hajj.

AN ISLAMIC REPUBLIC

AS THE END OF BRITISH RULE IN INDIA NEARED, THE MUSLIM LEAGUE SUCCESSFULLY CAMPAIGNED TO ESTABLISH MUSLIM-MAJORITY PAKISTAN. IT WAS DECLARED AN ISLAMIC REPUBLIC IN 1956.

The modern state of Pakistan was formed on 15 August 1947. British rule ended and the Indian subcontinent was partitioned into Hindu-majority India and Muslim-majority East and West Pakistan. Both Pakistan and India were initially dominions within the Commonwealth of Nations. India became a republic on 26 January 1950 and Pakistan was declared an Islamic republic on 23 March 1956.

THE CAMPAIGN FOR INDEPENDENCE

Within India, the Muslim League led by Allama Iqbal campaigned for an independent state in north-western India for Indian Muslims from 1930 onward. In 1933, Indian Muslim nationalist Choudhary Rahmat Ali put forward the name 'Pakistan' for the proposed country. In 1940, the Muslim League adopted the Lahore Resolution, which called for the establishment of 'autonomous and sovereign' states in those parts of north-western and north-eastern India where Muslims were numerically in a majority.

In June 1947, Muhammad Ali Jinnah, as representative of the Muslim League, agreed at a meeting with representatives of the Hindu Indian National Congress, the Sikhs and the Untouchables to the creation of Pakistan. The new country of West Pakistan comprised the provinces of Baluchistan, Northwest Frontier Province, Sindh and West Punjab; meanwhile, in the north-eastern corner of the subcontinent, the province of East Bengal formed East Pakistan.

Above In September 1947, Muslims wait to leave India in a protected convoy bound for the new country of Pakistan.

VIOLENT BIRTH

The decision to split the provinces of Punjab and Bengal was highly controversial and led to wide-scale rioting and as many as 500,000 deaths. In the Punjab, millions of Muslims migrated eastward into Pakistan, while millions more Sikhs and Hindus migrated westward into India; a similar cross-border migration took place in Bengal. In total, around 14 million people were forced to relocate.

Disputes arose over the princely states, which theoretically were free to remain independent or to join either India or Pakistan. Of enduring consequence was the disagreement over Kashmir, whose Hindu ruler chose to join India, despite having a Muslim majority population; this led to a long-running dispute between India and Pakistan over the territory. The countries fought two wars – in 1947–8 and 1956 – without resolving the issue.

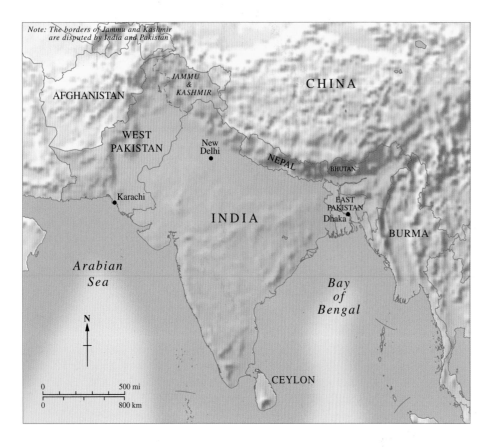

Note: The borders of Jammu and Kashmir are disputed by India and Pakistan

Left This map shows India with East and West Pakistan at the moment of their creation in 1947 as dominions within the Commonwealth of Nations.

Left Benazir Bhutto was twice Prime Minister of Pakistan, in 1988–90 and 1993–6, and was the first woman elected to lead a Muslim state.

CONSTITUTIONS OF PAKISTAN

Pakistan's first constitution was drawn up by the Constituent Assembly, a body established under the terms of independence from British rule in 1947. It declared the country an 'Islamic republic', provided for a parliamentary form of government and decreed that Muslims in Pakistan should be enabled to order their lives in accordance with principles in the Quran and sunnah, and that no laws 'repugnant to the injunctions of Islam' could be passed. Muslims would be required to study the Quran, and only a Muslim could be president of the country, but citizens of Pakistan would have the freedom to practise and propagate any religion they chose. It provided for parliamentary government.

In 1958, the constitution was abrogated and martial law imposed. A new constitution in 1962 renewed the majority of the above provisions; the form of government was to be presidential. Martial law continued until 1972, then a third constitution was agreed in 1973 under the rule of Zulfikar Ali Bhutto. For the first time, Islam was declared to be the state religion of Pakistan. At various times, these constitutions have been suspended and martial law imposed in Pakistan. Shariah law was introduced in the 1980s under General Muhammad Zia-ul-Haq.

THEOCRATIC RULE IN AN ISLAMIC REPUBLIC

Ayatollah Ruhollah Khomeini, Shiah Islamic scholar and an outspoken critic of the regime of the Shah of Iran, returned to Iran after 15 years of exile. Throughout his exile, he had continued to oppose the Shah's regime, and by the late 1960s, was established as a *marja-e taqlid* ('model to be imitated') by Shiah Muslims around the world. The country declared itself an Islamic Republic on 1 April 1979 and in December that year, adopted a theocratic constitution. Khomeini became Supreme Leader.

The system of government was based on the Shiah theory of *wilayat al-faqih* ('Guardianship by the Islamic Jurists'). According to this theory, Shariah laws are sufficient to cover all areas of life, and countries should be governed by a *faqih* (an expert in Shariah law). Such a system is deemed necessary to guard against oppression, injustice and corruption, and representative parliamentary systems of government are considered to be contrary to the teachings of Islam. Under the constitution of Iran, all political decisions have to be approved by the Supreme Leader before they become legal.

On Ayatollah Khomeini's death on 3 June 1989, Ayatollah Ali Khamenei became the Supreme Leader of Iran.

Right Khomeini was an ayatollah (Shiah religious leader) from the 1950s, and was in his late 70s by the time he became Supreme Leader of Iran in 1979.

RADICAL ISLAMISM

IN THE 20TH CENTURY, WHILE MANY MUSLIM GROUPS ENCOURAGED MODERNIZATION, SOME ISLAMIC ACTIVISTS URGED RADICAL POLITICAL OR TERRORIST ACTION TO REFORM SOCIETY AND GOVERNMENT.

Several groups over the course of the 20th century called for a revival of Islam through a return to the faith's central tenets and most ancient traditions. Writers and teachers proposed that Islam was more than a religion, and that social and political systems should be remade according to the faith. This theory was generally called *al-Islamiyyah* ('Islamism').

THE MUSLIM BROTHERHOOD

The Muslim Brotherhood, or the Society of the Muslim Brothers (*al-Ikhwan al-Muslimun*) was established in Egypt in 1928 to promote a return to the Quran and sunnah as the basis for modern Islamic societies. The Brotherhood spread quickly to Palestine, the Lebanon, Syria, the Sudan and North Africa.

In the late 1930s and 1940s, the Muslim Brotherhood became politicized, and in Egypt in 1952, it supported the coup led by Gamal Abdel Nasser, whom they expected to found an Islamic religious government. Disappointed by his development of secular nationalism, the Brotherhood attempted to assassinate him in 1954.

One of the leading figures of the movement in the 1950s and 1960s was the Egyptian intellectual Sayyid Qutb. While in prison for his involvement in the planning of the failed assassination (he was later hanged), he wrote a strongly anti-Western and anti-secular book

Below Mujahidun *are those who struggle in* jihad – *in opposition to* qaid, *a person who does not join* jihad. *These* mujahidun *were fighting in Afghanistan.*

Above *Shaykh Ahmad Yassin was co-founder, with Abdel Aziz al-Rantissi, of the militant Islamist organization Hamas in the Palestinian Territories in 1987.*

Ma'alim fi-l-Tariq (*Milestones*). In this influential book, Qutb denounced all existing governments, even those of the Muslim countries, as subject to *jahiliyyah* (ignorance). He appealed to Muslims to form a revolutionary vanguard that would

oppose *jahiliyyah* through preaching and by removing governmental systems that supported *jahiliyyah*, through 'physical power and *jihad*'.

HAMAS

In the Palestinian Territories, members of the Gaza wing of the Muslim Brotherhood founded Hamas, the *Harakat-al-muqawamah al-islamiyyah* ('Islamic Resistance Movement') in 1987. The organization is associated with suicide bombings and other attacks on the Israeli military and on civilians; its founding charter called for the state of Israel to be destroyed and replaced with an Islamic state. Hamas is also a political party and won a majority of seats in the elected council of the Palestinian Authority in Gaza in January 2006.

AL-QAEEDA

Qutb's writings were a direct influence on the international Islamic *jihad* movement of al-Qaeeda, which was behind the terrorist attacks on New York City and Washington on 11 September 2001 and subsequently became one of the central targets of the United States' 'war on terror'. Qutb's brother, Muhammad Qutb, became a professor of Islamic studies and

Above A propaganda billboard in the Lebanese capital Beirut promotes the armed struggle of the Shiah militia Hezbollah in the Lebanon.

promoted Qutb's theories. One of his students was Ayman al-Zawahiri, who was reputedly a mentor of al-Qaeeda leader Osama bin Laden and eventually a leading member of al-Qaeeda himself.

There is considerable debate over what al-Qaeeda actually is. Its name perhaps means the 'base' and, according to some accounts, it grew out of the organization set up to train *mujahidun* (Muslims fighting *jihad*) fighting against the Afghan Marxist regime and Soviet troops in Afghanistan in the 1980s.

In 1998, its emerging leader, Osama bin Laden, and Ayman al-Zawahiri issued a *fatwa* calling on Muslims to expel foreign troops and interests from Islamic lands, to 'fight the pagans…until there is no more tumult or oppression…and there prevail justice and faith in Allah'.

Many writers suggest that although training camps in Sudan and Afghanistan were reputedly run under its aegis, al-Qaeeda is not actually a centralized organization, but is, in fact, a loose-knit group of Islamists dedicated to *jihad*.

ISLAM'S RESPONSE TO TERRORISM

In 2005, at an international Islamic Conference convened by King Abdullah II of Jordan in Amman, religious leaders and scholars from 50 countries agreed that no declarations of apostasy could be made against a Muslim (as defined by one of the eight legal schools) and that a Muslim's honour, life and property were inviolable.

Muslims from mainstream viewpoints argued that radical Islamicists misrepresent the spirit of Islam and encourage Westerners to believe that Islam has no values in common with other cultures. Some liberal Muslims are keen to move away from fundamentalist interpretations of the Quran and sunnah in order to think critically about their religious heritage. Mainstream and liberal Muslims tend to agree that the most damaging aspect of promoting their religion as a political ideology is that this obscures Islam's beauty as a faith based on love for and submission to Allah.

Above Osama bin Laden, alleged founder of al-Qaeeda, ranked Shiah Muslims alongside heretics, the US and Israel as the four main 'enemies of Islam'.

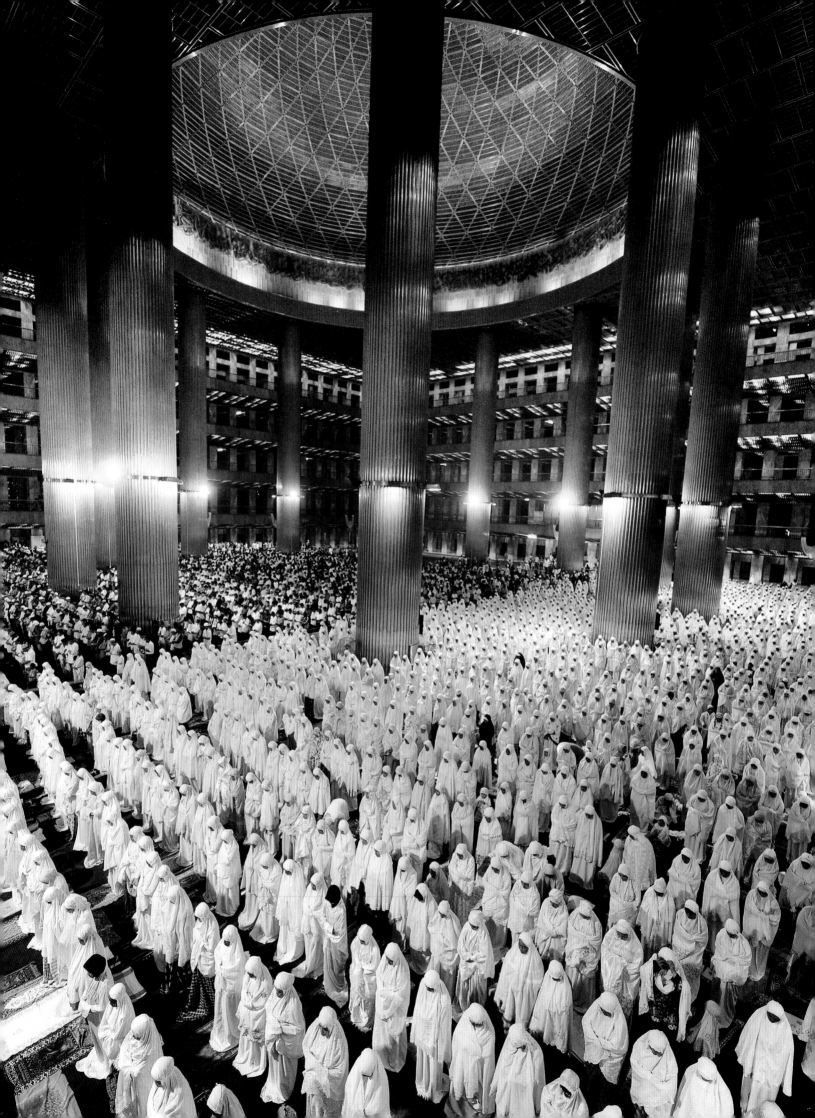

CHAPTER 3

ISLAMIC BELIEFS

There are a number of fundamental doctrines in Islam that all Muslims are expected to adhere to faithfully. Collectively known as the six articles of belief and the five pillars of faith, all are enshrined in the Quran.

The six articles of belief can be described as the core religious truths of Islam: belief in the oneness of God, his angels, his divinely revealed scriptures, his prophets and messengers, his predestination of all things, both good and bad, and resurrection and divine judgement after death. The five pillars of faith are the physical manifestation of Islamic beliefs: declaring that there is no God but Allah and Muhammad is his messenger, praying five times a day, fasting during the month of Ramadhan, paying the charity tax and making pilgrimage to Makkah.

Muslims believe that they will be held in individual account for their beliefs and practices on the Day of Judgement, when every action and thought will be recalled and judged by God.

Opposite Congregational tarawih, *optional prayers offered by devout Muslims, are observed in mosques throughout the world during the fasting month of Ramadhan.*

Above A 17th-century Mughal manuscript painting captures the beauty of nature and reflects the great diversity of God's creation.*

ONE GOD

ALLAH SIMPLY MEANS 'THE ONE GOD', AND PROFESSION OF THIS RELIGIOUS BELIEF SHOULD OCCUPY THE CENTRAL POSITION IN A MUSLIM'S CONSCIOUS THOUGHT AND ACTION AT ALL TIMES.

The *shahadah*, witnessing that 'there is no God but the one God' is the central Islamic creed. It is a doctrine that has transformed numerous civilizations across many continents, from Arabia to Africa, Asia and beyond. But monotheism is not new, and Muhammad was not calling his pre-Islamic Arabian society to a religious concept that was unknown to their civilization.

ISLAMIC MONOTHEISM

The ancient Arabs of Makkah were a Semitic people who traced their ancestry to Ibrahim's son Ismail. The belief in one God was therefore familiar to their history and civilization, while Ibrahim's temple, the *Kaabah*, was a constant reminder of their monotheistic heritage.

Linguistically, the idea of God's uniqueness is crystallized in the Arabic word *Allah*. To proclaim *Allah* in Arabic is to deny the possibility of any co-existing deities, which is why the pagan Arabs avoided using the term. Muhammad's call of *tawhid*, the 'oneness of God', was essentially a revival of the ancient teachings of Ibrahim and the other monotheist Semite patriarchs.

The concept of *tawhid* asserts that divine unity and divine truth are one and the same. This means that for Muslims to declare that the truth is one is to declare not only that 'God is One' but also that there can be 'no other God but God' (*la ilaha ilallah*). This combination of assertion and negation is contained in the *shahadah* (the Muslim declaration of belief).

THE PROPHETS

Connected to the notion of divine unity and truth is the concept of *risalah*, or 'divine communication'. In Islam, *risalah* is the means by which God reveals his nature, purpose and truth to men and women by the election of human prophets and messengers (10:47, 13:7, 35:24).

Muslims believe that God has sent many prophets to humankind, the first being Adam and the last Muhammad. According to a hadith, there have been 124,000 prophets, although the Quran refers to only 25 by name, among them Adam, Noah, Ibrahim, Ismail, Isaac, Moses, David and Jesus.

Islam teaches that all these prophets taught the same message of monotheism to their people.

Above Allah – 'The one God', written in calligraphic Arabic, adorns a high minaret in the former Turkish sultan's palace at Topkapi in Istanbul.

A number of them brought divinely revealed scriptures (2:213, 7:52), but Muslims believe that the Quran is God's final and perfected book of guidance.

THE NATURE OF GOD

Philosophers and theologians have argued about the exact nature of God for centuries. The arguments of Muslim philosophers were based on the cosmological order of things: the created realm is ordered by natural laws in which events happen by cause, and causes, therefore, cannot be without their proper effects, they argued. Like the ancient Egyptian, Greek and Mesopotamian thinkers before them, Muslim philosophers conceived that a world of both chaos and order must necessarily be inconsistent with the idea of a sublime, transcendent being.

Meanwhile, the Muslim theologians feared that an emphasis on the orderliness of the universe could result in the belief that God is detached from the apparent mechanical causality of his own creation. This could lead to the conclusion that either God is

Above A decorative brass plate that hangs in the Tanyal Mosque in Tripoli, Lebanon, declares 'Muhammad is the seal of the Prophets and Messengers'.

Right *The Blue Mosque in Istanbul, Turkey. Its huge domes tower high above the congregation in a symbolic portrayal of God's abode in the highest heavens.*

divinely unique, wholly 'other' and transcendent, or he is immanent and physical, if not human-like.

OCCASIONALISM

In the view of Muslim theologians, such reasonings regarding the nature of God compromise the doctrine of *tawhid* and seemed to echo not only pagan Arabia's polytheism, but also Judaism's reference to God in the plural as *Elohim* and Christianity's developed trinity – three persons in the deity, each of whom is fully God.

The theologians responded by rejecting the philosophers' views and developing the doctrine of 'occasionalism': at each moment in time, God continues to recreate the universe. In this way, the theologians made the notion of causality dependent on God's 'divine presence'.

Above *Ibrahim's belief and faithfulness is tested when God commands him to sacrifice his son, but Ismail is spared by the miraculous substitution of a ram.*

QURANIC TRANSCENDENCE AND IMMANENCE

'If there were therein Gods besides God then verily both (the heavens and earth) would be in disorder and chaos. Glorified be God, Lord of the Throne, Transcendent beyond all they ascribe to Him.' (21:22)

'We verily created man and We know what his soul whispers to him and We are nearer to him than his jugular vein.' (50:16)

117

THE ATTRIBUTES OF ALLAH

THE QURAN ASCRIBES 99 DIFFERENT NAMES TO ALLAH, EACH OF WHICH DESCRIBES A PARTICULAR ASPECT OF HIS NATURE. MUSLIMS LEARN ABOUT GOD AND GAIN MERIT BY MEMORIZING THESE NAMES.

Understanding the nature of God is important in helping Muslims to establish and submit to his will. For example, those who believe that God is *al-Aleem*, 'all-knowing', and *al-Sami*, 'all-hearing', will be convinced that God knows their innermost thoughts, hears all that they say, and sees all that they do. Such an understanding of God's attributes will have a direct effect on the way they live their lives, both publicly and in private.

THE POWER OF GOD

Muslims believe not only that God created the universe but also that he is the all-pervading (*al-Muhit*) controller (*al-Qadir*) and reckoner (*al-Hasib*) of all unfolding events, which have been predetermined by his *qadar*, or 'divine measure'. In other words, Allah knows the present, past and future of all creation because he is the bestower or giver (*al-Wahhab*) of all things.

However, Islam teaches that the fact that God has power and authority over all creation and events does not mean that human beings do not have free will or choice; for example, no one is compelled to obey God or believe in him. Freedom of action does not contradict the foreknowledge of God. An individual does not know his final destiny and is given the freedom of choice to take any course of action he wishes.

Nevertheless, Muslims believe that there will be a final Day of Judgement (*yawm al-hisab*, or 'the day of account'), when God will judge and reward or punish each action in accordance with its intention, with the ultimate reward of eternal heaven or hell.

THE 99 NAMES OF GOD

The Prophet Muhammad stated that there are 99 names of Allah and said that he who commits them to memory will enter paradise. For Muslims, to know or remember the names of God is to understand who he is. All of God's names are found in the Quran.

Left The 99 divine attributes of God are ornately displayed in a beautiful calligraphic style above an entrance to the Blue Mosque in Istanbul, Turkey.

Above Congregational prayer at the Great Mosque in Lyon, France. The prayer begins with Allahu Akbar ('God is Greatest'), an acknowledgement and declaration of God's ultimate authority.

Islam teaches that not only is each of these attributes of God complete in itself, but they are also perfect in their collective harmony. This means that, for example, while God is *al-Jabbar*, the 'compeller' or 'punisher', he is also *al-Ghafir*, the 'forgiver' or 'clement'. According to Nawawi's *Forty Hadith Qudsi*, Muhammad explained that 'when God decreed His creation, He pledged Himself by writing in His book that is with Him: My Mercy prevails over my Wrath.'

Muslims believe that by recounting and reflecting on the divine attributes of God, their hearts can find both solace and strength of faith (13:28).

REMEMBERING THE DIVINE

Dhikr means 'to remember' and refers to the particular devotional ritual of repeating or reflecting on the attributes of the divine (*dhikr Allah*). The practice of *dhikr* is usually associated with Muslim

Left An Egyptian Sufi twirls rhythmically in a trancelike state, accompanied by a religious devotional song, nasheed, *as he contemplates God and celebrates the Prophet's birthday.*

mystics or Sufis but is also observed by Muslims from various other Islamic theological expressions.

The Quran explicitly instructs Muslims to engage in remembrance of God as a means of spiritual self-development and attaining inner peace: 'And the remembrance of God is the greatest (of actions)' (29:45), 'O Believers! Remember God with abundant remembrances' (33:41). Muslims are assured that when they remember the Divine and give gratitude to him, he returns the favour with great blessings and rewards (2:152).

The Prophet Muhammad said that everything has a 'polish' and that the 'polish' of the heart is *dhikr*. Muslims engage in *dhikr* in many varied ways, from offering extra ritual prayers to attending special gatherings to recite the Quran, or to exclusively remember God, as with the Sufis. But Muslims also recall God while engaged in their everyday activities, whether they are at work or study, eating or undertaking a journey.

CELEBRATING THE DIVINE

Remembering God is a celebrated encounter that is manifested in various artistic forms across the Muslim world. The most obvious of these is the arabesque, a unique abstract form of interconnected symmetrical designs that have been applied to painting, architecture, calligraphy and horticulture. The arabesque is designed to represent not God himself, but rather his inexpressibility.

Modern calligraphic works by artists such as Ahmed Moustafa, whose work is derived from, and inspired by, the original Quranic text, are products of remembering and celebrating the Divine. Equally, devotional songs of *nasheed* (Arabian), *sama* (Turkomanic) and *qawwali* (South Asian) are the result of a musical contemplation and remembrance of the Divine.

Right Quranic verses in an earthenware mosaic are set around a 16th-century necropolis created by Sultan Ahmed al-Mansour in Marrakech, Morocco.

DIVINE WILL

MUSLIMS BELIEVE THAT THE SACRED TEXT OF THE QURAN REVEALS
GOD'S WILL TO HUMANS AND TEACHES THEM HOW TO ACHIEVE PEACE
AND HARMONY IN THIS LIFE AND ETERNAL REWARD IN THE NEXT.

Submission to God's will is a central teaching of Islam, and the relationship between God and human beings is presented as that of Lord (*Rabb*) (1:1, 51:56) and slave (*abd*). The term Abdullah means 'servant of God', and the concept of worship (*ibadah*) in Islam is derived from the root word *abd*, which means slave, servant or worshipper. Men and women are seen as completely dependent on their creator for all their needs, both spiritual and physical, yet they have been granted freedom of choice.

DIVINE SOVEREIGNTY

Islam teaches that God is sovereign over all creation, including the human realm, and that everything is subject to God's 'primordial and harmonious condition' (*fitra*), or universal natural laws. Because they have free will, people can choose to act in accordance with *fitra* or against it by rejecting God's will. This conscious rejection is known as *kufr*, meaning 'to cover'. *Kufr* is seen as the antithesis of Islam because it represents the 'covering' or denial of the truth of God's supremacy.

Above In Islam, gardens reflect the beauty of God's creation and represent paradise as an eternal abode for the righteous.

DIVINE PURPOSE

The Quran declares that God's purpose for creating human beings was so that they might worship him: 'And I did not create *jinn* [creatures of the unseen realm] and mankind except to worship me' (51:56). However, while the reason for human existence is explicitly given, the Quran teaches that God, in his infinite wisdom, compels no one to believe in him (2:256).

A prophetic tradition recounts that before God made human beings, he created both heaven and hell and decreed that both should have their fill. Muslims believe that only God knows who will dwell in paradise and who will dwell in hell,

Left A musallah, *an Islamic prayer mat, shows birds of paradise perched upon heavenly flowers, which symbolize God's promise for the faithful.*

but that there is no need for people to be fatalistic or resign themselves to hell; instead, they should endeavour to seek God's grace by submitting to his divine will.

ACHIEVING GOD'S WILL

Islam teaches that divine revelation exists so that men and women might learn and live in accordance with God's will. Muslims believe that in the process of revelation, the divine nature of God is also made known: throughout human history, God has communicated his will through prophets and messengers who translate God's will into practice, leaving a living example for people to follow.

These two means of establishing divine order – God's scriptures and his prophets – both invite and enable people to submit themselves to God and be of service to their fellow human beings. The idea of living in peace and harmony with the creator and the created is, in fact, what is understood by the word Islam, which means 'peaceful submission'.

THE END OF THINGS

According to Islamic theology, the idea that people have that they are self-sufficient is a result of them becoming detached from the divine will for human evolution. The Quran teaches that humankind is on a journey that originated within the presence of God, who then sent us down to earth as a means of testing our faith.

Islam teaches that on this journey through life on earth, men and women will be tempted by Satan, or Shaytan, 'the rejected one', before experiencing a physical death and thereafter an eternal resurrection, either with God in paradise or with

Below Qurans are not only written in beautiful calligraphic styles, but are also handled with great reverence by Muslims.

the devil in the hellfire. To this end, all deeds and thoughts of every person are scribed by two recording angels (*kiraman karibeen*) and will be presented before God on Judgement Day (50:17–18). He will then reward or punish according to the individual's account.

According to the Quran, each human being is the creator of his or her own destiny, which is determined at any given point in life by the exercise of freedom of choice – to do good and obey God or to commit sin in disobedience. 'This Quran guides one to what is more straightforward and reassures believers who act honourably that they shall have great earnings. Yet We have reserved painful torment for those who do not believe in the hereafter' (17:9–10).

Above A Turkish manuscript from the 16th century shows eternal damnation in hellfire for those who reject faith.

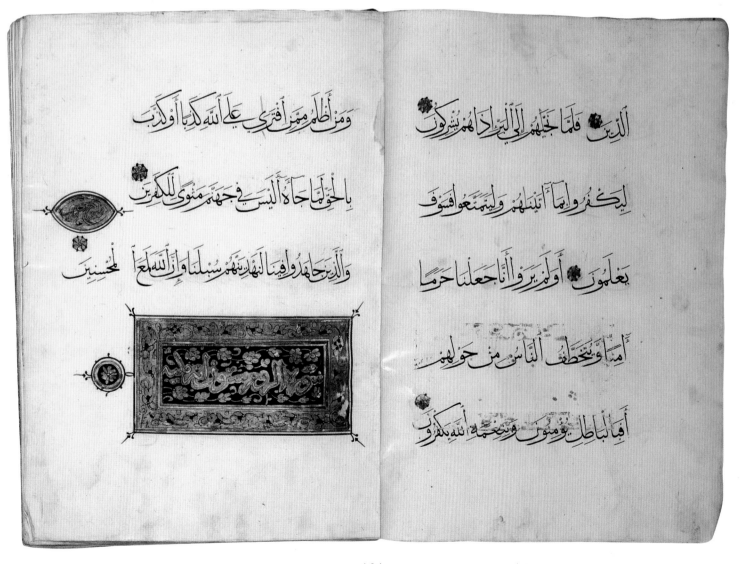

COSMOLOGY

THE QURAN INVITES ITS READERS TO REFLECT UPON THE CREATION OF THE UNIVERSE AS AN OBSERVABLE REALITY THAT REFLECTS THE GREATNESS OF GOD AS ITS CREATOR.

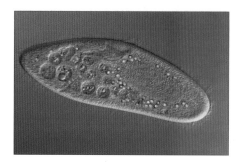

Above This micro-organism – Paramecium caudatum – *is part of God's beautifully proportioned creation.*

The genesis of humankind and the creation of the heavens and the earth is a recurring theme. The verses relating to creation are invariably linked to the idea that the world is a temporary abode and that believers will ultimately return to their Lord.

GOD, THE CREATOR
The Quranic narrative of the genesis of creation has many similarities to that of the Old Testament, but whereas the Bible alludes to the apparently human-like qualities of God, the Quranic text is devoid of all such descriptions. The Old Testament states that God created the heavens and earth in six days and on the seventh he rested. While the Quran confirms that God created all things in six days, it states that then he 'established Himself on His Throne' (32:4). In the Quran, a 'day' (*yawm*) is not viewed as one complete course of the earth around the sun, but refers to the conditions that existed before the creation. In one passage, it describes God's reckoning of a day to be equivalent to 1,000 of our days; in another to 50,000 (32:5, 120:4). Similarly, the word 'throne' is used symbolically, implying God's absolute authority, direction and control of the cosmos as the ever-living, immanent creator.

The Quran teaches that God is *al-Awwal*, the first, before whom there is nothing, and *al-Akhir*, the last, after whom there is nothing. He is also described as being ever-active within it as *al-Dhahir*, the 'outward', and *al-Batin*, the 'inward', privy to all that exists within the unseen realms of our being and what is around us.

FREE FROM EVIL
The Quran claims that God's creation is in itself good, beautifully proportioned and perfectly adapted for the functions it has to perform (32:6–7). This concept is known as *fitra*, or 'natural pre-disposition', and it includes the notion that all humans are born in a similar state to the rest of creation, that is free from evil (30:30). Dissension and disorder are believed to be the result of men's and women's excessive pride and practice of injustice leading to the harming of God's world (10:23) and their succumbing to Satan's temptation.

The Quranic worldview sees the creation as perfectly balanced and harmonized, on condition that men and women perform their appointed role as God's earthly vicegerents, peacefully submitting themselves to God's divine will. Muslims believe that at an appointed time in the future – the Last Day – God will reclaim his creation and the souls of men and women (15:85–6).

ABUNDANCE ON EARTH
The Quran's defined purpose for the creation of the earth challenges the idea that it is the result of cosmic chance. Instead, the earth is described as a place of abundant sustenance for human beings, with both animal and plant produce of incredible variety as a sign of God's bounty (15:20, 26:7). Ecological sustainability is implicated through the idea of agricultural cultivation

Left A medieval Islamic manuscript on astronomy illustrates shooting stars: 'light missiles to drive away the devils' (67:5).

and preserving the earth's natural resources. The earth's terrain is presented as a surface that men and women can easily travel across by land or sea. Its volatile landscapes are said to be fixed by lofty mountains, described as 'stakes' (*awtad*), like those of a tent, anchoring the deep foundational geological folds (78:6–7).

The earth is viewed as a temporary abode for humankind, which will eventually be brought to an end by God (99:1–3), and is always mentioned in the context of humankind's final destination and return to God (14:48).

INFINITE UNIVERSE

The Quran contains quite detailed information relating to the creation of the universe, referring to the existence of an initial, unique gaseous mass (*dukhan*), whose elements are fused together (*ratq*)

Right Islam teaches that human life and creation is not a chance occurrence but part of God's predetermined plan.

and subsequently separated (*fatq*) (41:11–12). The separation process resulted in the creation of multiple worlds in orbital solar systems.

The Quran teaches that 'God is the One Who created the night and the day, the sun and the moon, each one is travelling in an orbit with its own motion' (21:33). Specific celestial bodies are mentioned: the

Above The Horsehead Nebula in the Orion constellation is considered to be God's creation in Islam – like all the other stars.

sun, the moon, stars and planets. The universe is constructed of 'seven firmaments' (41:12), and its vastness is a testimony to the creator's power and greatness.

THE BIG BANG

RECENT SCIENTIFIC THEORIES REGARDING THE ORIGINS OF THE
UNIVERSE APPEAR TO HAVE MANY SIMILARITIES TO VERSES FROM THE
QURAN THAT REFER TO THE GENESIS OF THE HEAVENS AND EARTH.

The modern era is founded on scientific inquiry and the application of reason, which has brought humankind many benefits. But some people argue that the application of scientific analysis to sacred scriptures has increased religious scepticism and disbelief. Muslims conversely claim that the Quran, which was revealed more than 1,500 years ago, contains many verses that appear to agree with modern scientific discoveries.

ISLAM AND THE BIG BANG
The Quran does not provide a continuous narrative or an exact chronology for the origins of the universe, but Muslims claim that there are verses in a number of chapters that, taken together, could

Above A Turkish Muslim astronomer is shown consulting an armillary sphere and compass as he maps out the universe in this 16th-century manuscript illustration.

be said to offer a brief synthesis of the events that led to its formation: 'Then He directed the Heaven when it was smoke, saying to it and the Earth, merge you willingly or unwillingly; they said we merge in willing obedience' (41:11), 'Do not the unbelievers see that the Heavens and Earth were one mass, then we split them asunder and that we created every living thing from water; will they then not believe?' (21:30), and 'Then He ordained the seven Heavens in two periods and He assigned to each Heaven its duty and command, And We adorned the lower Heaven with lights and protection, Such is the decree of The Exalted, The Mighty' (41:12).

All of the above, many Muslims would say, appear to agree with scientific theories on the existence of primary nebula and the process of secondary separation of the elements that had formed in the initial unique mass of the 'Big Bang' theory.

INTERMEDIARY CREATION
It is generally accepted by scientists that the separation of the primary gases resulted in the formation of galaxies, which, after dividing, formed stars, from which the planets came into being. The Quranic verses on creation also refer to an intermediary creation existing between the heavens and earth: 'it is He who created the Heavens and Earth and all that is in between them…' (25:59).

Left The Milky Way constellation provides us with an illustration of how cosmic matter from the 'Big Bang' has scattered across the universe.

Muslims claim that this intermediary creation bears striking similarities to the modern discovery of bridges of matter, present outside organized astronomical systems. The Quran also accords with the modern theory regarding how the celestial organization is balanced by the particular orbits of stars and the interplay of gravitational fields related to their speed of movement and mass, each with its own motion: 'And it is He who has created the night, the day, the sun and the moon; each one is travelling in an orbit with its own motion' (21:33).

EXPANDING UNIVERSE
The first chapter of the Quran, *al-Fatiha* (the Opening), describes God as '*Rabb al-aalameen*' ('Lord of the worlds'), and the use of the plural term 'worlds' conveys both the spiritual and physical realms. The heavens are referred to as multiple not only because of their plural form, but also as a mystical and symbolic quantity of seven.

Right According to Islamic cosmology, the earth, although a complete and natural ecosystem, is only a temporary abode for humankind.

Other references to celestial bodies in the Quran suggest a fixed place for the sun within the solar system and the on-going evolution of the heavens, both of which are in agreement with modern science.

There is also an allusion to the universe being in a state of continuous expansion, with the idea that at the 'end of time' it will be 'folded in' and 'the Earth flattened' (84:1–3). The Quran also suggests the possibility of the conquest of space – though claims that this will be achievable only by God's grace: 'if you so wish to penetrate regions of the Heavens and the Earth, then penetrate them, you will not penetrate them except by [God's] power' (55:33).

SOLAR SYSTEM

The Quran describes the sun, which we know to be a celestial body in a state of continuous combustion and a source of heat and light, as a *siraj* (torch), and the moon, an inert body that reflects a light source, as *nur* (light). The rotations of the earth around the sun and the moon around the earth are eloquently portrayed in the Quran (39:5) by the use of the verb *kawwara* (meaning 'to coil' or 'to wind'). The word is that used to describe the way in which a turban is wound around the head, which, like the earth's orbit, is elliptical.

The contribution of Muslim astronomers to scientific progress has been widely acknowledged, but the details contained in the Quran are often overlooked.

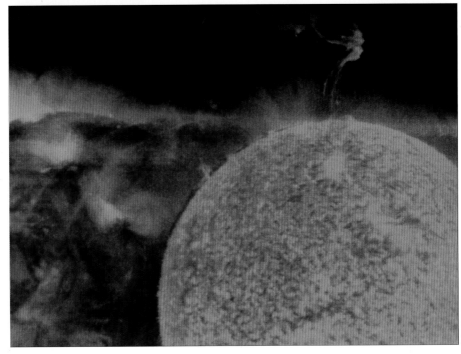

Right The planets revolve around the sun at the centre of our solar system. The Quran states that 'each floats along according to its own orbit' (36:37–40).

125

THE QURANIC GENESIS

THE STORY OF ADAM AND EVE IS COMMON TO THE TRADITIONS OF
JUDAISM, CHRISTIANITY AND ISLAM, BUT THE GENESIS ACCOUNT
GIVEN IN THE QURAN CONTAINS SOME SIGNIFICANT DIFFERENCES.

According to the monotheistic religions, Adam and Eve are the parents of the human family, who originally dwelled in the presence of God in his heavenly kingdom. The story of their temporary exile from paradise to earth becomes the primordial narrative of humankind, but the Quran does not refer to the 'Fall'.

IN THE BEGINNING

The Quran account emphasizes the common origin of men and women: 'O mankind! Be conscious of your Sustainer, who has created you out of one living entity, and out of it created its mate, and out of the two spread abroad a multitude of men and women' (4:1).

According to the Quran, the angels panicked when they saw God creating Adam, for they feared that he would make mischief on earth. However, God informed them they did not know his plans (2:30). According to a hadith, he then created Adam from soil taken from different parts of the earth and

eventually breathed into him. Later, when Adam was in need of a mate, God created Hawwa (Eve).

'MAN-MADE' WOMAN

Unlike the Old Testament story, the Quran relates that Eve was not derived from Adam, who, indeed, was not the first creation in male form. According to the Quran, God made a *nafs*, a soul, from which he then made Adam as a gendered male, then brought forth its female counterpart, Eve (4:1). Therefore, Adam and Eve share the same original source, one living entity, out of which both were made.

Eve's purpose in being created was, like Adam, to worship God. Yet, Adam desired her as a mate, 'so that he might dwell in peace with her' (7:189). The roles of men and women are therefore seen as wholly complementary in Islam.

THE 'ENEMY'

The Quran story relates that after God had created Adam, he asked the angels and *jinn* (genies) to bow

Above The Genesis narrative from a 16th-century Ottoman Bible illustrates Adam and Eve's rejection from paradise to earth to toil on the land and procreate.

to him, which they all did, except Shaytan (the devil, Iblis) (2:33–34). In his pride, Satan refused, arguing that he was made of a superior matter: smokeless fire. This disobedience led to his rejection from heaven (7:12). However, he vowed to lead men and women astray as revenge against God for this fall from grace. Adam and Eve enjoyed peace in heaven and closeness to God, until Satan seduced them to approach the forbidden tree. As a result of this, they earned God's displeasure and were sent to earth for a life of toil (7:16–21).

Islam differs from the Judaeo-Christian tradition, though, in teaching that Adam and Eve's disobedience did not result in the 'Fall' of humankind, because although they transgressed, Adam and Eve later repented for their sins and were forgiven by God (7:23). Nor do Muslims believe in original

Left This modern representation of Adam and Eve approaching the forbidden tree is by Egyptian artist Karima Ali.

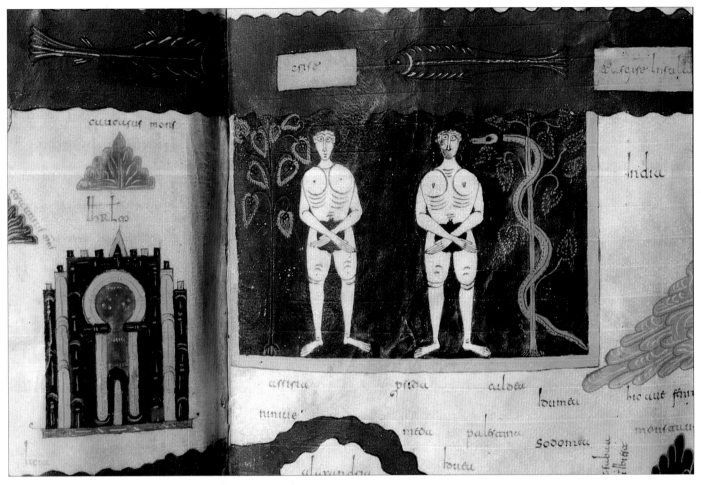

Above This 11th-century Spanish manuscript charts Adam and Eve's settlement on earth in the Middle East after their exclusion from paradise.

sin, rather that every man and woman is born free of sin. According to the Quran, God did not blame Eve as the temptress, but held both Adam and Eve equally responsible (2:36). (In fact, according to one verse, 20:121, Adam alone was judged to be guilty.) The Quran relates that Adam and Eve both turned to God in repentance and that God accepted their repentance, promising them guidance from him (2:38).

Muslims believe that men and women, as well as Satan, will live on earth for an appointed term, after which they will face a Day of Judgement before God. Thereafter, according to their beliefs and deeds, they will face eternal paradise in heaven or punishment in hellfire (7:24–5, 6:51).

Above Some Muslim scientists have used evidence of fossilized life, especially fish, to argue that humankind did not evolve.

THE THEORY OF EVOLUTION

Among Muslims there is no consensus on the theory of evolution – that all living things are made from simple cell structures, which mutated, evolved and transformed into other life forms by becoming complex cell structures – especially as many perceive that this theory is incompatible with a belief in God. Islamic literature upholds that all living things are made from water (21:30) and claims that creation came about through the will of God. The Quran decribes how Adam and Eve were made in perfect human form, and that different tribes and nations were then made to populate the earth (30:22, 49:13).

While many Muslims have rejected the idea that all creation was an accidental occurrence of cause and effect, some Muslim scientists have engaged with the theory.

ANGELS

ACCORDING TO THE QURAN, GOD CREATED ANGELS BEFORE HE
MADE ADAM. FORMED FROM DIVINE LIGHT, ANGELS SERVE AS THE
MEDIUM BETWEEN GOD'S HEAVENLY DOMAIN AND THE EARTH.

According to Muslim belief, Muhammad's first encounter with the divine was through Archangel Jibril, and believing in the existence of angels is therefore one of the six articles of faith in Islam. Angels are frequently referred to in the Quran in connection with a number of divine activities, from conveying holy scriptures and divine communications from God to his prophets and messengers, to aiding ordinary humans in their pursuit of righteousness.

THE NATURE OF ANGELS

In Islamic theology, angels (*malaaikah*) are celestial beings, who, according to prophetic hadith, are created from divine light (*nur*), in contrast with humans, who are said to have been formed from dried clay and black mud (15:28). Unlike men and women, angels have not been given free will: they can carry out only the duties and tasks ascribed to them by God and can never disobey him nor act other than in accordance with his command (66:6).

According to a hadith, angels never sleep, nor do they require sustenance or have needs as humans do. They are usually invisible except when they choose to appear to humans, as Archangel Jibril frequently did to Muhammad. In order to implement God's divine will and commands, angels have been given certain qualities and powers in accordance with their particular functions. The Quran describes the angels as generally possessing two, three or four sets of wings (35:1), though it is believed that some individual angels have hundreds of wings.

ANGELIC DUTIES

The Arabic word for angel, *malak*, literally means 'to send on a mission', as does the Hebrew *malach* and the Greek *angelos*.

In addition to conveying God's divine revelations and carrying out his will, Islam teaches, angels

Left Angels and demons surround the enthroned King Solomon, in this scene from a Manuscript of the Khamsa *of Nizami.*

Above A 16th-century Ottoman Turkish text, Ajaibul-mukhluqat, *contains this illustration of angels prostrating in ranks.*

also bring God's blessings to humankind (33:43) and his warnings of impending punishment or catastrophes (16:2). Angels communicate between the *dhahir* (seen) and *batin* (unseen) worlds, and the Quran promises angelic support to believers who commit themselves to righteousness and sincere faith (41:30–2).

Some angels are believed to have been created to assist humans in employing their free will: each person decides what he or she wishes to do and angels help them in that decision or task (82:10–12). Each human being is appointed two 'recording angels', known as *Munkar* and *Nakir*, each of whom records both good and bad deeds. According to a popular hadith, others roam the earth, searching to join gatherings where God is remembered, praised and

Right A Turkish manuscript painting depicts the Prophet's death: Izrail, the angel of death, seeks permission to take his soul, while Muhammad's daughter Fatimah stands by.

worshipped. There are also said to be hordes of angels that will both escort the wrongdoers to hell and greet those who enter paradise, whom they will welcome with the words 'Peace be unto you! Enter the Garden on account of the things you were doing' (16:32).

ARCHANGELS

Islam teaches that there are countless numbers of angels in existence with countless more constantly being created. From among these heavenly hosts, the Quran mentions a few angels by name that have a higher rank: Jibril (Gabriel), the archangel of revelation, who brought the divine message and scriptures to the prophets; Izrail, the angel of death, who is responsible for taking each human soul; Mikail (Michael), the angel of sustenance, who brings provision to the earth for humankind; and Israfil, the angel who is charged with blowing the trumpet at the 'final hour' before the Day of Judgement.

Above In Islam, jinn are unseen beings, created before humans and, like us, endowed with free will.

THE *JINN*

According to Islamic theology, Shaytan, also named Iblis, was not a 'fallen angel', but was one of the unseen spirit creatures known as the *jinn* (genies). In Islamic theology, the *jinn*, like humans, have been given free will and are divided into various categories and groupings: believers and non-believers, ethnic and racial groups, etc.

The Quran teaches that the *jinn* were created by God before humans (15:27), and while they are usually invisible to humans, the *jinn* are able to observe us (7:27).

The Prophet Muhammad taught that the *jinn* take one of three general forms: one type flies through the air, another type takes the physical form of an animal, appearing to humans sometimes as snakes and dogs, and the third is based in one place but travels around. The *jinn* do not normally interfere with the human realm unless they are disturbed or provoked by humans.

DIVINE REVELATIONS AND PROPHETHOOD

MUSLIMS BELIEVE THAT GOD COMMUNICATES TO HUMANKIND BY REVEALING HIS WILL THROUGH REVELATIONS AND HOLY SCRIPTURES BESTOWED ON SELECTED INDIVIDUALS KNOWN AS PROPHETS.

The process of communication between God and humankind is known in Islam as *risalah*, or 'prophethood'. According to Islam, divine communication began with the creation of Adam, the first man and prophet, and thereafter includes a series of divine messengers and holy scriptures to guide humankind from generation to generation in the straight path.

Muslims believe that God, in his infinite wisdom and mercy, has not only created men and women and given them a beautiful world in which to live, but that he has also provided them with guidance to enable them to follow the right course and live in peace and harmony with each other.

DIVINE MESSENGERS

Since the beginning of creation, Islam teaches, God has selected individuals to receive his divine guidance and act as perfect examples for men and women to follow. All of these divine prophets and messengers were human and all of them taught the same basic message as they called men and women to worship the One God. The Quran states that deprived of God's continued guidance, men and women would be lost and without purpose (103:1–3).

SENT TO ALL NATIONS

The Quran asserts that God has sent his divine prophets and messengers to every nation at different times (10:47, 13:7, 35:24). Muslims believe that not only did the prophets receive and transmit divine revelations and guidance to humankind, but also their lives serve as an example for believers on how to live a steadfast and virtuous life, in the face of both adversity and ultimate success.

Above Muhammad is believed to have received Quranic verses from Archangel Jibril. Other prophets, for example, Lot, also had angelic visitations.

According to the Quran, God guides his prophets in a number of different ways, including inspired dreams (Joseph), angelic visitations (Lot) and divine revelations (Moses). Muhammad said that the number of prophets sent to earth is 124,000, but the Quran mentions only 25 by name. Of these, 22 are also referred to in the Bible.

Islam distinguishes between prophets (*anbiya*), those who receive divine guidance, and messengers (*rusul*), who receive both divine guidance and holy scriptures. Thus, while all messengers are prophets, not all prophets are messengers; however, the role of both is to guide men and women to God. Muslims believe in all the prophets and messengers of God, from Adam to Muhammad, and the scriptures they received (2:285).

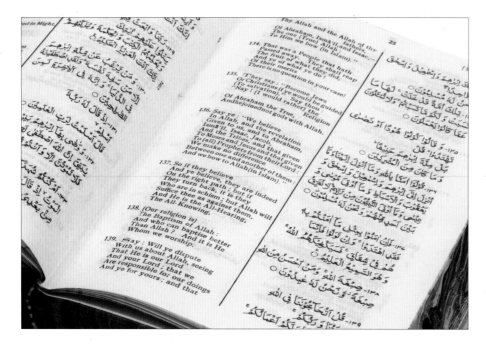

Left Quranic verses include 2:136, which confirms belief in the revelations and prophets that preceded Muhammad as mentioned in the Bible.

Above Muslim pilgrims offer prayers and blessings at the shrine containing the head of John the Baptist inside the Umayyad Mosque, Damascus, Syria.

SCRIPTURES

The Quran refers to a number of messengers and their scriptures by name, claiming that Moses (Musa) received the Torah (Tawrat), David (Dawud) the Psalms (Zabur), Jesus (Isa) the Evangel (Injil) and Muhammad the Quran. Muslims believe that while the details of how each of these scriptures was revealed differs, their purpose was the same: to carry God's guidance and laws for humankind to follow.

These scriptures have shaped and formed the religious and cultural practices of monotheistic faith communities throughout the ages. While some believers have strived to preserve their texts and religious laws, others have preferred to engage with the spirit of their religious scriptures, allowing for changes to translations, alternative interpretations and new meanings to the text. However, Muslims believe that of all the holy scriptures, only the Quran remains in its original form from the time of revelation (15:9). Nevertheless, the Quran claims that faithful believers from all the monotheistic traditions – Muslims, Christians and Jews, including the Sabians (possibly followers of John the Baptist) – will be rewarded by their Lord, without fear or grief, if they remain faithful to their original teachings (2:62).

Above A 16th-century bible showing Moses parting the Red Sea. Many Biblical narratives are considered divine and are replicated in the Quran.

OTHER HOLY BOOKS

In addition to the holy scriptures of the Torah of Moses, Psalms of David and the Evangel of Jesus, the Quran mentions the 'Scrolls of Abraham' (*Suhuf-i-Ibrahim*) (87:19). Although no record of Abraham's scriptures exists, the Old Testament recognizes Abraham as a prophet (Genesis 20:7). The Quran also refers to the Pentateuch, the first five books of the Old Testament, attributed to the original revelations of Moses.

The Quran does not rule out the possibility of revelations having been given to earlier religious figures in other traditions, such as Hinduism and Buddhism, because, it says, prophets of God were sent to every nation (10:47).

JESUS, PROPHET OF ISLAM

WITHIN ISLAM, JESUS (ISA IN ARABIC) IS CONSIDERED A UNIQUE AND IMPORTANT PROPHET. BOTH HE AND HIS MOTHER, MARY, ARE PORTRAYED IN SOME DETAIL WITHIN THE QURAN.

Mentioned by name many times in the Quran, Jesus is also referred to by other titles, including the *Masih* (Messiah). He is an important figure in the 'End of Time' events related in the Quran and hadith, and his mother, Mary, has a whole chapter of the Quran named after her (*Surah Maryam*, chapter 19).

MIRACULOUS CONCEPTION

The Quran calls Jesus (Isa) 'the word of God' (4:171, 3:45), 'servant of God' (19:30) and 'messenger of God' (61:6). In themselves the titles given to Jesus are not unique – for all of God's prophets are deemed to be his 'word', 'servant' and 'messenger' – but the miraculous birth of Jesus is exceptional.

The Quranic text compares Jesus' conception to that of the first man, Adam: 'Indeed, the likeness of Jesus in God's eyes is as Adam's likeness, he originated him from dust, and then said unto him "be" and he was.' (3:59). Many Muslim scholars of the Quran interpret this verse to explain Jesus as 'the word of God', because of the particular way in which he was conceived by God's simple word 'be'.

But the story of Jesus' birth as told in the Quran lacks elements of the Biblical narrative – there are no stable, wise men or stepfather Joseph. Instead, the story relates, Mary retreated to the desert and gave birth under the shade of a palm tree, in some considerable discomfort (19:22–6).

JESUS AND DIVINITY

Although the Quran affirms Jesus' miraculous conception (3:47), it rejects outright the notion of Jesus as divine or as 'the Son of God' (5:18, 19:88–92). To ascribe Jesus' divinity is a major and unforgivable sin in Islam known as *shirk* (associating partners to God).

While the Bible does not directly mention the Trinity (one God existing in three persons and one substance, Father, Son and Holy Spirit), the Quran refers to it in admonishment: 'They do blaspheme who say: "God is one of three, in a trinity: for there is no God except One God" '. (5:73)

Jesus is often referred to in the Quran as 'Jesus, son of Mary' (for example 19:34, 61:6) as a reminder of his humanity, and his genealogy is traced through the Israelites to Isaac, son of Ibrahim (Abraham), through his mother's lineage (the Bible, Luke 3:23–34). The Quran

Above A late 18th-century Ethiopian Christian liturgical parchment written in Geez, an ancient Ethiopian language, portrays Christ teaching his followers.

attributes a number of miracles to Jesus, but it gives details only of the first. The story tells that Jesus, as a newborn child, spoke in his mother's defence after she was accused of being unchaste by her people when she returned after giving birth to him (19:27–33).

THE CRUCIFIXION

As Islam is devoid of the notion of 'original sin' and the subsequent 'fall of man', so, too, the Christian theology of salvation of humankind through the sacrifice of Jesus as the 'Lamb of God' is absent. However, just as the Quran addresses the Christian claims of Jesus' divinity and the Trinity, it also contains verses relating to the event of his crucifixion. The Quran states: 'And they said, "We killed Christ Jesus, the son of Mary, the messenger of God" – but they killed him not, nor crucified him, but so it was made to appear to them'. (4:157)

This passage, although denying outright the crucifixion of Jesus and his death, continues to confirm his ascension to heaven: 'No, God raised him up unto Himself...'

Above Muhammad prophesied Jesus' return, claiming that he would appear at the Umayyad Mosque, Damascus, Syria, and would then defeat the Antichrist.

(4:158). The Islamic teaching, then, is that Jesus was not crucified (or killed in any other way) by his enemies, although it was made to appear as such, but rather, God raised him up to paradise, where, the Quran relates, he dwells alive until he will reappear just before the Final Day (4:159).

JESUS AND THE END OF TIME

There are many hadiths relating to Jesus that give descriptions of his appearance and details of his miracles and prophetic mission. In the prophetic narrations relating to the events of the 'End of Time', Jesus is featured as an important character, who, it is claimed in a famous hadith, 'will break crosses, kill swine and abolish the *jizyah* (an exemption tax for religious minorities under Islamic rule) and wealth will pour forth to such an

Right The Quranic narrative of Jesus rejects the crucifixion but accepts the ascension, as illustrated in this 16th-century Ottoman manuscript painting.

extent that no one will accept it and one prostration of prayer will be better than the world and what it contains.'

Jesus is also mentioned in connection with the appearance of the Antichrist and the upheavals of the events connected to him. Another hadith informs that after defeating the Antichrist, Jesus will marry, have children and remain for 45 years before his death, when he will be buried next to the Prophet Muhammad in Madinah.

Below A medieval painting of Jerusalem features the al-Aqsa Mosque – the third holiest shrine in Islam. The city is central to Christianity, Judaism and Islam.

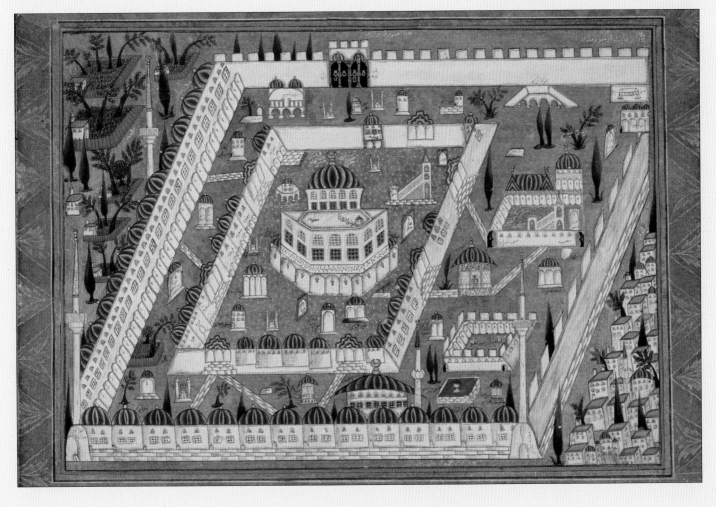

ISLAM AND OTHER FAITHS

RELIGIONS OFTEN EXCLUDE OTHER FAITHS FROM SALVATION AND HEAVEN. HOWEVER, THE QURAN HAS MADE SPACE FOR OTHERS, PARTICULARLY THOSE OF OTHER MONOTHEISTIC RELIGIONS.

The literate activity of polemics, where the world is seen in clearly divided black and white categories, has produced a spate of apologetic works, defending and explaining the faith for believers, that condemn other religions. This thinking has also featured in some Muslim societies through exclusivist interpretations of the Quran, in which only Muslims are considered worthy of heaven. However, there are also inclusive interpretations, which state that people of other faiths, as well as Muslims, are guaranteed a place in heaven.

Above A painting from 1686 depicts Muslim men in paradise. Debates about who goes to paradise have occupied many pages in Muslim writings.

THE QURANIC VIEW

As Islam presents itself as a continuation of previous divine religions, it is no surprise that it should encompass many people beyond its own religious tradition. The Quran affirms this in no uncertain terms: 'those who have faith, those who are Jews, Christians and Sabians (possibly followers of John the Baptist) – whoever has faith in God and the Last Day, and performs good deeds – will have their reward from their Lord. No fear will come upon them, nor shall they grieve' (2:62).

However, there is an apparent contradiction: while many Quranic verses include Jews and Christians, others chide them for the exclusive rights they claim over paradise: 'if the Last Home with God be for you specially, and not for anyone else, then seek ye death…' (2:94)

It also criticizes Jews and Christians for trying to make Muslims be like them, and instructs Muslims that their response should be 'Nay, (I would rather follow) the religions of Ibrahim, and he joined

Left A Christian service at the Chaldean Seminary in Baghdad. Christianity is a continued feature of the religious landscape of Iraq.

not partners with Allah' (2:135). The finality of Islam is confirmed by the Quranic revelation 'if anyone desires a religion other than Islam, never will it be accepted of him…' (3:85)

Scholars of the Quran have attempted to explain this apparent contradiction in several ways. Some have suggested, for example, that certain verses were applicable only until the faith of the early believers was strengthened, after which subsequent revelations were given that nullified the previous rule. This would mean that while Jews and Christians were initially accepted into God's heaven, they were eventually excluded, because God accepted only Islam as a faith and way of life.

INCLUDING OTHERS

This exclusive interpretation of the Quran has sat very uncomfortably with some Muslim scholars. Their argument is that whatever God has revealed must surely be applicable for all times and places, until the end of the world. Therefore, they claim, scholars must not take on the 'role of God' and limit the

Above A collection of Qurans in a bookcase in the Prophet's Mosque in Madinah. The Quran has many verses relating to people from other faiths.

application of those verses that include those of other monotheistic religions into the fold of faith.

Those that support this view claim that 'Islam' does not refer simply to the religion but to anyone submitting in peace to one God – 3:77 defines 'religion of Allah' as being that of everyone who submits to him. Muhammad's acceptance of *hunafa* would seem to corroborate this view – *hunafa* shunned paganism and believed in one God, but did not follow a formal religion.

Some historians of Islam have commented that the exclusivist interpretations of the Quran seem to have been in circulation and popular at times when Islam was strong as a ruling entity: it has been argued, in other words, a position of superiority has led some Muslims to exclude others.

Many other commentaries of the Quran note that verses that are hard to interpret (*mutashabihah*) should not be interpreted, on the grounds that only God knows their true meanings. Instead, they should be taken at face value.

While other religions may not accept Muslims as a believing people, Muslims have a clear instruction in the Quran to accept others. This viewpoint urges Muslims to treat 'others' as equals, with respect and affection. Islam teaches that the final judgement is

Right Jewish boys wearing kippas in Torah class in Tehran. The Jewish teacher is observing the Iranian dress code.

God's, as only he knows who is truly devoted to Him, regardless of religious structures. Ultimately, heaven is his kingdom and he alone decides who enters it.

FREE WILL

ISLAM TEACHES THAT HUMAN BEINGS ARE UNIQUE AMONG EARTHLY CREATURES IN HAVING BEEN GIVEN FREE WILL TO ENABLE THEM TO CHOOSE RIGHT OR WRONG AND TO BELIEVE OR DISBELIEVE IN GOD.

Islamic theology teaches that men and women are to exercise their God-given free will. However, being endowed with choice entails both accountability (*masulliyyah*) and responsibility (*caliph*). Islam asserts that human free will is best employed in the establishment of God's will as revealed to his prophets and their holy scriptures.

DIVINE ORDER

According to Islam, the universe has been beautifully and perfectly created and divinely ordered, with the whole of nature and its innate goodness placed at the disposal of humankind. The purpose of nature is to enable men and women to do good and achieve felicity by divine design and order: 'The earth is full of signs of evidence for those who have certitude' (51:20).

Islam teaches that God is the ultimate cause of every event (*al-Awwal*) and the end of all action and things (*al-Akhir*), and men and women should therefore deem his will to be greater in moral worth than their own. This is not to say that they are removed of individual responsibility or account, but rather that they should reckon all that they do and choose to be in accordance with God's divine initiative.

The Quran claims that to assist humans in pursuit of their purpose, God has continuously provided evidence of his will through divine revelations (30:30, 33:62, 40:85).

Above *The Quran teaches that although God knows everything, he has given humans free will over their beliefs and actions to test their obedience and faith.*

Below *A detail from a 14th-century Persian manuscript by al-Qazwini illustrates the endless possibilities of unlimited free will.*

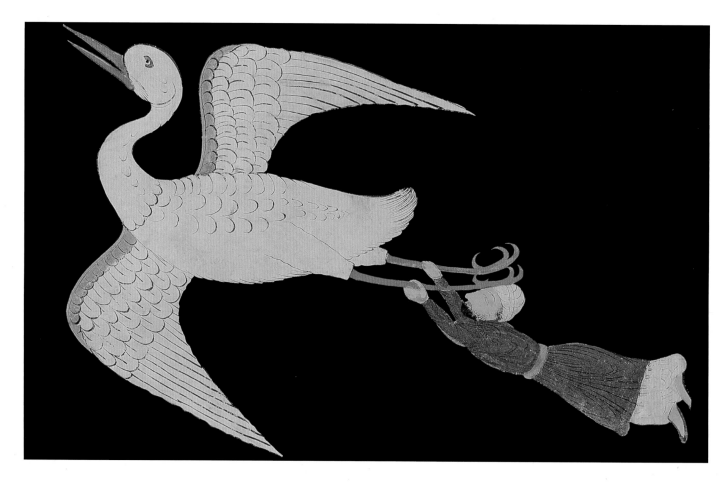

Indeed, Muslims see the universe itself as a living proof of God's sublime existence and predestined command (10:5–6).

PREDETERMINATION

Islam posits that the essential element of choice or free will in humankind results in only two outcomes, which are predetermined by God before each person's worldly existence. In God's schema, however, individual choice manifests itself as an exercise of free will that is devoid of divine predetermination. Because God knows that which angels and human beings do not, he alone has prior knowledge not only of what each man and woman will or will not do, but also of the final abode of every human being.

KNOWING GOD'S WILL

The Quran contains many passages concerning the divine attributes and names of God but offers little in the way of theological doctrine. Hadiths seem to advise against trying to fathom divine will (qadar): 'Do not cogitate on God, but on the creation of God' and 'earlier communities perished because they dwelled on discussions regarding qadar'.

Traditionally, Muslims have divided into two distinct – if not opposing – groups in their pursuit of knowing God. The first, the legates (fuqaha), have historically focused theological discussions on what is manifest (dhahir) of God's will through law (Shariah) and jurisprudence (fiqh): that is, they explore what God has permitted to be known about himself through the Quran and sunnah.

The second group, the Sufis, or ascetics, have maintained that God is best known through experience. They believe that God unveils his divine nature to those who seek to draw near to him through inner dimensions (batin) of worship. The medieval scholar Ibn Tamiyyah

(1263–1328) concluded that 'the truth [regarding Divine will] does not belong to one party exclusively but is divided among all groups'.

Neither the legates' scriptural conformity nor the inner spiritual purification of the ascetics could in themselves solve the problem of tensions that surfaced around the arguments about divine will. However, the classical scholar al-Ghazali (1058–1111) synthesized the rationalism of the legates with Sufi practices of 'living faith' in his *Revival of the Religious Sciences*, which set the Shariah in the context of an experienced religion, in which love of God was the main motivator.

Above This miniature Ottoman astrological zodiac chart dates from 1583. It neatly, if speculatively, illustrates man's divine predestination.

HUMAN WILL

Theological discussions regarding the correct understanding of divine will can detract from the Islamic teaching that every individual is in fact responsible for his or her own actions. Humankind's true vocation, according to Islam, lies in the moral realm, where fulfilment of God's will can take place only in freedom. In other words, to truly prosper, humankind must exercise free will in accordance with God's will.

THE STAGES OF HUMAN EXISTENCE

IN ISLAMIC THEOLOGY, THIS WORLD IS SEEN AS A TEMPORAL AND TRANSIENT ONE, THROUGH WHICH HUMAN BEINGS ARE JOURNEYING ON THEIR WAY TO THE PERMANENT REALMS OF THE AFTERLIFE.

The Quran reminds humankind that 'to God we belong and to Him is the return' (2:156), and the reality that, 'every soul shall taste death' (3:185). But death is not seen by Muslims as the final end, only the termination of worldly life and physical existence.

THE ABODE OF SOULS
Muhammad taught that there are stages of human existence that both precede and succeed this worldly life. The first stage is said to be the 'abode of the souls' (*dar al-arwah*), the place where the spirit (*ruh*) of every human being abides before the creation of its physical body.

Muhammad said that when a person senses familiarity on first meeting someone, it is because their souls have recognized each other from the previous abode, suggesting a continuum and direct connection between the abode of the soul and earthly existence.

Muslim scholars have concluded that the ego-self has three states of being, which are determined by the Quranic terms: *ammarah* (12:53), prone to evil; *lawwamah* (75:2 – *wa la uqsimu bin nafsil lawwamah*, 'And no! I swear by the accusing soul'), aware of evil but resistant through patience, faith and repentance; and *mutmainnah* (89:27), the highest

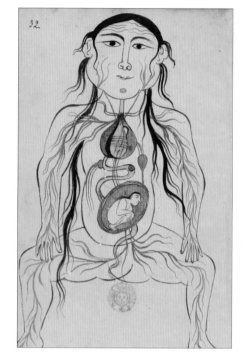

Above This 15th-century drawing by a Muslim artist shows a woman carrying a baby. A hadith explains the soul is blown into the foetus by an angel.

stage of belief, satisfaction and peace. Islamic theology teaches that the soul's earthly struggle is largely believed to be that of the contesting desires between his or her ego (*nafs*), which yearns for worldly materialism, and his or her soul (*ruh*), which seeks the higher spiritual state of being.

EXISTENCE IN THE WOMB
The Quran refers to the creation of human beings in stages (*atwara*) (71:14), drawing attention to several points in the reproductive process (75:37, 23:14, 39:6). A hadith explains the connection between the pre-existing soul and the physical body: 'Verily the creation of each one of you is brought together in his mother's belly for forty days in the form of seed, then he is a clot of blood for a like

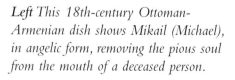

Left This 18th-century Ottoman-Armenian dish shows Mikail (Michael), in angelic form, removing the pious soul from the mouth of a deceased person.

period, then a morsel of flesh for a like period, then there is sent to him an angel who blows his soul (*ruh*) into him.'

WORLDLY EXISTENCE

According to the Quran, when God declared that he was about to create humankind, he commanded the angels: 'When I have fashioned him and breathed into him of my spirit, then obediently prostrate before him' (15:29). The verse is taken to imply that only when the spirit was breathed into Adam's body did he become superior to the angels and God's befitting vicegerent (caliph) (6:165).

In Arabic, worldly life is termed *dunya*, which means something lowly, insignificant, without value. The Quran makes a value distinction between this life and the afterlife, or hereafter, which is seen as the first as well as the final resting place of humankind: 'What is the life of this world but play and amusement? But best is the home in the hereafter, for those who are righteous, will you then not understand?' (6:32)

EXISTENCE IN THE GRAVE

Death is the inevitable end of worldly life, but the Quran teaches that 'He [God] created death and life, that He may try which of you is best in deeds' (67:2). According to hadith, Muhammad claimed that the soul is taken from the body at the point of death, but that it is reunited with it after burial.

Some Muslims believe that in the grave, the human soul is visited by angels, who question it about its religious beliefs and its deeds. If the soul has believed and worked righteousness, it is given a view of paradise as a reward to come. However, if the soul has denied God and committed evil, it is tormented and punished in the grave as a taste of the eternal punishment of hell (6:93–4).

THE AFTERLIFE

For Muslims, death is seen not as the end but merely as a transition from one state of being into another in the soul's journey back to the creator, who will reward righteous believers and punish evil wrongdoers (10:4).

The Quran claims that at the 'Final Hour', a trumpet will sound and all souls will be resurrected and recreated in their original physical

Above The city of Najaf, Iraq, has one of the largest cemeteries in the world and is a preferred place of burial for Shiah Muslims globally.

form to stand in rows before their creator (18:99–101, 78:17). Each person will then be questioned by God regarding what he or she believed and did, and will be rewarded accordingly with either paradise or hellfire.

FRIDAY: DAY OF CONGREGATION

THE IDEA OF GOD RESTING ON THE SEVENTH DAY AFTER CREATING THE WORLD IS REJECTED IN ISLAMIC THEOLOGY. RATHER, THIS IS SEEN AS THE DAY ON WHICH HE ESTABLISHED HIS THRONE OF AUTHORITY.

Above In Christianity, Sunday is the traditional day of corporate worship and rest and it is observed from the teachings of the Old Testament creation story.

In Muslim countries, Friday is the day of congregation (*Jumuah*), but it is not a day of rest. While many people may not attend work on the day of *Jumuah*, working or earning a living on this day is not prohibited by Islamic law. This reflects the Muslim belief that, for God, 'no tiredness can seize Him, nor sleep' (2:255).

THE 'SEVENTH DAY'

Although Friday is the day of congregation in Islam and is even *Jumuatul Mubarak* ('Blessed Friday') in some hadiths, it is not equated with the Judaeo-Christian concept of the Sabbath as the 'seventh day' or a 'day of rest' (Genesis 2:1–3).

Islamic theology terms God as *al-Kahliq* (the creator), who is also *al-Hayy* (the ever-living) and *al-Qayyum* (the self-subsisting), and, as such, he is transcendent and wholly other. That is, God as creator is far removed from the qualities of his creation and the frailties of humankind (2:55). The Biblical concept that God exists as a 'Heavenly Father' (Matthew 23:9, 24:36 and 26:39) suggests that he may possess human-like qualities or traits: anger, jealousy, hunger and tiredness. The notion that God would have human attributes or that he would need to rest after the creation, or even at all, is contrary to the concept of God in Islam.

In the Quranic accounts of the genesis story, after God created the world, he established his Throne of authority over his creation as the final act of his supremacy over it.

THE 'THRONE' OF GOD

A number of verses in the Quran refer to the 'Throne of God' (*al-arsh*), and one verse is known specifically as *ayat al-kursi*, or 'the verse of the seat' (2:255). Here, God's 'Throne' symbolizes his authority, the seat of his power and knowledge. The Quran asserts that to imagine the realm of the ever-expanding universe and everything contained within it is a totally unfathomable task for any human being, yet so great are God's power, will, wisdom and authority, that they encompass everything within the cosmos and beyond.

According to Islamic theology, the expansive infinity of the universe is a reflection of God's absolute reality (16:12, 22:18). God's activity, eternal nature, perfection and self-sustenance represent his constant and direct involvement with all the realms of his creation.

ADAM AND FRIDAY

The Quran implies that Adam was the last of creation because God informs the angels 'I will create a vicegerent on Earth', to which the

Left Friday is the day of Jumuah or congregation in Islam, but business and social interactions are not prohibited, either before or after prayers.

Left Adam and Eve are depicted playing innocently in paradise. Muslims believe they were created on a Friday and that Judgement Day, too, will occur on a Friday.

hadith relates that Satan, Adam and Eve were sent down to earth from paradise on a Friday.

A DAY OF WORSHIP

The monotheistic traditions of Judaism, Christianity and Islam each have a day of congregational worship: the Jews celebrate Shabbat on Saturday, Christians worship together on Sunday and Muslims participate in *Jum'a* on Friday.

Beyond the theological and canonical justifications for the different days of congregation within these three religious traditions, the overarching principle is that each religious community should meet together to remember, celebrate and praise God on a weekly basis. The instruction in Islam to suspend work and trading in order to attend *Jumuah* is prescribed in the Quran, in a specific chapter entitled *Al-Jumuah*. The passage continues 'and when the prayer is ended, then disperse in the land and seek God's bounty, and remember God much that you may be successful' (62:9–10).

angels ask, 'will you not place therein a thing that will cause much bloodshed while we praise and glorify Your hallowed name?' In his reply, God affirms his all-encompassing knowledge and wisdom: 'Indeed, I know that which you know not' (2:30).

In a hadith, Muhammad said that God had created Adam on a Friday, and that he then taught Adam the names of all things, something the angels could not do. He then commanded all created things to bow before Adam in acknowledgement of his supremacy. All did so except for Satan, a *jinn* (a genie, or creation of the unseen, who, like humans, has been endowed with freedom of choice), who chose to disobey God because he was jealous of Adam (2:34).

According to the Quran, human beings have been created in the 'best of moulds', but those who follow their temptations and lusts become debased, whereas the righteous shall have unfailing rewards (95:4–6). A prophetic

Right Muslim men attend Friday prayers at the Prophet Muhammad's Mosque in the holy city of Madinah, Saudi Arabia.

THE DAY OF JUDGEMENT

THE QURAN SPEAKS OF A 'FINAL HOUR' — THE END OF THE WORLD — WHEN MEN AND WOMEN WILL BE RESURRECTED FROM THEIR GRAVES AND GATHERED TOGETHER TO STAND IN JUDGEMENT BEFORE GOD.

Belief in the Day of Judgement (al-yawm al-akhir) is a fundamental creed and one of the six articles of faith in Islam. Muslims believe that on this day, every person who has ever lived will be called to give individual account in front of their creator for what they believed and did during their life on earth.

The Day of Judgement is an aspect of Islamic faith that belongs to the unseen realm (al-ghayb) — as do God, his angels, resurrection and the hereafter of paradise and hellfire. All the Islamic prophets taught their people to worship God and to believe in the hereafter with certainty of faith.

END-TIME EVENTS

The Prophet Muhammad taught that a number of minor and major events, or signs, will precede the Day of Judgement. According to sayings attributed to him, minor events would include a change in the male–female ratio, with women outnumbering men by 50 to 1, the construction of lofty buildings by the Bedouin Arabs and a decrease in religious knowledge among the general populace.

Major events that are mentioned in the Quran include the appearance of the Gog (yajuj) and Magog (majuj), wild people who, it is said, will break free from the barrier that restrains them and swarm the world, spreading mayhem (21:96). The Quran also refers to a 'beast' that it says will come out from the earth and address humankind with lies and falsehood, which they will believe because they doubted

the promise of God (27:82). Other hadiths also inform and warn of the Antichrist (al-Masih al-Dajjal), who will misguide humankind and create wars and strife.

According to hadith, other major catastrophic events will include the appearance of the promised Muslim Mahdi ('guided one'), who will fight the Antichrist; the eruption of volcanic fires in Yemen; the rising of the sun from the West, and the descent of the prophet Jesus from heaven.

SIGNS IN NATURE

Although the Quran does not make clear the precise chronology of these events, it does tell of signs in the natural world that will precede the 'Final Hour', including 'gales that rage on and on, scattering things around…'. It also promises that it will be a day 'when stars fade away and the sky splits open, when mountains are pulverized…'. (77:2–3, 8–10) According to the Quran, once all of the above events

Above An illustration of the beast of the Apocalypse taken from Zubdat al-Tawarikh *by Sayyid Loqman Ashuri.*

have occurred, the angel Israfil will blow a trumpet. Every person (except martyrs) will then be brought from their graves (78:17–20), where, Islam teaches, they will already have experienced a form of reward or punishment in a transient spiritual state — either al-araaf (heights) or al-barzakh (purgatory) — that will have been decided by what they believed and how they lived during their worldly existence.

The pre-Islamic Arabs mocked Muhammad's warning of a bodily resurrection, and in the Quran are quoted as saying, 'What! When we are reduced to bones and dust, should we really be raised up as

Left This medieval French painting shows the three-headed Antichrist being aided by the devil and by humans. The Antichrist is central to Islamic — as well as Christian — eschatology.

a new creation?' (17:49) But the Quran gives the reply that he who created humankind in the first instance will do so again (17:50–1).

JUDGEMENT BOOK

The Quran says that on the Day of Judgement, most of humankind will be lined up in ranks and every person will be brought forward to be judged by God, and a 'book' accounting for every deed will be placed before them. The sinful will be terrified, saying, 'Ah! Woe to us! What a book this is! It leaves out nothing small or great, but takes account thereof!' (18:49). The verse continues, 'They will find all that they did, placed before them: and none will thy Lord treat with injustice.' For this reason the Day of Judgement is also known in Islam as 'the Day of Absolute Truth' (*yawm al-haq*) (78:39).

Above Muslim martyrs await the Day of Judgement with Ali – depicted symbolically as the 'Lion of God' – watching over their graves.

HEAVENLY MARTYRS

Islam teaches that anyone who dies in the path of God, pursuing righteousness and defending justice in the service of humanity, should be considered a martyr. It is believed that these martyrs will enter paradise directly, without experiencing death as others do (2:154, 3:169), and without being judged. Muhammad said that they will be allowed to intercede on behalf of their loved ones on Judgement Day and will have lofty mansions with many spouses in paradise near God.

The Quran warns that while successful believers will be rewarded by God with eternal paradise, disbelieving wrongdoers will be punished for ever in hellfire.

Below Medieval representations of the damned commonly depict horrific scenes of eternal blazing torture and punishment, often based on the descriptions of divine texts.

HEAVEN

IN ISLAM, HEAVEN IS SEEN AS THE DOMAIN OF ALLAH, AND THE ETERNAL RESTING PLACE AND ULTIMATE REWARD FOR ALL HIS RIGHTEOUS SERVANTS. IT IS THE GOAL OF EVERY MUSLIM.

The Quran and hadith contain many descriptions of heaven, but it is a place that belongs to the unseen aspects (*al-ghayb*) of Islamic beliefs and as such can be imaged only by analogy. Indeed, Muslims believe that its realities are far removed from any descriptions of worldly language and the limits of human imagination.

ORIGINAL ABODE

Muhammad foretold that God has prepared for his servants delights that 'no eye has seen nor any ear has heard and has never occurred to a human heart'. Paradise, or heaven, is the place where God and his Throne are believed to exist, surrounded by countless angels singing his praises and extolling peace (23:86, 39:75).

Islam teaches that the righteous and faithful who attain paradise will find that the desire of their soul will be fulfilled, because they will be returning to their original abode and that of the primordial parents of humankind, Adam and Eve. The Quran teaches that before Satan's jealousy led him to tempt Adam and Eve to take fruit from the forbidden tree, this first man and woman lived in peace and bliss within the Garden of Paradise (2:35). Ever since the momentous event of their expulsion from this garden, their believing and righteous descendants have been striving to return to their original abode in the company of Allah and his angels (6:60, 10:45–6).

DWELLERS OF PARADISE

The reward of returning to the Garden of Paradise is not open to all, however, and the rightful dwellers, according to the Quran and hadith, need to be very worthy souls. Entrance to heaven is not automatic simply on profession of a religious creed or doctrine. Indeed, the Quran warns against such complacency: 'it is not by your wishes, nor by the wishes of the People of the Book [Jews and Christians]: whoever does wrong shall be punished for it, and he will not find other than God as protector or helper' (4:123). Paradise, therefore, is believed by Muslims to be reserved for those who have pure faith and good deeds (2:62).

DESCRIPTIONS OF HEAVEN

The reward promised to the righteous is clearly presented in the Quran, but there is no structure

Above In this 10th-century drawing from a Persian manuscript, Adam and Eve are depicted in the Garden of Paradise – they spent the first part of their lives in heaven.

to paradise suggested in the text. However, it is generally believed to consist of various realms – and some Muslims conclude that people are admitted to each realm depending on their righteousness.

Both the Quran and hadith offer descriptions of heaven's features. It is said to have eight entrances, one of which, the gate of *rayhan*, is as an exclusive entrance for those who were faithful in their religious fasting. The Quran describes its gardens having rivers and fruits of every kind and desire (47:15) and says that it will be neither too hot nor too cold and will provide shade for its inhabitants (76:13–14). There are special fountains of pure water, milk, honey and heavenly wines free from intoxicants and drinks of camphor and *zanjabil* (a

Left This Indian carpet displays the many pleasures of paradise. Faces have been obscured, as some Muslims prohibit figurative art.

Above In Islam, paradise is believed to have various levels of rewards, as shown in this 11th-century Persian painting.

and *talh* (thought to be a fruit similar to plantain or banana) trees in abundance (56:28–9). Other food delights will include inexhaustible selections of meats, particularly the flesh of fowls (56:21).

LIVING IN PARADISE

As a reward for their goodness, proclaims the Quran, the dwellers of paradise will have all that they desire (9:21–2), and describes how they will spend their time. They will wear musk and clothes of the purest silk, with gold and pearl jewellery (22:23) and, reclining on raised thrones, they will be greeted by their Lord (36:56–8) in an atmosphere free of idle or vain talk (19:62). They will be served by youths with plates and goblets of silver and gold (56:17–18) and will live in tents 97km (60 miles) high and made of pearls. The Quran also refers to heavenly companions (2:25), wide-eyed maidens (56:22–4) and beautiful, pure spouses for the righteous (55:70).

Above A beautiful green bird perches on a rock by flowers at a riverside. A hadith states the souls of Muslim martyrs will be housed in the bodies of green birds in paradise.

ginger-based beverage), all served from ornate golden goblets (47:15, 76:15–17). It is said that the fruits of the Garden of Paradise are in pairs (55:52), with pomegranates, dates

HELL

ISLAM TEACHES THAT AS GOD CREATED HEAVEN, SO HE ALSO MADE HELL, WHICH THE QURAN DECLARES IS PREPARED FOR ALL THOSE WHO REJECT FAITH AND COMMIT SINS AND GRAVE INJUSTICES.

When God granted humans free will, teaches the Quran, it was conditional to a covenant that they would faithfully worship none but God and live in accordance with divine will (2:38–9). Muslims believe that while the faithful will live forever in paradise, disbelieving evildoers will have their recompense in hell (3:131, 78:21–2).

DESPISED ABODE

Prophetic sayings regarding hell imply that it already exists as a place of punishment waiting to receive wrongdoers. The Quran confirms this: 'truly Hell is lying in wait' (78:21), and says that it will be filled with *jinn* and men (11:19).

Where hell is positioned in relation to heaven is not made clear, but it is described as a bottomless pit of fiercely burning fire (101:8–11), into which evildoers will be thrown, suggesting that it lies some way underneath heaven. Like heaven, it is believed to have different levels, which relate to the quantity and gravity of the sins of its inhabitants (6:123).

The Quran vividly describes hell as a place of unimaginable terror and suffering, in which dwellers receive no respite from their eternal punishment. Hell also appears to be an abode of continuous purgatory, whose inhabitants 'will neither die nor live' (20:74).

Above A 15th-century painting provides a gruesome insight into the punishments of hell.

DWELLERS OF HELL

Compared with other sacred texts, the Quran contains far more descriptions of heaven and hell, particularly in the earlier revealed verses from the Makkan period. This increased focus on the hereafter appears to underline the central theme of inevitable divine judgement. While there are numerous depictions of the abodes of heaven and hell in the Quran and prophetic traditions, it would be wrong to interpret them literally. This is because the real nature and exact descriptions of the hereafter are known only to God. However, Islam teaches that there definitely will be compensation and reward for good deeds and punishment for all evil ones.

On the Day of Judgement, relates the Quran, hell will be asked if its blazing eternal fire has been satiated with the souls of men and women as its fuel, to which it will reply, 'Are there some more (available)?' (50:30)

Left This painting from the 16th century gives a frighteningly graphic and detailed portrayal of the torments and fires of hell.

The response will be that hordes of humans will be dragged in chains into the fire by cursing angels (69:30–2). The Quran names a few dwellers of hell, including: the Pharaoh who drove out Moses and the Israelites (7:103–41, 11:96–9); and Abu Lahab (the disbelieving uncle of Muhammad) and his wife (111:1–5).

DESCRIPTIONS OF HELL

There are various different words used in the Quran to describe hell: *al-hutamah* (human crusher), *al-jaheem* (ferocious fire), *jahannam* (hellfire), *ladha* (fire of hell), *saeer* (burning fire) and *saqar* (flaming inferno). In addition to these six terms, the generic Arabic word for fire (*an-nar*), is also used, and, collectively, the passages create an acutely disturbing and horrifically graphic idea of the place of hell.

According to a hadith, the depth of hell is such that a stone thrown into it would take 70 years to reach the bottom, and so vast that it will be dragged forth on the Day of Judgement by 70,000 angels pulling 70,000 reins. The Quran teaches that hell has seven gates, suggesting seven levels, each assigned to a different class of sinner (15:44), and that 19 angels guard it (74:30). At the centre of hell, its fiercest point, is said to be a tree called *az-zaqqum*, bearing fruit of flaming fire that is served as food to the worst evildoers (37:62–7, 44: 43–6, 56:51–6).

PUNISHMENTS OF HELL

The Quran claims that the fuel of the fire of hell will be humans, *jinn* and stones (2:24, 72:14–15). Hell's punishments will be in relation to the sins committed (15:43–4). Scholars are keen to point out that once in heaven, the fear of being removed does not hang over a dweller, but once in hell, the hope of escaping is always possible – God's mercy is infinite. The allegorical

interpretations which stress God's love also indicate that despite evil actions, a person may escape the torments of hell, if God so wishes. Those who used money belonging to orphans will be made to eat raw fire (4:10), as will those who changed or tampered with the scriptures of God for a small profit (2:174).

Above A vision of hell on earth as a volcano erupts. Prophetic narrations describe hellfire as being 70 times hotter than any earthly fire.

Below A detail from an 18th-century Geez manuscript shows sinners burning in the eternal fire as hell's guardians hold them in chattels and taunt them.

CHAPTER 4

WORSHIP AND RELIGIOUS PRACTICE

An oft-quoted hadith states that Islam is built upon five pillars: the declaration (*shahadah*) that there is no God but the One God, Allah, and that Muhammad is his final messenger; the five daily prayers (*salah*); paying alms to the poor (*zakah*); fasting in the month of Ramadhan (*sawm*); and performing a pilgrimage (*Hajj*) to Makkah, if resources permit.

Festivals capturing the essence of these pillars are celebrated throughout the year. The most frequent is the celebration of *Jumuah*, Friday, the day of congregational prayer. The greatest Muslim festivals of the year are the two *Eids*, marking the end of Ramadhan and *Hajj*. Several others, such as *Mawlid*, the birthday of the Prophet, and *Miraj*, Muhammad's night journey to heaven, are widely celebrated in some parts of the Muslim world.

Because worship and prayer are the central purposes of life, places of prayer are an important part of Muslim civilization. The mosque, as both a building and an institution, is a proud place of gathering.

Opposite The five pillars are the realization of faith in Islam. Prayer is central, and when combined with celebration, as here on Eid ul-adha *in al-Abbas Mosque in Kerbala, Iraq, all the family attend.*

Above Nepali Muslims attend the last Eid ul-fitr *prayer at the Kashmiri Mosque in Kathmandu, which marks the end of the holy fasting month of Ramadhan.*

SHAHADAH: DECLARING BELIEF IN ONE GOD

THE CENTRAL DOCTRINE IN ISLAM IS THE *SHAHADAH*, WITNESSING AND DECLARING THE BELIEF THAT THERE IS NO GOD BUT THE ONE GOD (*ALLAH* IN ARABIC), AND THAT MUHAMMAD IS HIS MESSENGER.

Religious civilizations can often be summed up by one central doctrine or figure: in Islam, the *shahadah* embodies *tawhid*, the doctrine of belief in one God, and *risalah*, that of the prophethood of Muhammad, the central figure of Islam. These two facets of the creed are connected and interdependent; for Muslim belief to be present, both parts of the declaration must be affirmed.

NEGATION IN BELIEF

For Muslims, belief in God cannot exist without first negating the possibility of any other form of deity. Thus, the conviction in one God is first by the negative statement 'there is no god…', followed by the affirmation '…but Allah'. This briefest of affirmations is the richest in meaning in Islamic life, and, according to a hadith, it is also the weightiest in God's eyes. The entire body of Islamic civilization is seen as being encapsulated in the phrase *la ilaha illal-lah, Muhammad rasulul-lah*.

SHAHADAH AS LIFE

As a recitation, or declaration, the *shahadah* constitutes the first words that a Muslim baby hears, and the

Below An oil painting by Jean-Léon Gérôme from 1865 depicts Muslim men declaring their faith through prayer.

Above An Iraqi Muslim holds up his prayer beads after Friday prayer in Baghdad, as he recites the shahadah *as praise of God.*

last words heard by a dying Muslim. In between these points of birth and death, the entire circle of life hinges on these words, which a Muslim will recite countless times in one day – when waking up, when washing, in the five daily prayers, in supplication. In fact, the opening words of Muslim speeches

THE HADITH OF THE PILLARS OF ISLAM

'Islam is built on five pillars: declaring that there is no god but Allah and that Muhammad is the messenger of Allah; establishment of the five daily prayers; payment of the poor due; pilgrimage to the House (Makkah); and fasting (in Ramadhan).'

Bukhari's hadith collection

and documents are usually the *basmalah*. Even in conversation in social settings, Muslims will often intersperse their talk with this declaration, as a reminder of the presence of God, his existence, his oneness and his love.

MUHAMMAD IN THE *SHAHADAH*

For a Muslim, the belief in God is via Muhammad the Messenger. It is therefore incumbent upon Muslims to affirm Muhammad's prophetic mission. In order to follow God's laws, a Muslim must

study the life example and teachings of the Prophet, as he is believed to embody the perfect way to live. It is impossible for a Muslim to separate belief in God and his Prophet.

Uttering the simple sentence of *shahadah*, devoid of any other ritual, brings people into the fold of Islam, and, regardless of their actions, they are henceforth considered 'Muslim', meaning 'submitting to God's will'.

CERTAINTY OF KNOWING

However, some scholars believe that the best form of Muslim life is that where the *shahadah* is not just orally uttered, but practised, held in the heart and translated into peaceful actions.

Indeed, a true confession of faith should not be an intellectual activity exclusively – but also an emotional, sensory (hence physical), rational and spiritual one. Muslims believe that experiencing the declaration of faith on all four levels leads one to *yaqin*, the absolute certainty of knowing, seeing and believing the truth (69:51 and 102:5–7).

While the other four pillars of Islam are ritual acts of worship, evolving around this declaration, the *shahadah* is a pillar of belief.

Left A silver vessel bearing the shahadah: la ilaha illal-lah, Muhammad rasulul-lah *(there is no God but God, and Muhammad is his messenger).*

SHAHADAH AS A PRACTICE

The *shahadah* is illustrated in practice through the Treaty of Hudaybiyah, where peace was concluded between Muslims and the Makkan pagan Arabs. Many then came to pledge their allegiance to the Prophet and God, with him placing his hand over theirs (48:10).

Muhammad was instructed later that if pagan women came to him, swearing belief in one God, obeying the Prophet and vowing not to commit major sins, he should accept their oaths (60:12). However, the women would hold the end of a cloth that he held, rather than taking his hand.

In modern times in the West, *shahadah* often takes place by confirming belief in the one God and in the prophethood of Muhammad in both the vernacular and Arabic. The declaration of a convert is often witnessed by two people, although this is not regarded as strictly necessary, as God Himself is believed to be a witness to belief.

Above A South Korean soldier converts to Islam. Conversion is a private matter before God, but many new Muslims choose to recite the shahadah *before witnesses.*

SALAH: THE FIVE DAILY PRAYERS

SALAH IS THE MEANS WHEREBY, FIVE TIMES A DAY, MUSLIMS HOLD COMMUNION WITH GOD. IT MUST BE CARRIED OUT IN A STATE OF RITUAL PURITY, AND WITH THE INTENTION TO WORSHIP HIM ALONE.

Salah, the second pillar of Islam, has both individual significance and communal importance. While often translated as 'prayer', the Arabic word *salah* specifically refers to 'communication'. The worshipper is therefore believed to be in direct communion with God: a hadith claims that *salah* is the ascension to heaven for the believer. The purpose of *salah* is solely to worship and remember God (20:14).

THE FIVE PRAYERS

Salah is compulsory, offered five times a day – at dawn (*fajr*), noon (*dhuhr*), late afternoon (*asr*), sunset (*maghrib*) and night (*isha*) (11:114) – facing the *Kaabah*. It is always recited in Arabic, the language of the Quran: Muslim brotherhood is central to *salah*; thus, Muslims can join *salah* in mosques in any part of the world.

Salah is preceded by the *adhan*, the call to prayer, which pours out of mosque minarets with the melodious voice of the *muadhdhin*, the caller. In many cities, such as Istanbul, one *adhan* is joined by another until the whole city rings with God's call. *Salah* itself is made up of units of prayer, *rakaah*, which vary in the prayers. The opening chapter of the Quran is recited in every unit, followed by other verses. God is praised and his blessings are invoked on Muhammad.

Performed standing, bowing, prostrating and sitting, *salah* can be offered individually or, preferably, in congregation. While it can be recited at home, at work, in the open or when travelling, *salah* carries most spiritual rewards when offered in a mosque.

WUDU

Salah can only be performed in a state of ritual bodily purity. This means that Muslims and their clothes must be clean at the time of prayer. *Wudu*, ritual ablution, therefore precedes *salah*,

Above Minarets of the al-Azhar Mosque in Cairo, Egypt. The adhan, *call to prayer, which precedes* salah, *is heard from the minarets ringing across cities throughout the Muslim world.*

and consists of washing the hands, mouth, nose, face, ears, head, arms and feet. Without sacred purity, and without intention, *salah* cannot be offered.

While *wudu* suffices for general purity, such as after waking up or using the toilet, a full bodily wash (*ghusl*) is required after sexual intercourse or menstruation.

PRAYER AS DISCIPLINE

Salah offers Muslims discipline and the chance to empty the mind entirely of its preoccupations. For Muslims, *salah* can be a powerful reorientation both spiritually and physically, as the body is engaged in prayer just as much as the soul. For believers, each movement of prayer carries deep spiritual significance,

Left Before prayer, ritual ablutions, wudu, *are performed from a fountain at Qarawiyyin Mosque in Fez, Morocco.*

where every limb is seen as turning its attention to its Creator. Muslims demonstrate their belief in God's greatness and their dependence on him in the act of prostration, of putting the most noble and prized part of the body, the head, before God, in submission to his will.

ORDAINING OF *SALAH*

When Muhammad was chosen as a prophet, he was at first told to purify himself and stand before God in worship. Eventually, he was asked to encourage his followers to do the same. However, it was not until 620, the tenth year of Muhammad's prophethood, that *salah* was institutionalized. This is said to have happened during the Prophet's night ascension to heaven (17:1), when, Muslims believe, he was miraculously transported to Jerusalem and then to the heavens via al-Buraq, a winged horse.

A hadith states Muhammad had conversations with God, during which 50 prayers a day were ordained. However, the story relates that on his way back through heaven, Muhammad met Moses, who told him to return to God and ask for the prayers to be limited in

Above A group of Muslims bowing in prayer at a mosque in Ibadan, Nigeria. In the Muslim world, all of life is organized around salah.

Above Sunset prayer (maghrib) is offered in the Haram Mosque in Makkah. The Kaabah sits in the centre.

number. God reduced the required prayers to five a day, but promised that those offering them would receive the rewards of at least 50.

ORGANIZING THE DAY BY THE PRAYER CYCLE

Salah naturally imposes discipline on believers, for each day is divided and regulated by prayers. Whether Muslims are studying, working or playing, they will stop at intervals to remember God. Everyday life is temporarily suspended by a natural rhythm of 'taking time out' from the world and its pressures. In the Muslim world, people plan events and meetings according to these set prayer times.

ZAKAH: GIVING ALMS TO THE POOR

ISLAM AIMS TO PRODUCE AN EGALITARIAN SOCIETY, WHERE THE SOCIAL AND ECONOMIC GAP BETWEEN THE RICH AND THE POOR IS REDUCED THROUGH THE PAYMENT OF *ZAKAH*, OR ALMS-GIVING.

Islam teaches that wealth is a blessing from God, and those who lawfully amass wealth are entitled to enjoy it. However, to prevent one person living in total luxury while others suffer in abject poverty, *zakah*, alms-giving, is an obligatory requirement for Muslims.

SOCIAL JUSTICE

This third pillar of Islam requires a portion of one's wealth to be distributed among the needy (9:103). It is a reminder to Muslims that all wealth is ultimately God's, and that people are merely trustees of it. *Zakah* is a fiscal policy through which social justice can be secured.

The Arabic word *zakah* means to purify, to bless and to increase. Giving alms is believed to purify wealth from greed: a hadith states that a man came to Muhammad, asking him, 'O Messenger of Allah,

I have plenty of property and wealth, tell me how to conduct my life', whereupon he was told to pay *zakah* to purify it. The Quran warns against amassing wealth and not spending on others (9:34–5) and promises that whoever spends for Allah will find an increase in what Allah bestows on him (2:245).

Alms-giving is fundamental in Islamic life and is mentioned 82 times in the Quran, in conjunction with *salah*. It is also recorded as having been observed by earlier prophets, such as John, Jesus and Ismail (chapter 19).

WHO PAYS *ZAKAH*?

Zakah is to be paid by any Muslim – minor or adult, male or female – who has held money, gold, silver, property or capital (including cattle and crops) above a determined amount, the *nisab*, for a year. The

Above A zakah *collection box from Shiraz, Iran.* Zakah *requires all Muslims to give 2.5 per cent of their substantial savings in charity per year.*

nisab is a minimum calculation: gold must weigh at least 85 grams for *zakah* to be payable, and cash must be above the minimum value of 595 grams of silver. The rate of *zakah* also varies depending on the property: for gold, silver and cash, it is 2.5 per cent; for agricultural produce, it is 5 per cent.

THE SOCIAL WISDOM BEHIND *ZAKAH*

Although sometimes collected by governments, *zakah* is seen to be the responsibility of the individual. *Zakah* avoids the tension that often exists between the state and the citizen in matters of tax payments

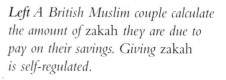

Left A British Muslim couple calculate the amount of zakah *they are due to pay on their savings. Giving* zakah *is self-regulated.*

because it is not a tax levied by the state, but a social and legal obligation fulfilled by the individual, who takes personal control over their wealth and pays the money due themselves. This is important, because for the benefits of *zakah* to be truly felt, there should be no resentment in the heart of the giver.

WHO RECEIVES *ZAKAH*?

The Quran states eight categories of people who may receive *zakah*. They are the poor, the needy, the officials collecting the *zakah*, those recently converted to Islam whose hearts still need reconciling to the faith, those in captivity or bondage, debtors, those working in the cause of Allah (running community or education projects, for example) and the wayfarer.

Non-Muslims and Muhammad's descendants are forbidden from receiving *zakah*, as too are a donor's direct relatives, because the believer already has an obligation to maintain them.

ZAKAH IN HISTORY

During Muhammad's lifetime, the Islamic state collected *zakah*, but after his death, there was resistance to it. The first caliph, Abu Bakr, declared those resisting *zakah* as apostates and fought them until they acknowledged its legal status. *Zakah* continued to be collected under the Umayyad and Abbasid

Above A teenager in Birmingham, England, gives charity through the well-known Islamic Relief clothing bank system.

Above Food, as a form of charity, is distributed at the end of a fasting day in Ramadhan. Here, bread is being given to women in Peshawar, Pakistan.

dynasties, but it was eventually abandoned at state level. Payment of *zakah* is now generally upheld on voluntary moral grounds by individual Muslims.

SADAQAH: CHARITY

Like *zakah*, *sadaqah* is charitable giving, and is mentioned many times in the Quran and in hadith. Muslims are told that *sadaqah* must be practised, but when and how much is up to the individual. *Sadaqah* means to give truthfully, lawfully and with sincerity, and it should therefore be given whenever possible, in addition to *zakah*. It need not be money: even smiling or removing something harmful from the road can be considered as *sadaqah*.

SAWM: FASTING

FASTING DURING THE MONTH OF RAMADHAN IS BOTH AN INDIVIDUAL AND A COMMUNAL ACT OF WORSHIP AND SPIRITUAL EXERTION, WHICH HAS THE AIM OF BRINGING MUSLIMS CLOSER TO GOD.

Above Palestinian women pray in front of the Dome of the Rock Mosque in the Old City of Jerusalem at the last Friday Prayers during Ramadhan.

Sawm, meaning abstaining, is the fourth pillar of Islam, and refers to fasting from sunrise to sunset in Ramadhan, the ninth month of the Muslim calendar. Healthy Muslims abstain from food, drink and conjugal relations during these hours. The end of this testing month is followed by the *Eid* celebrations. As the Islamic lunar calendar is ten days shorter than the solar calendar, Ramadhan falls ten days earlier each year, travelling through the seasons.

Outside Ramadhan, people are free to fast voluntarily, though not on the days of festivities or on Friday. Fasting was prescribed in 623, after migration to Madinah, purely as an act of obedience to Allah. The Quran states, 'O you who believe, fasting is prescribed for you as it was prescribed for those before you, so that you might remain conscious of God' (2:183). For Muslims, the only reason for *sawm* is to attain piety and God-consciousness (*taqwa*).

THE IMPORTANCE OF RAMADHAN

The month of Ramadhan is known by Muslims as 'Blessed Ramadhan' because it is the time in which they believe that the Quran was revealed, and in which Muhammad stated that the gates of heaven are opened and those of hell closed and the devils chained. According to the Quran, fasting is solely for God's sake; therefore, he will reward it how he sees fit in this world and the next.

Muhammad said that in the first ten days of Ramadhan, Allah's mercy descends on believers; in the next ten days, his forgiveness is showered on them; while, in the final ten days, immunity from hell is promised. It is a time for Muslims to exercise forgiveness and patience and to think of the less fortunate – so empathy with the poor, feeding them and giving daily charity is extolled. Muslims hasten to feed

Left Indonesian women pray the tarawih *prayer in the nights of Ramadhan in Bali. Prayer is segregated in Islam, as this women's section shows.*

fasting neighbours at the time of *Iftar*, breaking the fast, in order to gain God's blessings. The meal is supposed to be simple, nutritious and not too filling.

THE BENEFITS OF FASTING

Muslims believe that fasting is a shield from wrongdoing, because abstention leads to self-control – whether from over-eating or from gossip. Muhammad said that whoever fasted in Ramadhan and abstained from all forbidden things would have all their sins forgiven.

Supplicating is recommended at *Iftar*, as Islam teaches that God answers the fasting believer. (A hadith relates that Muhammad comforted his companions by telling them the odour from a fasting person's mouth was more pleasing to Allah than the smell of musk.)

Abandoning normal life, Muslims engage in far more worship than they can usually manage, reciting the Quran, remembering God and meditating. It is a month of intense spiritual renewal and reflection for Muslims, when they call upon God and re-establish their covenant with him. The nights of Ramadhan are marked by an extra prayer, the *tarawih*, where the whole Quran is recited over the month.

CONDITIONS OF FASTING

Children and the elderly are not expected to fast, though the latter are required to feed the poor instead. For those who are ill, travelling, menstruating, pregnant or breastfeeding, fasting can be postponed until a later date (2:185). Muslims can enjoy ordinary life during the nights of Ramadhan, but must begin fasting at sunrise. Eating the *suhur* meal at dawn was a

Right More than 100,000 people break their fast with the Iftar *meal at sunset in the Prophet's Mosque in Madinah, Saudi Arabia.*

prophetic tradition that carried many blessings, and it is still faithfully emulated the world over.

Deliberate eating or drinking will break a fast, but eating or drinking through forgetfulness does not constitute a break in the fast.

THE LAST TEN DAYS AND *EID*

The Quran is believed to have been revealed on one of the last ten odd nights of Ramadhan, known as the *Laylat al-Qadr*, the Night of Power/Decree. As it is not clear when this night occurs, Muslims spend all ten nights in prayer, and some believers retreat to mosques to excel in their worship.

Above A family taking an Iftar *meal in the privacy of their home. While* Iftar *is a time for sharing, it is also an important family time for Muslims, when children are taught the importance of Ramadhan.*

As the crescent is sighted and Ramadhan ends, the *Eid* festivities follow. The poor are remembered throughout the celebrations, as *zakat ul-fitr*, alms to end Ramadhan, are paid by every Muslim to help the poor enjoy the celebrations. *Eid salah*, a communal prayer, is offered, new clothes are worn, gifts are exchanged and celebration follows. All this, however, is with a tinge of sadness that Ramadhan has ended.

HAJJ: THE PILGRIMAGE

THE FIFTH PILLAR OF ISLAM IS *HAJJ*, THE PILGRIMAGE TO MAKKAH, WHICH TAKES PLACE IN THE LAST ISLAMIC MONTH, *DHUL-HIJJAH*. MUSLIMS AIM TO PERFORM *HAJJ* AT LEAST ONCE IN THEIR LIFETIME.

Prescribed in 631, the year before Muhammad's death, the *Hajj* is elaborated in the Quran (22:26–33), where it is ordered as a symbol of devotion to God in the footsteps of Ibrahim. Whoever fulfils this pillar of Islam, 'for them it is good in the sight of their Lord' (22:30).

PREPARING FOR *HAJJ*

Hajj is perhaps the most complex of Islamic rites as it requires a great deal of preparation. It is considered a calling from God, but Muslims must ensure that they possess the financial means to go, have paid off all debts, distributed *zakah* and left no dependents unprovided for. *Hajj* demands intention and purity of heart, so pilgrims are encouraged to cultivate an attitude of repentance, mercy and God-consciousness.

THE RITES IN *HAJJ*

Muhammad showed how the rites of *Hajj* were to be performed, and clarified that he himself was emulating the practice of Ibrahim. As Islam teaches that all people are equal before God, Muslims are required to shed any symbols of their social status when making *Hajj*, so the same *ihram*, *Hajj* clothing, is worn by all as far as possible. For men, this consists of two unsewn pieces of cloth, often white, which represent the shroud. For women, it is any simple plain clothing that covers them fully, according to Islamic dress codes.

Right The white tents at Mina where pilgrims camp for four days during Hajj in Makkah. The three million pilgrims are grouped in tents according to nationality: these are European ones.

No jewellery or perfume is worn during *Hajj*. On approaching the stations around Makkah (*miqat*), all pilgrims assume a 'state of death', where only necessary physical acts are allowed: even nail-clipping is prohibited. A rigorous state of consciousness follows, where no disagreement or violation of any living thing must take place.

According to the Quran (22:27), God asked Ibrahim to proclaim the pilgrimage to the House of God (*Kaabah*) that he built. Ibrahim responded by climbing on a rock and calling the *talbiyah*, 'I am at your command, O Lord, I am at your command.' Pilgrims continuously repeat the *talbiyah*.

On the eighth day of *Dhul-Hijjah*, the pilgrims camp at Mina, one of the eastern entrances to the Makkan valley, where they offer *salah* from noon to dawn. They then travel to the plain of Arafah, 16 km (10 miles) south-east of Mina. This is the most important day of the

Above A manuscript painting by al-Hariri shows a caravan of Hajj pilgrims on camel and horseback. In the past, the Hajj was arduous and often perilous.

rites, as Muhammad said that Arafah is the pinnacle of the *Hajj*. This is where, according to Islam, Adam and Eve met after their descent to earth, and beseeched God for guidance. Here, Muslims spend the entire day in prayer close to the Mount of Mercy (*Jabal-al-Rahmah*).

At sunset, the pilgrims retrace their steps 8km (5 miles) north to Muzdalifah, where Muhammad is said to have camped for the night.

Right Pilgrims ritually walk seven times between the two 'hillocks' of Safa and Marwa, which are now enclosed within the Great Mosque in Makkah.

Here, they offer prayers and collect pebbles for the following rituals. The morning of the tenth day of *Dhul-Hijjah* sees pilgrims returning to Mina to ritually stone three stone pillars that represent the devil, who is said to have tempted Ibrahim and his family away from God. A sacrificial animal is slaughtered in recollection of the Ibrahim story, pilgrims clip or shave their hair and the final rites at the *Kaabah* begin.

The pilgrims circle the *Kaabah* seven times, kiss the Black Stone, which they believe came with Adam from heaven, and offer prayers at Ibrahim's Station, the place where he is said to have raised the *Kaabah* and prayed to God. Finally, they run between the two hillocks of Safa and Marwa as, according to tradition, did Hajar in her search of water for Ismail. Water from the Well of Zamzam is drunk, and after the stoning of the devil at Mina, the *Hajj* is complete.

Most pilgrims then make their way north to Madinah, where they offer their salutations to the Prophet and seek to absorb the blessings of his city. Muslims believe that performing the *Hajj* purifies them from sin, and they return home amidst great celebrations of their new sinless status.

SPIRITUAL SYMBOLISM

Hajj is one of the world's largest religious conventions, with more than three million people gathering at Arafah. The experience of brotherhood is breathtaking, as Muslims from every corner of the world flock to worship together.

Hajj is very complex, for while it is outwardly physical, it is laden with spiritual symbolism. To make sense of all the rites, Muslims must search for meaning deep within their hearts. According to Islamic tradition, even Ibrahim was asked by Archangel Jibril whether he understood the meanings of *Hajj*.

The majority of Muslims do not manage to perform the *Hajj*, but they are nevertheless equally valued and included, for on the day of Arafah, they fast, and the day after, they celebrate *Eid*.

Below Pilgrims on the day of Arafah, on the Mount of Mercy, Jabal-al-Rahmah, *beseeching God, as, according to hadith, did the prophets Adam, Ibrahim and Muhammad.*

MAKKAH AS A PLACE OF WORSHIP

MUSLIM HISTORIANS CONSIDER MAKKAH TO BE THE CENTRE OF THE EARTH. AND FOR MUSLIMS IT ALSO HAS MODERN SIGNIFICANCE: IT IS TO THIS CITY THAT THEY TURN THEIR ATTENTION DAILY IN PRAYER.

Makkah is important for Muslims not just because the Prophet Muhammad was born there and spent most of his life in the city, but also because it houses the *Kaabah*, the cubelike edifice that is known as *Bait-Allah*, the first House of God established for his worship. Throughout the *Hajj*, there are rites that take pilgrims back in history to the roots of the city.

ADAM'S MAKKAH

Makkah as a place of worship is thought by early historians to have been first established by Adam, who, Muslims believe, was guided to Makkah after he descended from heaven. It was there that he is believed to have found God's Throne, and honoured it, on the site of the present-day *Kaabah*. It was also in Makkah, on the plain of Arafah, that he is said to have been reunited with Eve and, together with her, sought God's forgiveness and guidance, as do millions of Muslim pilgrims on the *Hajj* today.

Muslims believe that the *Hajar al-Aswad*, the Black Stone in the eastern corner of the *Kaabah*, was brought by Adam out of heaven, and that after Adam's death and burial in Makkah, his son Seth continued to honour God's Throne until it was recalled to heaven.

According to hadith, Noah's Ark later sailed through the area in which the city now stands, and many years afterward, Ibrahim is believed to have taken Hajar and her son Ismail to settle in this land.

Below Al-Masjid al-Haram in Makkah, commonly known as the Grand Mosque, is the largest mosque in the world.

Above Pilgrims are depicted performing the Hajj *rituals at Makkah in a painting produced for Timurid prince Iskandar Sultan, c.1410–11.*

IBRAHIM'S MAKKAH

The rites associated with Ibrahim and his family are immortalized in the *Hajj*, from circling the *Kaabah*, which Muslims believe he rebuilt with his son Ismail, to praying at the Station of Ibrahim, where his footprints are said to be preserved in the stone slab, and drinking from the Well of Zamzam, which is believed to have quenched the thirst of his son Ismail as a babe.

According to Islamic traditions, the rite of running between the two hillocks of Safa and Marwa was begun by Ibrahim to remember his wife Hajar's search for water. The curved arch by the side of the *Kaabah*, the *Hajar Ismail*, is included in its circling, as it is believed to have once been part of the holy house as well as the place where Hajar and Ismail are buried. A story tells that before building the *Kaabah*, Ibrahim visited Ismail when he was a boy, for he had a vision to sacrifice his son to God. On their way outside Mina, Ibrahim, Ismail and Hajar were tempted by the devil, whom Ibrahim stoned. Again, Muslims

remember the great patriarch as they stone the pillars of *jamarat* at Mina. Finally, to pay homage to Ibrahim's willingness to sacrifice Ismail, all pilgrims offer a sacrificial animal and feed the poor.

MUHAMMAD'S MAKKAH

It is in this mystical city that the Prophet Muhammad was born, and his endorsement of the Ibrahimic *Hajj* rites gave it new authenticity. His life also added new sites to visit during pilgrimage: many Muslims visit the places where he lived and walked, in order to retrace his spiritual footsteps. However, this custom is not part of the *Hajj* rites, and the present Saudi authorities' fear of pilgrims practising innovative worship, and thus compromising their attention to God, has almost completely erased any monumental historical sites from Makkah. Although the place of Muhammad's upbringing with his wet nurse, Halimah, is preserved (albeit surrounded by a market), other sites, such as where he lived with his wife Khadijah, her burial place and his wife Ayesha's house, though believed to be known locally, are not officially marked.

Many Muslims visit the Cave of Hira, where Muhammad is believed to have received the first revelation, and the Cave of Thawr, his hiding place on the migration to Madinah. Some scholars claim to know the whereabouts of the pillar in the precincts of the al-Haram, from where Muhammad is believed to have been taken on the night journey to Jerusalem. Leaving Makkah, pilgrims can see the mountain that the Prophet is said to have miraculously split with a gesture from his finger.

Memories of the old Makkah of Adam and Ibrahim mingle with the newer Makkah of Muhammad, who brought new meaning to the city.

Above A view of the Kaabah, *the surrounding mosque, and the city of Makkah in the distance.*

Left Worshippers kiss the Hajar al-Aswad, *the Black Stone set in the eastern corner of the* Kaabah. *The stone, according to hadith, is from heaven, and was brought to earth by Adam.*

JUMUAH MUBARAK: BLESSED FRIDAY

FRIDAY, *JUMUAH*, IS THE DAY OF CONGREGATIONAL PRAYER, WHEN, AT NOON, THE MUSLIM COMMUNITY GATHERS IN THE LOCAL MOSQUE TO HEAR A SERMON AND TO PRAY TOGETHER.

Chapter 62 of the Quran, named *al-Jumuah*, is said to have been revealed to Muhammad during the first few years after migration to Madinah. In it, God commands Muslims to pray the congregational prayer: 'O you who believe, when the call is proclaimed to prayer on Friday, hasten to the remembrance of Allah, and leave off business…' (62:9). Friday is named *Jumuah* from the Arabic *al-Jam*, meaning 'gathering'. This day of congregational prayer is considered honoured in Allah's sight.

BLESSED FRIDAY
Muhammad said that as the Jews have Saturday and the Christians Sunday, so Muslims have Friday as their special day. However, it is not a day of rest as such, but rather a day of collective worship and particular remembrance of God. It is the day,

Muslims believe, on which God created Adam, the day Adam was sent to earth from heaven, the day he died, the day when the Final Judgement will come and the day on which there is an hour, toward the end, just before sunset, when all prayers are answered. Islam teaches that all prayers are witnessed by the angels, but that on Friday, the angels record all those who go to the mosque and pray. As a reward, they are forgiven all sins committed between that Friday and the next.

Friday is also a day on which Muslims pray for blessings on the Prophet, and recite chapter 18, *al-Kahf* ('The Cave') specifically, for its esoteric message of guidance.

Below Muslims pray in Malaysia during the Friday prayer. Offering collective worship in mosques is an important part of Muslim community life.

Above The Friday prayer at al-Azhar Mosque. Built in the Fatimid city of al-Qahira (Cairo), it claims to be the oldest university in the world.

PREPARING FOR *JUMUAH*
In Muslim countries, preparations for *Jumuah* usually begin after sunset on Thursday, when groups assemble to sing God's praises and blessings on the Prophet. Friday is normally a holiday in the Muslim world, with families preparing for time together in a spirit of worship. Muslims take an obligatory bath on Friday, wear

Left As well as giving Friday sermons, imams give religious instruction on other days – as shown in this painting of the Mosque of the Metwalis, Cairo.

second *adhan*, the imam leads those present into two *rakaah* (units) of prayer, from a niche at the front of the mosque. Afterward, people usually spend some time greeting each other and catching up with their news, for *Jumuah* is just as much an opportunity to come together as a community and socialize as it is to remember God.

AFTER THE PRAYER

The Quran teaches that all business and worldly affairs should be put aside for the remembrance of Allah, but that afterward, people are free to disperse and go about their businesses (62:10). This means that trade in the Muslim world does not stop on a Friday. In fact, it is a day when most Muslim families relax and spend time eating and shopping together, thus boosting trade on a Friday.

Jumuah Mubarak is, in essence, a day of joy, peace and community spirit – a holiday as well as, most importantly, a holy day.

their best attire, perfume themselves, pay attention to oral hygiene and then make their way slowly and peacefully to the mosque.

Jumuah prayer is compulsory for all adults, except women who may find it difficult to go out due to family duties, the infirm, travellers and those under environmental constraints, such as extreme hot or cold temperatures or rain.

THE *JUMUAH* PRAYER

Jumuah replaces the noon *salah* when prayed in congregation. It is preceded by an *adhan* (call to prayer) and a *khutbah* (sermon), given by the imam from the pulpit, facing his congregation. The sermon praises God and his Prophet and quotes verses from the Quran, encouraging people to do good. The theme varies from week to week and may address contemporary concerns of the congregation. The imam then sits and the congregation offers silent supplications before he gives a second *khutbah*, ending in prayers for believers globally, and for all who are oppressed and poor.

The congregation is asked not to speak at all during the sermon, and to reflect on the words. After a

Right Friday prayers at the mosque of Shaykh Abdul Qadir al-Gailani, Baghdad, Iraq. The women enjoy the prayer as spiritual time, but also as social bonding.

THE TWO *EIDS*

THE END OF RAMADHAN AND THE PERFORMANCE OF *HAJJ* ARE EACH MARKED BY A MAJOR FESTIVAL, *EID*, WHEN MUSLIMS THE WORLD OVER CELEBRATE, EXCHANGE GREETINGS, SING AND SHARE MEALS.

Festivals in Islam are a time for great joy, but at the core of the celebrations is devotion to God, for Muslims believe that all happiness and joy emanate from him. The two great festivals in Islam, the *Eid*, are a testimony to this: both events take place after rigorous devotional training programmes – fasting and pilgrimage – and both are imbued with thanksgiving throughout.

EID UL-FITR:
THE END OF RAMADHAN

After an arduous month of fasting and self-control, Muslims mark the end of Ramadhan with great festivity. They begin the day by bathing, perfuming themselves and putting on their best clothes, usually new ones for children. (It is said that Muhammad himself wore his best clothes on *Eid*, including a special cloak.) Believers then eat something sweet, such as dates or milk pudding, before going to pray.

A congregational *Eid salah* is normally offered early in the morning, in an open space if possible. The whole community – men, women and children – is required to attend, as it is seen as a day of joy for all. Thanks are given to God in a *khutbah*, or sermon, for the blessings of Ramadhan, and supplications are offered for the month's efforts to be accepted and the spirit of the month to be carried throughout the year. People then greet and congratulate each other.

Above Members of a Palestinian family in the West Bank city of Nablus share a modest Eid *meal to celebrate the end of Ramadhan.*

Below Eid *prayers are offered at the Regent's Park Mosque in London, a racially and ethnically mixed community.*

Above Meat is distributed during the Eid ul-adha in Senegal. Animals are slaughtered and the meat divided between family, friends and those in need.

As this is usually a holiday of three days, a wonderful array of food is prepared, which is shared with friends and family. Muslims visit each other and give gifts to the children, and play and singing are encouraged. According to hadith, Muhammad and his community enjoyed watching Abyssinians perform in the Prophet's mosque during *Eid* festivities, and, later, girls sang in the Prophet's house.

Remembering those who are less fortunate is incumbent upon Muslims with enough money to be able to celebrate. It is therefore compulsory to pay the *zakat ul-fitr* on the days of *Eid* or just before. This is a nominal amount, paid by the head of the family for each family member, to be distributed to the poor and needy so that they can also enjoy the celebrations of *Eid*.

EID UL-ADHA: THE END OF *HAJJ*

Those unable to participate in the *Hajj* can nevertheless join in the great ritual through celebrations.

On the day of Arafah, only those not performing the *Hajj* are encouraged to fast. The day after, *Eid* is declared and festivities begin. Again, Muslims will bathe, beautify themselves and wear their best clothes. It is customary on this occasion to eat after the morning *Eid salah*. Many Muslims offer a sacrifice, in honour of Ibrahim's readiness to sacrifice Ismail, and they will therefore eat part of that, rather than sweet pudding, on returning from the prayer.

PRAISING GOD

As in *Eid ul-fitr*, the prayer is offered in congregation and is followed by a sermon, praising God for the opportunity of pilgrimage for humankind and extolling the benefits of sacrificing an animal and distributing the meat among family, friends and the poor. Finally, God is praised in abundance. Afterward, the congregation spends time greeting and congratulating each other, giving gifts to children and sharing lavish meals.

During the two *Eids*, praising God with *takbir* – singing that he is great – is prescribed as a way of thanking God for his guidance. It is sung intermittently from going to

GIFTS AND THE MEANING OF *EID*

Celebrating on the *Eid* is encouraged, particularly with good food and gifts. However, in this age of materialism, Islam is keen to guide Muslims away from extravagant celebrations, and to remind them that no joy is devoid of the presence of God. Gift-giving is meant to please and satisfy children, but making it the centre of the day is discouraged. The day must begin with the prayer, and should be filled with prayers and thanks, and thoughts and charity given to the poor, so that God is the focus, not material objects.

Above Young British Muslims exchange gifts with their friends on Eid. *While* Eid *is a joyous occasion and gifts are part of the celebrations, the emphasis is on spiritual aspects of the festivals.*

prayer until the sermon begins on *Eid ul-fitr* and on the *Eid* marking the end of *Hajj*, for three days from the day of Arafah. Men and women all join in: '*Allahu akbar, Allahu akbar, la ilaha illal-lah. Allahu akbar, Allahu akbar, wa lillahil-hamd.*' ('God is the greatest, God is the greatest, there is no god but the one God, God is the greatest, God is the greatest, and for Him is all Praise.')

MUHARRAM: THE MARTYRDOM OF HUSSAIN

THE MARTYRDOM OF IMAM HUSSAIN IN THE MONTH OF MUHARRAM IS THE PIVOTAL EVENT OF THE ISLAMIC YEAR FOR SHIAH MUSLIMS, WHO COMMEMORATE AND MOURN HIS DEATH WITH GREAT PASSION.

Muharram is the first month of the Islamic calendar, and one of the four months in which fighting has been prohibited in the Quran. However, it carries another significance for Shiah Muslims, for it is the month in which Hussain, Muhammad's grandson, along with 72 others, was killed in Karbala, Iraq, by the forces of the second Umayyad ruler Yazid I (645–83).

THE 'PRINCE OF MARTYRS'

After Muhammad's death, many followers of Ali believed that he was the rightful successor for, being from the Prophet's family, he preceded all others in his claim to succession. The fact that he was not chosen as first caliph is considered a usurpation of his power by Shiah Muslims. This tragedy was replayed in the life of Ali's son Hussain, who stood up against the corruption of the second Umayyad caliph Yazid.

Hussain set off in 680 with his family and small band of followers in Muharram toward Karbala in Iraq, where he was promised support. However, at Karbala, their water supply was cut off and eventually, on the tenth day of Muharram, the day of Ashura, Hussain, along with his family, was killed in battle. His head was

Below The narrative of Imam Hussain's life and death – the focal event in Shiah history – is depicted in this tapestry at the imam's shrine in Karbala, Iraq.

Above Shiah Muslims inside the inner sanctuary of Imam Hussain's shrine in Karbala. Nearly two million pilgrims visit Najaf and Karbala during Muharram.

severed and taken to Damascus, and the children and womenfolk were taken there as captives.

Imam Hussain's head is thought by Sunnis to be buried in Syria, his body being interred in Karbala.

However, most Shiahs believe that his family, on being freed from captivity in Syria, took the head with them and had it interred either in Najaf, at his father Ali's mausoleum, or indeed with his body in Karbala.

Shiah Muslims consider the event to be the most heinous crime ever committed, because the blood of Muhammad's family was spilled by Muslims, and they view Hussain as the 'Prince of Martyrs'.

KARBALA MOURNING

Many Sunni Muslims, too, consider the events at Karbala to be a tragic blot on the history of Islam. However, they prohibit mourning, as the Prophet Muhammad himself forbade people from ritual and passionate displays of bereavement. The Shiahs, however, think it is a duty of believers to commemorate the event, and to mourn Hussain. Indeed, they claim that this will bring redemption to humankind.

From Iraq to Pakistan, Iran and Indonesia, elaborate lamentation ceremonies are held, usually in buildings known as *Hussainiyyas*, or in the open. Recitations, elegies, dirges and public processions are common. Professional reciters sing and recount the life of the martyrs. While the scholars familiarize those gathered with basic Shiah doctrines, this is essentially a time to arouse people's emotions at the injustice of Hussain's death. Rather than being presented as a willing martyr, Hussain is seen as a tragic victim, and his killers and enemies are openly cursed.

Taziyah, passion plays by theatrical re-enactors, were common until the early 20th century, but, since 1940, these have not been seen as much. Instead, models of the scenes of Hussain's martyrdom and of his mausoleum, along with representational banners of his army, are carried in processions. As

Above A procession by Iraqi Shiahs to mark Imam Hussain's martyrdom in Karbala, Iraq. Many more will join in on the day of Ashura itself.

emotional accounts of the events lead gatherers to cry in mourning, they are promised redemption, for Shiah Muslims believe that it is only through mourning Hussain that sinners will be forgiven. Believers also recount miracles attributed to Hussain – his severed head allegedly recited the Quran – as a testimony of his righteousness as opposed to Yazid's wrongdoing.

EXPRESSIONS OF GRIEF

An important feature of the gatherings is *matam* (chest-beating and self-flagellation), with men

Above Shiah Muslims in Peshawar, Pakistan, self-flagellate during a procession on the ninth day of Muharram.

often incorporating knives, chains and swords, whether in India, Iran or Lebanon. Some Shiah scholars allow this controversial part of the mourning rituals, but others have declared it unlawful.

The mourners at the gatherings are provided with meals by donors. Finally, on the tenth day of Muharram, the day of Ashura, mourners will fast. (It is interesting that Muhammad also ordered fasting on this day. However, this was not in prediction of the Karbala tragedy, but because it is believed to be the day on which God delivered Moses and his people from Pharaoh across the Red Sea.)

Muharram is a time of great community bonding and sharing for Shiah Muslims, as well as an opportunity for renewing their faith, when they reflect over the injustices of the world and vow to stand up for what is right.

MAWLID: THE PROPHET'S BIRTHDAY

MAWLID (OR MILAD) COMMEMORATES THE PROPHET MUHAMMAD'S BIRTHDAY. CELEBRATIONS ARE HELD THROUGHOUT THE MUSLIM WORLD, PARTICULARLY IN EGYPT, SYRIA AND PAKISTAN.

The celebration of *Mawlid* is held on the day believed to be the Prophet's birthday – the 12th day of *Rabi al-Awwal*, the third month of the Islamic calendar – with great pomp and ceremony. Passages from the Quran are recited, along with poetry in praise of the Prophet, and meals are distributed as charity.

THE HISTORY OF *MAWLID*

Mawlid is not universally marked in the Muslim world, but generally it is celebrated in Sufi circles. According to historical sources, the Prophet's birthday was first observed in Makkah by the mother of the famous Abbasid caliph Harun al-Rashid, who turned the house in which her son was born into a place of prayer. However, it was not publicly marked until the 11th century, when the ruler of the Shiah Fatimid dynasty in Egypt played a major role in the public procession and celebrations, laying claims to descent from the Prophet's family, and also thereby securing popularity.

By the 12th century, the Sunnis of Syria and Iraq had also begun to celebrate *Mawlid*. As the practice grew in popularity – as a way of renewing faith and remaining connected with the Prophet – it assimilated local customs and practices, notably in India and Egypt. The Ottomans observed it from the 16th century, and, in 1910, they gave it the status of a national holiday throughout the empire. Today, *Mawlid* remains an official holiday in many Muslim countries.

MAWLID CELEBRATIONS

In India, Pakistan and Egypt, *Mawlid* is often commemorated with public processions. Banners are made; homes, mosques and official buildings are decorated; and poems and songs in praise of the Prophet ring out from

***Above** A view of a mosque in Pakistan on the eve of the* Mawlid *celebrations. In Pakistan, it is the norm for mosques to be decorated and illuminated like this.*

loudspeakers. People are encouraged to reconnect with the Prophet Muhammad and his message, and to celebrate his birth and life on earth with great fervour. Believers wear their finest clothes to attend gatherings, where the Prophet's life story is recounted.

***Below** The Muslim world celebrates the Prophet's birthday in many ways. This man in Egypt is displaying his strength at a family talent entertainment show.*

Right Throngs of Pakistanis take to the streets in celebration on the Mawlid. *This man has dressed his son as an Arab, as a way of claiming a link with the Prophet.*

Children play a significant role in *Mawlid* and spend weeks beforehand rehearsing poetry and songs, which they perform at gatherings. Distributing food and charity is a significant feature of the festivities, particularly in poor countries, where people are fed en masse in the name of the Prophet.

Among the poems recited are those that honour the Prophet's birth and miracles surrounding it – Muhammad's mother, Amina, reportedly suffered no labour pains and was nursed and attended to by heavenly beings. Both Muhammad's mother and his foster mother, Halimah, are praised and revered.

The Sufi circles (spiritual brotherhoods) have traditionally played a major role in *Mawlid*. In Syria, men and women attend single-sex gatherings to sing Sufi poetry, such as the *Qasidah Burda* of Busayri, the 13th-century Sufi mystic. In Turkey, particularly in Konya, the Mevlevi Sufi order of whirling dervishes perform and sing poetry from Jalal-ud-Din Rumi's famous *Mathnawi*. These

Right Throngs of Pakistanis take to the streets in celebration on the Mawlid. *This man has dressed his son as an Arab, as a way of claiming a link with the Prophet.*

cultural expressions have also entered into *Mawlid* celebrations in the West via settled Muslim communities, particularly in Britain and Canada.

Although *Mawlid* started life as an elitist celebration initiated by the Fatimids, it has since spread among the masses, and, in fact, it gives many poor communities a cause to be hopeful as they look toward the Prophet Muhammad for salvation and escape from the difficulties of daily life.

MAWLID CONTROVERSY

Although *Mawlid* is widely observed, there is controversy as to whether it is a genuine Islamic celebration. Muhammad himself never initiated it, nor did the following generations of Muslims. For this reason, scholars from countries such as Saudi Arabia, as well as some from India and Pakistan, forbid the festivities as an innovation that corrupts the purity of the religion.

However, many Muslim scholars support *Mawlid* on the basis that it brings people closer to the roots of their faith, providing an occasion when believers can reflect on the importance of the Prophet and his message of peace and submission to God. Provided that great pomp, free mixing between the sexes and over-indulgence in food, drink and singing be avoided, they claim that the celebrations should be encouraged as spiritually uplifting.

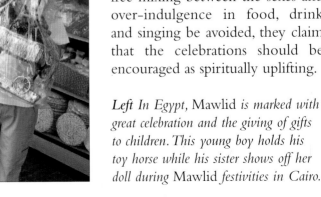

Left In Egypt, Mawlid *is marked with great celebration and the giving of gifts to children. This young boy holds his toy horse while his sister shows off her doll during* Mawlid *festivities in Cairo.*

THE NIGHTS OF POWER AND ASCENSION

TWO OTHER MUSLIM CELEBRATIONS, *LAYLAT AL-QADR* (NIGHT OF POWER) AND *ISRA WAL MIRAJ* (NIGHT JOURNEY AND ASCENSION TO HEAVEN), MARK IMPORTANT POINTS IN THE PROPHETIC MESSAGE.

Muhammad's life is said to have carried many miracles, but Muslims consider two of the greatest to be the revelation of the Quran, which according to the Quran began on the Night of Power, and Muhammad's miraculous Night Journey to Jerusalem and then Ascension to Heaven. Both events are celebrated throughout the Muslim world with special prayers, meditation and contemplation.

THE NIGHT OF POWER

According to chapter 97 of the Quran, it was on *Laylat al-Qadr*, the Night of Power or Decree (*qadr* means both power and decree), that Archangel Jibril visited Muhammad,

bringing the first revelation. *Laylat al-Qadr* is seen as a night of great power, when Muslims believe that all the matters for the coming year are decreed by Allah, and that Jibril and other angels descend from heaven, to spread peace on earth. The Quran declares that worship on this one night is equal to that of a thousand months (that is, more than 80 years), and Muhammad said that anyone who spent this night in worship would have all his previously committed sins forgiven.

Below Pakistani Muslims offer prayers at a mosque in Karachi on the night of Laylat al-Qadr, *when they believe the first verses of the Quran were revealed.*

Above Men and women praying (separately) during Laylat al-Qadr *in Kuwait's grand city mosque. Muslims spend the entire night in worship.*

The night falls on one of the last ten days of Ramadhan, on an odd night. Muslims view Ramadhan as a tremendously holy month, but this night adds further spiritual importance to it. As believers intensify their spiritual worship toward the end of the month of fasting, they combine it with their search for the Night of Power.

It is not clear on which of the odd nights *Laylat al-Qadr* falls; therefore, Muslims spend the last ten days of Ramadhan in constant worship. Many retire to mosques to sit in isolation, while others spend the night at home, praying, reciting the Quran and meditating. Some believers claim that they experience a spiritual awakening or 'happening' on a particular night that convinces them that this is the Night of Power.

THE NIGHT JOURNEY AND ASCENSION TO HEAVEN

Laylat al-Isra wal Miraj is Arabic for the night of the journey and ascension to heaven, an event that Muslims believe occurred on the 27th of Rajab, the seventh month of the Islamic calendar, in the tenth year of *hijrah*. It is said that having lost his wife Khadijah, and suffered in the town of Taif in the same year, Muhammad was consoled and strengthened in his mission by this timely miracle.

According to Islamic tradition, Muhammad spent the evening with his family and then went to visit the *Kaabah*, where he fell asleep in the *hijr Ismail*. He was woken by the Archangel Jibril, who led him to where a white winged beast named al-Buraq stood. He mounted the beast and they sped toward Madinah and Jerusalem. There, according to hadith, Muhammad led

all the previous prophets in prayer at the site of the farthest mosque, al-Masjid al-Aqsa. He was offered two cups of drink – wine and milk – but chose to drink the milk. Jibril approved of his choice, confirming that wine was prohibited.

Finally, it is told, al-Buraq flew him up to heaven from the site of a rock, now the Dome of the Rock Mosque. Muhammad met all the prophets again, but they were now in their heavenly forms. He went as far as the 'lote tree of the uttermost end', mentioned in the Quran (53:14), beyond which no one has ventured. God's divine light descended on the tree, and unlike Moses, Muhammad was able to gaze at it. Muslims believe that God

Above A tapestry of al-Buraq, the winged horse that, according to Islamic traditions, took Muhammad from Makkah to Jerusalem and thence to heaven.

instituted the five daily prayers here, first as 50, but finally reducing them to five. Muhammad claimed that he revealed only a part of what he and Allah discussed that night, and even that only over time.

While returning to Makkah, Muhammad saw trading caravans, which he later described to his companions. The caravans arrived just when he predicted, exhibiting all the details that he had described.

Like the Night of Power, this night is marked by Muslims with devotion, prayers and shared meals.

Above This is the rock, in the Dome of the Rock Mosque in Jerusalem, from where Muhammad is said to have begun his ascension to heaven on al-Buraq.

THE NIGHT OF FREEDOM

Laylat-ul-Bara, the Night of Freedom (from hell), occurs on the 15th day of Shaaban, the eighth Islamic month. Some Muslims believe that God's mercy and blessings descend on this night, and in many countries, including Yemen, they mark the event with prayers, remembrance of God and recitations from the Quran.

According to hadith, Muhammad said that Allah forgives all his servants on this night, except those who do not forgive each other and have malice in their hearts. While there is no evidence to support the popular belief that all matters for the forthcoming year are decreed on this night, many renowned scholars have extolled the virtues of observing prayers on this night and fasting on the following day.

MASJID: THE MOSQUE

MUSLIMS CAN PRAY ANYWHERE, SO THE WHOLE EARTH COULD BE SEEN AS A *MASJID* ('PLACE OF PROSTRATION'). THE TRADITION OF THE MOSQUE BEGAN WITH THAT ERECTED BY MUHAMMAD AT MADINAH.

Above The mihrab, *or prayer niche, at the Gurgi Mosque in Tripoli, Libya. The striking tile work of this* mihrab *reflects its central purpose in the building.*

The mosque is a focus for congregational worship and community affairs. *Masjid* in Arabic means a place of prostration; therefore, a *masjid* is primarily a place for *salah*, a place where Muslims kneel and prostrate themselves before God. The word 'mosque' is derived from the Spanish *mesquita*, which is the Latinized form of *masjid*.

OWNERSHIP OF MOSQUES

No matter what their size or location, all mosques fulfil the same function, which is to serve the Muslim community as a house of God. No one is allowed to own a mosque, for all mosques are considered to belong to God; those who fund them are viewed as donors, while those who 'own' mosques for legal purposes are simply trustees. The mosque is considered a *waqf*, or endowment, where any Muslim is free to enter, pray and participate. Muhammad encouraged people to fund the building of mosques, declaring that anyone who did so would find a home built for him in paradise.

MOSQUE DESIGN

As Muslims are commanded to pray toward the *Kaabah*, so mosques in Muslim countries are designed facing the *qibla*, the direction of the *Kaabah*, and the imam will lead the prayers from the back wall, the one facing the entrance.

Most mosques are virtually identical in the basic architecture of the back wall, which houses a *mihrab*, an arched, curved niche, usually featuring very subtle decoration. The imam will stand in front of this niche when leading his congregation in prayer.

To the right of the *mihrab* is the *minbar*, or pulpit, which is made from either wood, stone or mud, depending on the materials used in the mosque's construction. It has a flight of steps leading to the top, where the imam will stand to deliver his Friday sermon.

Most large mosques in Muslim countries have a huge entrance that opens on to a central courtyard. The courtyard is not only an important place where individuals and families can sit and reflect, but also houses fountains, taps and basins, where the ritual ablutions are performed.

Mosques invariably have at least one *midhanah*, a tower or minaret, attached to them. The minaret is the place from which the *muadhdhin* calls the faithful to prayer. The *Kaabah* has many minarets, but the Blue Mosque in Istanbul, Turkey, is the only mosque to have six.

As Muslim men and women pray separately, mosques will provide women with either a prayer space at the back of the main hall, as in the Sultan Ahmet Mosque, Istanbul, or separate prayer rooms from which they can hear the imam, as in the Prophet's Mosque in Madinah.

Left The simplicity of the interior of the Red Mosque in Islamabad, Pakistan, means that worshippers are not diverted from the mosque as a place of prostration.

FUNCTIONS OF A MOSQUE

As well as furnishing prayer spaces for men, women and children, mosques also need to fulfil other community functions in order to be officially designated as such. Each mosque must have kitchen facilities, so that guests and wayfarers can be fed, as well as washrooms, because ablutions are a compulsory requirement before prayer. Finally, mosques must

Above A muadhdhin *calls Muslims to prayer from an ornate* midhanah *(tower) of a Chittagong mosque, Bangladesh. Its style and colour are typical of this country.*

provide facilities for washing and shrouding the dead. Some mosques also contain an accommodation unit for the imam and his family, where they can live if it is convenient and comfortable for them to do so.

THE PROPHET'S MOSQUE

The first mosque to be constructed by Muhammad was in Madinah, where he is now buried. Although now extremely grand, with an advanced air-conditioning and sunshade system, the mosque started life very humbly.

The simple mud-brick enclosure had a courtyard, open at one end, with two rows of palm-trunk columns and a roof of mud and palm leaves. A small roofed area at the front was reserved for the poor, and rooms were built off the courtyard, with doors opening on to it, to house Muhammad and his family.

The mosque was a vibrant, community place, where both people and animals sought shelter, and where religious instruction was given and guests entertained.

Above A Turkish manuscript painting of the Prophet's Mosque in Madinah. This early layout shows the simplicity of the mosque as a functional prayer and meeting space.

173

MOSQUE PERSONNEL

THE MOSQUE IS A VIBRANT COMMUNITY CENTRE, OFTEN PHYSICALLY SITUATED IN THE MIDDLE OF A TOWN, AROUND WHICH ALL OF MUSLIM RELIGIOUS AND SOCIAL LIFE IS CONSTRUCTED.

There is no ordination of 'clergy' in Islam as every Muslim is considered 'ordained' by virtue of the covenant, mentioned in the Quran, that God made between himself and all people, when Adam's descendants recognized Allah as their Lord (7:172). The Quran also states that humans are trustees of the earth (27:62), which means that every Muslim is believed to be endowed with a certain amount of authority.

However, learned scholars have jurisdiction over the community as a whole, particularly those who are imams and mosque personnel. They play a significant role in running mosques, and serving and teaching the community.

IMAMS

Every mosque, whether large or small, has an appointed imam. The imam will be a person of letters – that is, qualified and well-versed in Quran and hadith studies and Islamic law – and will need to have good social skills, to equip him to lead the community.

The imam's main functions are to lead the five daily prayers, the Friday sermon and the *Eid* prayers. Other duties include officiating at weddings and funerals, dealing with domestic matters and representing his congregation in the wider community. The imam is always male, as traditional Muslim teaching claims only a man may lead a male or mixed-gender congregation.

Above The muadhdhin *plays an important role in the daily functioning of the mosque. This one calls the* adhan *from the Aqsunqur Mosque in Cairo.*

Below The imam, the most important of the mosque personnel, fulfils a religious as well as a pastoral role.

Above *Teaching the Quran in mosque* madrasas *is a daily activity. These young children are studying the religion in a mosque in Xian, China.*

OTHER MOSQUE PERSONNEL

The imam's pastoral and religious work is supported by other mosque personnel, which often include women. In the West, mosque personnel are usually elected on to a mosque committee, which deals with a range of matters, from organizing study circles (*halaqah*), youth learning and recreational events and children's Quran classes to local public relations and interfaith work. In the Muslim world, mosque personnel are also usually elected. Their responsibilities include facilitating study circles and social and political events, as well as dealing with finances.

In addition, each mosque has an appointed *muadhdhin*, who calls the *adhan* five times a day. The tradition of being a *muadhdhin* is often kept in one family, each generation taking great care to train the next to call the prayer. In Makkah, one family has supplied the *muadhdhin* at the Sacred Mosque for the last three generations.

THE *MADRASA* SYSTEM

A main function of the mosque is to educate the Muslim community in matters of the faith. This is usually through single-sex *halaqah*, or study circles. However, the education of children is one of the most important roles of the mosque. Learned men and women, approved by the mosque, hold classes to teach boys and girls from the ages of five to seven years onward. In these classes, some of which are held privately in homes, the children learn Quranic Arabic, prayer and the basic tenets of the faith.

In the 11th century, *madrasas* – colleges of learning – were set up, independent of mosques, to train scholars. These community colleges were primarily governed by the ruling authorities. Today, many *madrasas* still exist, and while the majority of them provide free education, they tend to be funded by donations rather than by governments. Most are attached to local mosques.

Over recent years, *madrasas* have received negative media attention as being terrorist 'boot camps' with anti-Western rhetoric. Many have been linked with terrorist organizations and extremist views,

THE IMPORTANCE OF EDUCATION

A prophetic hadith states that seeking *ilm*, or knowledge, is an obligation for every Muslim, man or woman. This means that every Muslim ought to have enough knowledge of the Quran and Islamic law to be equipped to lead a life by the precepts of Islam. Manners and social etiquette (*talbiyah adab*) are also seen as part of education, as is knowledge in any field serving the wider community, such as religion, sciences and engineering.

Above *Young children study the Quran in Arabic at Brick Lane Jami Mosque, London, England.*

often with little evidence. This misconception, however, does not do justice to the majority of *madrasas*, whose primary concern is the nurturing of Muslim children in the tenets of religion, to equip them for daily life.

While Muslim countries do not generally deliver free education through the school system, the mosques and *madrasas* do provide free religious instruction. This means that while official figures may indicate low literacy rates in the vernacular, many poor Muslims are literate in Quranic Arabic.

MOSQUE DIVERSITY

THE GLOBAL MUSLIM COMMUNITY IS UNITED BY THE MOSQUES, YET THESE CENTRAL PLACES OF COMMUNITY WORSHIP ALSO DISPLAY THE CULTURAL AND HISTORICAL DIVERSITY IN THE MUSLIM *UMMAH*.

The wide variation in mosques throughout the world can be seen by comparing, for example, the humble converted terraced buildings in England with the grand mosques of Turkey and Indonesia. The differences in size, architecture and cultural expression of these mosques and others provide a rich testimony to Islamic piety and civilization, where houses of worship have often been the epitome of artistic beauty.

VARIED STYLES

The historical evidence of former Muslim power and rule is spectacularly preserved in many buildings, especially mosques. The three most important of these – breathtaking in their architecture, spiritual importance and splendour – are the sacred mosques in Makkah, Madinah and Jerusalem. In addition to these, Islam has a legacy of varied architectural styles in the mosques of Mali, Iraq, Spain, Pakistan and Egypt, among many other countries.

The different periods of Muslim rule and civilization are reflected in the design of mosques, but while they display distinct historical and cultural styles, all mosques are united in their attempt to reflect something of the beauty of Allah as perceived by Muslims throughout the ages. Because they believe God to be incomparable and, therefore, beyond any form of representation, Muslims avoid any pictorial depictions of Him in either the simple or the ornate houses of worship they have dedicated to Him.

MAGNIFICENT MOSQUES

In most countries, the major congregational mosques, the *jami*, have huge courtyards to house all the worshippers, and these are often very regal. In Turkey, many mosques lack these but do have towering

Above The Dome of the Rock Mosque in Jerusalem has unique bold blue colours and impressive calligraphy. The verses are from chapter 36 of the Quran.

minarets. Elsewhere, domes and columns have played a major role, for example, in the Great Mosque in Córdoba, Spain, which has arcaded columns.

For Muslims, the aesthetic beauty of mosques serves one function: the remembrance and worship of Allah. To reflect his infinite nature, Muslim architects developed Quranic calligraphy and arabesque abstract art, which has no beginning or end. Small composite parts of the designs add to their often-complex sum total. The aim of such designs is to lead the eye – and the soul – into a creative expanse, where there is nothing but God. Floral and geometric arabesque patterns are reinforced by Quranic calligraphy, the divine words of Allah's guidance etched into the stone walls and the domes. Thus, wherever worshippers turn in a mosque, they can find reminders of the presence of God.

Left Muslims pray in Ramadhan at the largest mosque in India, the Jama Mosque in Delhi, an imposing mosque with a huge courtyard.

Above An aerial view of the Ali Saifuddin Mosque in Brunei, which unusually is built over water. Its architecture reflects the local culture.

HUMBLE MOSQUES

The great *jami* mosques are equal in purpose to humble neighbourhood mosques, for the practical function of a mosque is to provide prayer space. Local mosques tend to be very simple buildings, but are heavily used, particularly in districts in Turkey and Pakistan. The simplicity of these structures gives them a beauty of their own.

In England, local mosques are often not purpose built, but rather converted houses or churches. The thoroughly English architecture of such buildings highlights the unique acculturation of Islam. Just as the Seljuk mosques of Turkey and the Mughal ones of India reflect their time and place, so, too, do the newer mosques in England. In addition to converted buildings, there are now also several purpose-built mosques in England, notably the Shah Jahan Mosque in Woking, Surrey.

Right Constructed in 1889, the Shah Jahan Mosque in Woking, Surrey, was the first purpose-built mosque in Britain. Although not large, it is striking.

THE THREE SANCTIFIED MOSQUES

The three sacred, inviolable mosques (*haram*) in Islam, which Muslims are encouraged to visit, are the *Kaabah* in Makkah, the first house of worship; the Prophet's Mosque in Madinah, the first mosque built by him; and the al-Aqsa in Jerusalem. According to Islamic tradition, Muhammad travelled to Jerusalem in his Night Journey, and this was the first *qibla* (direction of prayer), until revelation changed it to Makkah.

All mosques are sanctified, but these three sites convey special religious significance. A prayer offered at the *Kaabah*, for example, carries far more reward than *salah* offered elsewhere. All three mosques are inviolable, which means there must be no blood shed there. It is the collective duty of Muslims worldwide to preserve all three sites – each of which is unique architecturally – as houses of worship.

EXTRA RITUAL PRAYERS

FOR MUSLIMS, A MAJOR PURPOSE OF LIFE IS TO WORSHIP GOD.
MUHAMMAD GAVE MANY FORMULAE FOR PRAYER SO THAT
BELIEVERS COULD HAVE CONSTANT COMMUNICATION WITH ALLAH.

Countless Muslim scholars have reflected on life comprising of many dimensions, in which internal (*batin*) and external (*dhahir*) aspects of life are fused together. To maintain balance, worship must reflect all dimensions, therefore outer forms of worship (*salah*) must have an inner reality.

SUPEROGATORY *SALAH*

In a classical treatise on prayer, Imam al-Ghazali (1058–1111) writes about the different forms that prayer takes, but he begins with the premise that 'prayer is the pillar of religion, the mainstay of conviction, the chief of good works and the best act of obedience.'

The minimum that is required from any Muslim in terms of prayer is the establishment of the five daily *salah*, which should be performed properly and on time. In fact, Islam teaches that if a Muslim fulfils this obligation with God-consciousness and humility, that would be acceptable to God, even if he or she offers no further prayers.

However, believers may also offer optional *salah*. The first kind consists of extra units of prayer (*rakaah*) that are offered along with the five canonical prayers. In this way, the *salah* can be extended, allowing worshippers to spend longer in communion with Allah.

Many devout Muslims pray four further *salah*, offered in the times between the five prayers. The most valuable of these is believed to be the night prayer, *tahajjud*, which is said to be highly rewarded as it involves great commitment to forsake the comfort of sleep and bed for worship. Keeping a night vigil of prayer, *qiyam-ul-layl*, is especially recommended, because Islam teaches that it will enable believers to draw closer to God. Certain times are believed to be particularly auspicious for the granting of prayers, the middle of the night being one of them. Devout Muslims will therefore spend a part of the night asking for forgiveness and guidance and offering other personal prayers.

At any point during the day or night, Muslims may pray for God's blessings in fulfilling a need (*hajah*), His divine intervention and guidance in making important decisions (*istikharah*), or His mercy in a prayer of penitence (*tawbah*).

Along with these individual prayers, there are several optional *salah* that can be offered in congregation. These include the *tarawih* prayer in Ramadhan, the *kusuf salah* at the time of solar or lunar eclipse, and indeed a prayer for rain, *istisqa*, which was often

Above This 19th-century painting by Carl Haag shows a Muslim raising his hands in supplication, an important aspect of devotional prayer.

performed by Muhammad. During times of fear or war, the *salah* of *khauf* allows half the congregation to pray while the rest keeps watch.

DUA

The formal prayer of *salah* is supplemented by *dua*, supplication, which is prayer in its wider sense, that is calling upon God at any time either to sing his praises or to beseech him. Making *dua* to seek God for his blessings is highly recommended as it is an essentially held belief in Islam that there is great power in prayer. Muslims will make *dua* for those that they love, for their deceased, for the world at large and for themselves. The Quran teaches that Allah will never turn away anyone calling upon him, though it states that when and how he answers *dua* is up to him.

Left Famous philosopher, Sufi and theologian, Abu Hamid al-Ghazali (1058–1111), wrote extensively on the nature of worship and prayer.

DHIKR AND MEDITATION

Remembrance of God, *dhikr*, is a further way of communion. The Quran refers to itself as *dhikr* (15:9), and it urges people to glorify God morning and evening (33:41), for it claims that only 'in the remembrance of God do hearts find satisfaction' (13:28).

The practice of *dhikr*, which involves inner dimensions of love, humility and sincerity with God, is meant to purify hearts and souls. It can be performed individually or in gatherings. Hadiths assert that God remembers those who remember him, and that the angels seek out *dhikr* gatherings in order to join them. Praising God, reciting the Quran, repeating his 99 names and invoking peace and blessings on the Prophet form the core of *dhikr*.

In the Sufi practice of meditation, worshippers shut their minds off from the sensory world and focus on their breath – the divine breath of life – and on God's holiness.

LIFE AS PRAYER

For Muslims, all life can be an act of worship: a deed done to help another person, earning money to support the family, even peeling vegetables can be prayer. Muslims believe that all actions are sacred if they are performed for the sole pleasure of God, so eating and sleeping are also acts of worship.

Above Two men praying in the desert in Afghanistan. Muslims often claim that those who live and call on God in harsh terrains do so with especial devotion.

Below Sufis gather to recite prayers and praise of God as extra ritual worship. At this Friday dhikr *session in Omdurman, Sudan, they recite and jump in unison.*

CHAPTER 5

MUSLIM LIFE

The home is the heart of Muslim life and the family the bedrock around which the rest of society is moulded. The Prophet's life is taken as the best example of human conduct and is emulated in rites of passage and life in the home. The family as a social institution provides not only a home as haven, but also the first site of learning and experiences. Harmony in marriage leads to peaceful relationships between parents and children, in which the rights and responsibilities of each member are clear.

The life cycles of birth, marriage and death are celebrated by rituals that mark the occasions as worthy of God's praise: newcomers are welcomed into the family and the souls of the deceased are returned to God.

Each aspect of life is regulated by laws of permissibility (*halal*) and prohibitions (*haram*), which are to be applied in spirit, not just literally. Many of these laws relate to dietary requirements and modesty in social relations. Islam regulates social interaction between people, especially between men and women, and, for this reason, rules on dress for men and women are considered an important part of Muslim observance.

Opposite The family is at the heart of Muslim life, and the home is the place where daily life is shared and where children are raised in accordance with the teachings of Islam.

Above Three girls in traditional Islamic dress converse at a Muslim school in central Tehran, Iran. The co-operative school is funded through government subsidies, donations and tuition payments.

THE FAMILY

THE FOUNDATIONAL INSTITUTION AROUND WHICH MUSLIM SOCIETY IS ORGANIZED IS THE FAMILY, AND ISLAM ESTABLISHES RESPECT AND HONOUR AS A HALLMARK OF FAMILY LIFE.

Great emphasis is placed on Muslim family life, where all members participate together to form a peaceful and cohesive community. Although family is the nucleus of society, Islam does not limit this to parents and children, but extends the understanding of family to include grandparents, uncles, aunts and cousins.

Above In Islam, the wider family plays an important role and several generations will often share one family home.

Left This image of the marriage of the three daughters of Serv, King of Yemen, from Shahnameh (The Book of Kings), an epic poem written c.1000, endorses the importance of marriage.

MARRIAGE AND SEX

The life of Muhammad elevates marriage as the best way of life; therefore, Islam discourages celibacy. Couples who enter into marriage are blessed by God. As Adam and Eve were created to live together in peace and love, so each couple entering into a marriage contract emulate that practice. Sex outside marriage is not allowed; therefore, Islamic traditions teach that marriage completes half of your faith, and that sex and procreation within marriage are not base physical acts, but natural pleasures like eating and drinking. Indeed, they carry spiritual rewards.

Choosing a pious partner is encouraged, and because the *nikah*, or marriage, is a civil contract (*aqd*), both consenting parties are bound by its terms. The husband carries the responsibility of financial maintenance, and the wife, while she is free to pursue a career, is seen as the source of peace and comfort in the home.

HOME AS HAVEN

At home, the door can be shut on the pressures of the outside world, and peace and love can rule. In this vibrant place, husband and wife

Right A mother fulfils the duty to raise children according to Islamic values by teaching her daughter the Quran.

find comfort in each other, women are free to celebrate and enjoy their daily lives, grandparents are respected and cherished and children flourish and are nurtured with love. Muslim family life, therefore, centres on the home, the private sphere, rather than public places. Here, taking meals together and socializing are just as important as prayer. The Prophet encouraged his companions to spend time with their families.

THE RIGHTS OF CHILDREN

One of the first responsibilities of parents is to raise their children according to the teachings of Islam. Within the family, children are introduced to an Islamic way of life through love and kindness. Parents are encouraged to set a good example themselves. As one hadith states, there is no better gift from a father to his children than a good education and behaviour. Socializing children with good

manners and training them how to function in a Muslim society is important, and teaching them the Quran, prayer and basic knowledge of God and his prophets is obligatory, but this ought to be done in an environment of love and play.

The obligation to raise children as good Muslims, however, must not be put over and above children's basic rights to food, shelter, love and gentle nurturing. In fact, the spirit of Islam makes love and kindness a condition for nurture, and the beauty of the extended family is that children are naturally socialized and eased into social relations, where everyone has a companion from their generation.

THE RIGHTS OF PARENTS

Parents also have rights due to them, for the Quran states that 'We (God) have made it a duty for humankind to be good to his parents. His mother bears him with strain upon strain...' (31:14) (Mothers are elevated higher than fathers.) Chapter 17 states that God has decreed kindness to parents, and that when they attain old age, they should not be pushed aside.

While parents are expected to give their growing children the right to make decisions regarding their own lives, parents nevertheless hold a position of experience, and seeking their advice is therefore highly recommended.

Above A father in Afghanistan spends time with his son. The parent–child relationship is fundamental in Islam.

HADITHS RELATING TO THE FAMILY

The Prophet said that the most perfect of believers were those who were most considerate to their wives. Kind and moral relations between husband and wife are considered to spread goodness in the family, and in society at large. It is said that a desert Arab came to Muhammad and asked him if he kissed his children, for his people did not. The Prophet replied sadly, 'What can I do for you if God has taken mercy away from your heart?'

RITES OF PASSAGE

EACH TRANSITIONAL STAGE IN THE LIFE OF A MUSLIM – FROM
BIRTH, TO MARRIAGE, THROUGH TO DEATH – IS SEEN AS IMPORTANT
AND IS ACCOMPANIED BY A SIGNIFICANT RITUAL CELEBRATION.

The special rituals that initiate the Muslim into each new phase of his or her life provide an opportunity for the community to come together, celebrate life and offer thanks to God, as people continuously remember him throughout life. God's laws are upheld in the rites of passage as life is dedicated to him.

BIRTH

A newborn child is welcomed into the Muslim community with much joyful celebration. The parents or elders pronounce the *adhan*, the call to prayer, in the newborn child's ear, testifying that 'there is no God but the one God', and that 'Muhammad is his messenger'. This ritual signifies the child leading a life in accordance with God's laws. Sweetmeats are then distributed in celebration of the birth.

Birth is later followed by a naming ceremony – in which the child is given a good, meaningful name – and an *aqiqah*, or meal, where an animal is sacrificed. Friends and family are invited to partake in thanking God for the child.

Newborn Muslim children often have their heads shaved. The hair is then weighed and charity is given, according to the weight of the hair, in the child's name. The baby thus begins life through good deeds of generosity.

Boys are circumcized, to honour the tradition of the prophet Ibrahim. This is usually done between seven days and a few months after birth. However, in some countries, such as Turkey, boys are circumcized when they are much older – at about seven years – with great ceremony.

PUBERTY

While there is no particular ritual ceremony to mark its onset, puberty is a time of a fundamental change in the life of a Muslim boy or girl, as he or she begins to enter adulthood. At this time, the age of innocence is left behind and life as an accountable and responsible Muslim begins. The five daily prayers become incumbent, as do fasting and other religious obligations. For both sexes, the correct rules of modest dressing now need to be observed.

Above An image of a procession in honour of the circumcision of the Turkish prince Mehmed. In Turkey, boys are often circumcized much later than they are elsewhere in the Muslim world.

MARRIAGE

As sex outside marriage is not allowed, young marriages are generally encouraged in Muslim societies, so that morality can be upheld. To assist in the choice of a good partner, families have traditionally aided the process by introducing prospective couples. Marriage brings together families, not just two individuals; therefore, several people are often consulted. Ultimately, the decision lies with the couple, however, and force can never be justified. The Prophet himself annulled forced marriages.

Marriage is marked by the *nikah* contract, where both parties give consent and the groom pays the bride a dowry, watched by two witnesses. The groom's family then

Left Kuwaiti children pray and read the Quran. While prayer is not compulsory for children, it becomes obligatory after puberty.

184

Right Marriage is a monumental rite of passage, in which two families are united by a couple taking vows to live in peace together.

Right Marriage is a monumental rite of passage, in which two families are united by a couple taking vows to live in peace together.

invite friends and family to a *walimah*, the marital meal. The marriage is thus made public, and thanks are given to Allah.

While marriage is important, it sometimes fails, and, in such cases, divorce, also, is a rite of passage. Again, the community is involved, as the Quran urges both parties to appoint arbitrators and to part with goodness and justice. The divorce must be witnessed, and any outstanding dowry must be fully paid to the wife.

DEATH

As birth brings a soul into the physical world, so death is seen as a positive experience, where life on earth ends and the soul returns to God. Despite knowing that death is decreed by God, it nevertheless represents a great loss for the family. Burial rites are therefore required not only to prepare the body and soul for return to its Lord, but also to allow closure for the family. Muslims will gather at the house of the deceased to offer their prayers and condolences, and the whole community will provide food for the grieving family for the first few difficult days.

The body is treated with great respect, and at no point is it exposed in its entirety. Close family and friends ritually wash the body, perfume it and shroud it, with reverence and prayers. A funeral prayer is then offered by the whole community – men, women and children – as they return the soul of the departed to God.

Muslim burials are eco-friendly as no coffin is used, unless local laws require it, which is usually the case in non-Muslim countries. The Quran and prayers are recited to aid the soul's passage to the next world.

Below Death completes the cycle of life, with the soul returning to its Lord. Here, the community pays its respects and says prayers at a burial in South Africa.

THE LAWFUL AND THE PROHIBITED

MUSLIMS BELIEVE THAT GOD HAS GUIDED HUMANKIND BY PROVIDING RULES THAT CLEARLY STATE WHAT IS ALLOWED AND WHAT IS PROHIBITED, IN ORDER TO BALANCE LIFE AND CREATE HARMONY.

The notion of lawful (*halal*) and unlawful (*haram*) has been used as a way of regulating societies since time immemorial. What constitutes these two categories of permissible and prohibited lifestyles has varied throughout time as individuals and societies have carved out their own understanding of good and evil.

Muslims believe that people need laws from God in order to carry out his divinely appointed role as God's vicegerents on earth. These laws therefore exist for the regulation and good of humanity.

SHARIAH
The word 'Shariah' literally means 'road' but is taken to mean Islamic law. Islamic scholars have elaborated that Shariah is a wide road, whose boundaries are quite far apart, allowing a great deal of movement and freedom. The edges of the road represent the limitations and prohibitions that exist in different spheres of life. For the Muslim, all actions are lawful unless expressly prohibited by Shariah.

WORSHIP
While Islam is considered to be a *din*, or way of life, a clear distinction is made in Islamic law between matters of worship and other aspects of life. Daily habits, lifestyle and cultural norms are all considered lawful unless expressly prohibited, but in matters of worship, the only actions and rituals permissible are those that are expressly affirmed by the Shariah.

In worship, there are five categories, which have been developed by jurists. Firstly, there are those acts, such as *salah*, which must be performed (*fard*) and that carry a reward. At the other extreme, those which are prohibited and carry a punishment are *haram*: for example, compromising on God's oneness by giving precedence to

Above A painting (c. 1675–1725) shows legal scholars discussing and formulating juristic opinions. For Muslims, living righteously involves observing the laws.

other things. In between are three graded stages: *mandub* acts are rewarded and recommended but not compulsory: for example, voluntary fasts; *mubah* acts are those on which the law is silent – they are allowed

Below A horse race at the Equestrian Club in Baghdad, Iraq – betting on horse-racing is perfectly acceptable under Islamic law.

but do not carry any merit; and *makruh* acts, which are not *haram* and therefore are not punished, but neither are they encouraged: for example, fasting on a Friday not followed or preceded by a day or more of fasting.

DAILY LIFE

Shariah categories of *haram* are far more limited in scope on matters of lifestyle and habits. This law is not formulated by jurists: the Quran itself explains what is prohibited and no one can add to this category. The Prophet Muhammad stated that what Allah allowed in his book is lawful, what he forbade is prohibited, while what he was silent on is also allowed.

Muslims believe that God prohibits certain actions because they are harmful and impure; in this way, he aids humans in controlling their base appetites and the ego and thus in nurturing the soul. For example, a Muslim man may lawfully marry a Jewish or Christian woman because she is monotheistic,

Right Shariah and the Quran strictly regulate finance, especially interest-free banking. This bank in Indonesia follows Islamic banking laws.

but is prohibited from marrying a polytheistic woman because her ideology would be in contradiction to Islam and it would, therefore, be difficult to establish peace and harmony in the family home.

However, certain matters are not clearly stated as either *halal* or *haram* and are therefore 'doubtful'. Muhammad advised caution in such 'grey areas', saying that it was better to steer clear of them in order to strengthen one's faith. For example, while eating pork is forbidden, using the skin of pigs is considered a grey area: while some

Above Muslims eating at Beurger King Muslim, a halal fast-food restaurant in Paris. ('Beur' is a French slang word for North African.)

jurists allow it, maintaining that only the consumption of animal meat is forbidden, others argue that all pig products should be avoided. Smoking is another such area: some Muslims argue that it is close to being *haram* as it is effectively self-violation and can cause illness; others claim that smoking in moderation is allowable as a social habit and a relaxant.

EAT OF THE GOOD THINGS

THE QURAN URGES MUSLIMS TO EAT THOSE FOODS THAT ARE *HALAL*, LAWFUL, AND *TAYYIB*, GOOD (2:168), IN ORDER TO UPHOLD GOD'S COMMANDS AND LIVE A LIFE OF PURITY.

Islam takes a holistic view of human life, believing that the mind, body, emotions and soul are all interconnected and, therefore, interdependent. Food and drink directly affect the body, and spiritual worship very much depends on a healthy body. Islam, therefore, has clear laws on eating and drinking.

TAYYIB, HARAM AND *HALAL*

The Quran commands, 'O ye who believe, eat of the good things that We have provided for you, and be grateful to Allah: it is Him you worship' (2:172). In Islam, good, or *tayyib*, foods are all those fruits, grains and vegetables that are naturally produced by the earth. Their goodness lies in their nutritional benefits and in the different pleasing colours and tastes that have been created by God. Some Muslims argue that *tayyib* in its purest sense means organic, non-genetically modified foods.

The Quran prohibits the eating of carrion, blood, pig and any animal that has not been slaughtered in God's name (2:173). Further categories of prohibited, or *haram*, foods are carnivorous animals, birds of prey and those partly devoured by wild animals. Islam teaches that the logic behind *haram* foods is simply that God prohibits only those things that are not good for health and wellbeing. All other meats – beef, lamb, fowl and fish – are accepted as lawful, or *halal*, foods.

SLAUGHTERING

Recent controversies over animal welfare have questioned methods of killing animals for food. Islam has always promoted animal welfare, and so prohibits any methods of slaughtering that cause pain or distress to the animals. Slaughtering is sanctioned only by the cutting of the animal's throat in one swift knife action, in which the windpipe and jugular vein are severed.

Above *Painting of a meal being prepared from the anthology of Hafiz, a 16th-century poet. Food should be prepared with prayers, peace and love.*

Kindness to the animal is paramount – both in life and at the time of its death. It is important that it is reared correctly and freely, is treated kindly at the time of slaughtering, does not see the knife, is not seen by other animals when being slaughtered and has Allah's name invoked over it.

ALCOHOL AND DRINKS

Water, milk and all fruit juices are highly recommended. The only prohibition is fermented drinks: that is, alcohol, or *khamr*. *Khamr* means 'a cover', for alcohol and drugs 'cover' (cloud) the mind through intoxication. As they can impair mental and physical faculties, they are prohibited.

Left *Eating* tayyib *and* halal *food is a requirement of Muslim life. Animals should be reared organically and treated with kindness in life and at their death.*

Above Eating together carries many blessings and is always preferred to eating alone. Here, a traditional meal is shared in a Yemeni home near Taizz.

Because drinking alcohol was such an embedded practice in pre-Islamic Arabia, the Quranic verses prohibiting it were revealed in three phases. Firstly, around the 16th year of Muhammad's prophethood, people were told that there were some benefits in it, but that the harm was greater (2:219). The year after, Muslims were instructed not to approach their prayers when intoxicated (4:43). Finally, in the 17th year of prophethood, the total ban on alcohol was revealed, linking it with the works of the devil (5:90).

NECESSITY NEGATES PROHIBITION

The Quran is emphatic, and the Muslim community is united, in the view that if a person will otherwise die of hunger or thirst, and there is no other food or drink available but the *haram*, or if a person is forced to eat unlawfully under oppression, then such food and drink are to be treated as lawful, without any blame being laid on the consumer. Preserving life is seen as a more sacred duty than obedience to dietary laws.

MANNERS AND ETIQUETTE OF EATING

Not only what but how Muslims eat is important. Muhammad encouraged people to eat with their right hand, and to start with a prayer in God's name. He also recommended that people eat slowly, and from what is nearest to them on their plates first. He emphasized that only a third of the stomach should be filled with food, another third with water and the final third left empty. This is so that overeating, and all the problems associated with it, can be avoided. Finally, praise and thanks to Allah should complete the meal. For attaining further blessings, Muslims believe that it is better to eat in company, rather than alone.

THE QURAN AND HEAVENLY FOODS

The Quran mentions many earthly foods, including lentils, corn, onions, dates, olives, water and milk. But in heaven, the Quran states, there are fountains and flowing springs, and drinks that will be sweet but without any headiness. There are also pomegranates, dates, other fruits, the *talh* tree, bearing perhaps a kind of plantain, and the flesh of fowl.

Above Referred to several times in the Quran, dates are believed to be one of the foods of paradise.

MODESTY, MORALITY AND THE VEIL

MUSLIM FAMILY LIFE IS ORGANIZED AROUND RULES OF ETIQUETTE AND APPROPRIATE SOCIAL INTERACTION. THE MOST QUOTED RULES PERTAIN TO DRESS, PARTICULARLY FOR WOMEN.

Morality plays a significant role in social interaction in Islam, so that Muslims are aware that all social relationships are affected by how people behave toward each other. The first rule in social interaction therefore is modesty, and this is encouraged in speech, behaviour and dress.

MODESTY IN BEHAVIOUR

The bond of brotherhood links all Muslims, but beyond this, every person's life and property is considered sacred. The Quran stipulates that believers must not mock, slander or revile each other, call each other names or be mistrusting and suspicious (49: 10-12). Friendliness and the safeguarding of people's honour are divine instructions.

Muslims believe that the best way to achieve this propriety is through modest, kind and polite behaviour, and by remembering God during all social interactions. The Prophet Muhammad instructed his companions to greet each other in peace, to sit and talk politely, and not to outstay their welcome. To socialize together was encouraged by him in order to strengthen the ties of brotherhood.

Some elements of the Muslim community are very conservative about men and women interacting socially, and therefore segregate society to the extent that men and women do not usually associate with each other unless they are directly related. Total segregation means that they will not come into contact in the marketplace, or in the spheres of health and education. For example, Saudi Arabia has separate educational campuses for women, and Iran has instituted separate health facilities.

The majority of Muslims take the view, however, that interaction between the sexes should be

Above Women are often seen in the marketplace in Marrakech, Morocco, where interaction between men and women in public is considered natural.

allowed, provided it is conducted with decorum. So women in Pakistan are often seen in the marketplace buying from men, and are taught by both men and women in higher education institutions. Muslims who believe that interaction should be allowed cite examples of Muhammad greeting and conversing with women.

Dress codes need to be observed with modesty at all times, however, and polite social interaction should not degenerate into intimate chitchat. Most Muslims therefore prefer single-sex social events. Indeed, it is believed that a man and woman should never be alone together, in case sexual feelings are aroused, and to prevent the reputations of individuals being harmed by malicious gossip.

Left Male and female students have a picnic together in Iran. Such interaction is not considered immoral, provided rules of dress and etiquette are adhered to.

The Quranic injunctions that encouraged Muhammad's wives to talk to men in a formal, business-like manner are often extended to all women. Social interaction is in the spirit of brotherhood, not of free mixing.

MODESTY IN DRESS

While women's dress is usually the focus of attention, the Quran first addresses men, urging them to 'lower their gaze and guard their modesty: that will make for greater purity for them' (24:31). Islam decrees that while the private parts must be covered at all times, the eyes do not have to be covered, simply lowered, as it is sometimes necessary to look at the opposite sex. What is being asked is that the believer control a lustful gaze. Men are required to cover themselves, as a minimum, from their navel to their knees.

Without doubt, the most controversy regarding modesty in dress arises when discussing women. The Quran instructs: 'Tell the believing women that they should lower their gaze and guard their modesty, and not display their adornment except what is apparent. And that they should draw their coverings over their bosoms...' (24:31)

Although women are instructed as men initially, it is generally believed that they are also required to cover their heads, neck and chest, and only to uncover those in front of their immediate family – husbands, fathers, uncles, sons and brothers. Another verse stipulates that women should cover themselves with their outer garments when going outside the home (33:59).

Right While some Muslim women wear the head covering, others veil their faces with a niqab, *like four of these women in the Netherlands.*

Above This late 14th-century painting on the leather ceiling of the Sala de los Reyes in Granada, Spain, depicts a meeting of Arab chiefs. The rich variation and modesty of their dress reflect the appropriate attire of the period for Muslim men.

THE VEIL

How such verses are interpreted has varied. No particular cultural dress is stipulated: all that women are told is what to cover, not how. Some Muslim women believe that they should have the choice not to cover if they so choose, while others even argue that hair does not need to be covered, claiming that the Quran urges modesty, not literal full covering. Others interpret the verses to mean a headscarf, and loose-fitting, but beautiful, tidy clothes.

Those who argue against total segregation maintain that it cannot be considered part of God's will, otherwise he would not have stipulated the need to cover in front of non-familial men. However, in traditional societies that insist on full segregation, women remain fully covered and it is believed that women's clothing should not be attractive in style or colour, with the full *burqa* (long garment) being worn. Conservative cultures often also insist on the face being veiled.

191

SOCIAL REALITIES FOR WOMEN

THERE ARE A VARIETY OF OPINIONS REGARDING WOMEN'S POSITION IN SOCIETY. WHILE ISLAM APPEARS TO GIVE WOMEN MANY RIGHTS, THE SOCIAL REALITY IS QUITE OFTEN VERY DIFFERENT.

Women in some Muslim societies do not have the safety and freedom of movement enjoyed by others, but appearances can be deceptive: in the early period of Islam, Muslim women had far more rights than were enjoyed by women under English law, even up to the 20th century, as regards property and education. Muslim women in the West are free to choose a public or private life. While many have excelled in education and the workplace, others have chosen a domestic role.

PATRIARCHY AND WOMEN
Muslim societies, like many other societies throughout the world, are traditionally patriarchal: that is, they

are organized and run by men. This has meant that Muslim women's movements have often been restricted. For example, in Saudi Arabia, women are banned from driving, and cannot usually leave their home without the company of a male relative. Not only has this curtailed women's movements in the public sphere, but it also contradicts the Prophet's teaching that all Muslims, whether male or female, should be able to ride a horse, which implies the use of any means of transport.

In Afghanistan, the Taliban closed many girls' schools, claiming that if girls were out in society they might freely mix with men, thus corrupting society. (In so doing, they squarely

Above In 2003, a Pakistani Muslim female politician outside the Parliament building in Islamabad calls for an end to Pervez Musharraf's dictatorship.

placed the blame for immoral behaviour on women's shoulders.) This again contradicts the prophetic teaching: in this case, that seeking knowledge should be compulsory for men and women. These erosions of women's rights are cultural malpractices that are oppressive to women, not religious injunctions, as Islamic teachings clearly state the opposite.

MOSQUE SPACES
Although the Prophet Muhammad said that women should be allowed to go to mosques to offer prayers, he is also reported as saying that it is better for women to pray at home. Though seemingly contradictory, these two statements can be reconciled from the perspective that it is not compulsory for women to pray in the mosque: that could be an imposition for those

Left In many countries, Muslim women are free to pursue whatever career they want – such as this teacher at a primary school in London, England.

Above Dr Amina Wadud leads mixed-gender Friday prayer in New York. Women imams of mixed congregations are not usually permitted.

who would find it difficult, such as mothers with young children. Unfortunately, the second teaching has been interpreted so literally in some Muslim communities that mosques do not always provide prayer spaces for women.

This extreme position, and the discomfort of some feminist scholars with male-only imams in mosques, led to Dr Amina Wadud, Professor of Islamic Studies at Virginia Commonwealth University, conducting, to much controversy, a mixed prayer congregation in New York in 2005.

DIVERSITY IN MUSLIM SOCIETIES

Such problems for some women, however, must be balanced with the fact that many Muslim societies are surprisingly diverse and egalitarian. Official statistics show that Iran's higher education population is made up of 65 per cent women. In Morocco and Tunisia, women make up 20–25 per cent of judges, compared with 22 per cent in

Britain at district judge level and 8 per cent at appeal level. In Pakistan, 17.5 per cent of politicians in the lower house are women, which compares favourably with 18 per cent in Britain's House of Commons, yet Pakistan is often viewed as a less progressive society than Britain. This illustrates that while some Muslim societies are very traditional and insist on strict

dress codes and segregation, others, such as Malaysia, for example, are not so curtailing of women and allow them free movement.

As Islam puts great emphasis on the home providing a stable life, some women have chosen home-making as a vocation. What might appear as an imposed private life for some Muslim women is, in fact, an expressed choice.

WOMEN IN EARLY ISLAMIC HISTORY

Seeking knowledge is a must for all Muslims, according to a prophetic tradition. This injunction was taken particularly seriously in the early centuries of Islam: after the Prophet's death, his widow Ayesha was often consulted for her wisdom and knowledge of Muhammad's life. Further, women appear in records of Islamic universities from the 8th century.

Many of the early compilers of hadith record female scholars as their source of authority. The same women were renowned teachers, their popularity reflected in records detailing the large numbers of students in their classes. One such distinguished woman was Karima al-Marwaziyya (d.1070), who was considered the best commentator on Bukhari's hadith.

Dr Muhammad Akram Nadwi has written that in the 13th century, Fatima bint Ibrahim, a famous teacher of the Bukhari collection, travelled for *Hajj* to Makkah. On reaching Madinah, she was asked to teach in the Prophet's Mosque. Because she was elderly, she taught while leaning on the Prophet's grave. This is enlightening, considering that some mosques do not allow women to enter. Similarly, Shaykha Shuhda, from the same period, was a renowned lecturer at Baghdad University, the Oxford and Cambridge of its time, yet Britain did not permit women into its universities until the late 1870s.

WOMEN IN THE QURAN

MUSLIM WOMEN CAN ASPIRE TOWARD AND LEARN FROM A WIDE
RANGE OF FEMALE CHARACTERS FEATURED IN THE QURAN, FROM
THE PRIVATE AND PEACEFUL TO THE POWERFUL AND PASSIONATE.

The many women portrayed in the Quran are admired for various reasons, and show clearly that there is no one ideal woman. Different character traits are depicted so that Muslim women can draw inspiration from the characters that most resemble them.

EVE THE HELPER
The narrative relating to Eve in the Quran presents her as Adam's mate and helper, the one with whom he sought to live in peace. Eve therefore represents domestic harmony and bliss, the other half of Adam, and she is not solely blamed for the couple's subsequent descent from heaven (7:19-25).

MARY THE DEVOUT WORSHIPPER
Mary the mother of Jesus is likewise presented as a peaceful character, but one who is a model of spirituality. Although she is living under the care of her uncle Zakariyya, her life is dedicated to serving God through the temple.

Because of Mary's great piety, her communication with God is very direct. Indeed, whenever her uncle approaches her in the temple with provisions, he finds that she already has food. When he questions her about where this food comes from, Mary simply replies that it has been brought to her from God (3:37).

Above Archangel Jibril appears in human form to Mary, to announce the birth of Jesus, from The Chronology of Ancient Nations, *al-Biruni, 1307.*

Perhaps the most unique event in the narrative of Mary is that angels speak to her directly. (Only men called as prophets are usually addressed by angels.) She is told that she has conceived a child as a virgin and that he will be devoted to God, and is later instructed to withdraw from her people to give birth to the child, then to bring him to her people.

Mary is a figure whom Muslim women aspire toward: she is pious, sincere in her worship of God and innocent – the perfect image of femininity and tenderness. She is so revered in the Quran that chapter 19 is named after her.

BILQIS THE RULER
While both Eve and Mary are very private figures, Bilqis, the Queen of Sheba, is the opposite. In the Quranic account, a hoopoe brings King Solomon the news of a queen from Sheba, a city in Yemen prided for its civilization and produce

Left Adam and Eve and their twins in earthly paradise, from The Fine Flower of Histories, *by Sayyid Loqman Ashuri, 1583.*

Above Verses from chapter 19 of the Quran narrate Mary's story. Mary is highly revered in Islamic thought.

Right Bilqis, the Queen of Sheba, walks through (illusionary) water in this manuscript painting, Majalis al-Ushshaq, *from 1552.*

(27:22). The extent of the queen's power and status can be judged from her magnificent throne. However, the kingdom worships the sun, and Solomon therefore invites Bilqis to Islam via a letter.

The narrative shows her to be both a diplomatic and a well-liked ruler – she seeks advice from her ministers regarding Solomon's letter (27:32), but they show allegiance to her by submitting to her decision. She prudently avoids war by sending gifts to Solomon, and eventually accepts the one God.

ASIYA THE OPPRESSED

Most of the women presented in the Quran are married to God's devout prophets, but women who are tyrannized by oppressive men are not to be seen as weak. The wife of Pharaoh, Asiya, is seen as the epitome of women who suffer in such circumstances but who are still striving toward goodness in their silent struggles. Not only does Asiya raise Moses with love (28:9), but she is also devoted to God, asking him to free her from Pharaoh's crimes and build a house for her in paradise close to him. She is shown in the Quran to be exemplary for both men and women: 'And Allah sets forth as an example to those who believe, the wife of Pharaoh' (66:11).

ZULAIKHA THE PASSIONATE

The wife of the Aziz of Egypt, Zulaikha, is a passionate character. The Aziz has given shelter and work to Joseph, son of Jacob, in Egypt, but as Joseph grows up, Zulaikha falls in love with him and pursues him with passion. On being caught in her pursuit, she pleads innocence, crying (attempted) rape. Joseph's innocence is acknowledged, but Zulaikha still manages to ensure he is imprisoned (12:21–32). She is seen as a woman blinded by anger and passion, bent on making Joseph suffer. Although the story makes it clear that Zulaikha is helpless in being attracted to Joseph, it is also made plain that natural desires can be contained and purified only by a belief in God. Joseph is saved by his God-consciousness (12:24).

While discouraging unlimited passion, the Quran acknowledges that passion is a human trait. In this story, Zulaikha eventually repents and seeks God's forgiveness.

CHAPTER 6

MORALITY, ETHICS AND LAW

In Islam, morality and ethics are not abstract concepts that are defined simply by individual conscience. Rather, they are concrete values that are enshrined in the Quran and regulated by the Shariah. Muslims believe that because moral and ethical concepts are prescribed by Islamic laws and teachings, Muslim society is able to function with harmony and cohesion.

This does not deny the importance of conscience, however, which Islam teaches has been given to every individual by God. Rather, the norms are determined by the Shariah for certain basic actions, while individuals have the responsibility of applying the moral teachings and ethical dictates of Islam to each human interaction, in accordance with their conscience. For Muslims, such an approach is seen not as the product of mechanical instruction, but as a set of clear directives that appeal to a person's intellect (*aqd*) and sense of social justice (*adl*). There is a balance (*mizan*) between man as spiritual being and social actor: God is obeyed and others served.

Opposite An imam studies the Quran before prayers in the Larabanga Mosque, Ghana, West Africa. The Quran contains a blueprint for moral and ethical values.

Above A man and his child attend prayers in Dhaka, Bangladesh. Family values and practices are shaped by the ethical teachings of Islam.

ACCOUNTING FOR THE SOUL

ISLAM TEACHES THAT INDIVIDUALS HAVE MORAL AND ETHICAL DUTIES TO GOD, THEMSELVES, THEIR FAMILIES, THEIR COMMUNITY, THE WIDER SOCIETY, HUMANITY AT LARGE AND EVEN OF THE WHOLE CREATION.

Above Muslims believe that giving zakah *purifies one's possessions and deeds, as well as ensuring that poverty is addressed through wealth distribution.*

Humankind is seen as the best of God's creation, and as such has a moral responsibility to establish God's will on earth. Muslims believe that God has instructed men and women in their responsibilities by sending a series of divinely guided prophets, some with holy scriptures, to show them the 'straight path'.

Islam teaches that humankind's divinely appointed task is to establish prayer and charity in the service of God and to forsake all evil in thought and deeds, to be morally upright and ethically principled in accordance with God's decrees.

INDIVIDUAL RESPONSIBILITY

The Shariah sets down clear instructions concerning the duties of men and women at every level. Firstly, it maintains, they should worship God as the owner of all creation. The Quran teaches that God has given humankind unique faculties – reason, intelligence and free will – in return for earthly vicegerency (caliph).

Each individual has responsibility for himself or herself – to nurture his or her body and soul, be morally upright and ethically conscious and accept God's divine decree for his or her life. Each person has a duty to love, respect, protect and provide for the material, emotional and spiritual wellbeing of his/her family, which includes extended family.

Individuals also have duties in respect of their community and neighbours (defined as those living within a radius of 40 houses). Responsibilities toward society include issues of allegiance and loyalty, distribution of charity, community service and civil participation. The Shariah gives both specific rulings and general guidelines in terms of Muslims' wider responsibilities toward humanity, which vary depending on the community's theological and cultural proximity to Islam.

Left This early 17th-century Persian painting shows a Safavid princess in the tranquillity of her garden. Islam calls for humans to look after the natural world.

Above A Muslim family in Britain visit the local mosque. Children are encouraged to attend congregational prayers and other religious events.

Finally, Islam presents itself as an environmentally friendly religion: the Shariah enshrines laws relating to water wastage, destructive tree-felling and the rights of animals, among other ecological issues.

TRUSTEESHIP

A Muslim's thoughts and actions are regulated by a set of moral values and ethical actions bound by the Shariah. Islam teaches that God is unique (the doctrine of *tawhid*) and therefore all creation belongs to him, but that he has given the earth to humankind as a sacred trust. This concept of trusteeship is fundamental in Islam.

The Quran describes trusteeship as 'enjoining what is good': that is, establishing what God has permitted (*halal*) and 'forbidding evil', or stopping transgression and what is harmful (*haram*)(3:104). In doing so, Muslims believe that divine peace (Islam) will be established.

In Islam, men and women are duty bound to co-operate with each other to meet their religious

Right Thai Muslim civilians and soldiers are observed as God's caliphs, or vicegerents, as they plant grass seeds together to protect the soil from erosion.

obligations, and are both considered caliphs on God's earth. As such, they have an equal responsibility in preserving the natural order of God's creation and the ecological balance of their environment.

This sacred trusteeship is bound with accountability, and Islam teaches that abuse or injustices to fellow humans, animals and plants, or the landscape and atmosphere will be judged and punished by God accordingly, both in this world and the hereafter. Human injustices and inequalities cause strife and conflict, and abuses of nature, such as pollution, upset the divinely ordained balance and result in ecological catastrophes.

ESTABLISHING JUSTICE

Another moral responsibility is establishing justice (*adl*). It could be argued that the purpose of all the prophets was to establish divine justice, and, in Islam, the concept begins with the individual. Muslims are taught that they must be mindful of the needs of their own body, mind and soul, avoiding any activity that harms the self. Justice must also be shown to others, particularly to those who are poor and vulnerable.

The Quran and hadith make many references to the status of women. Cultural malpractices can impose a dominant patriarchy on some Muslim societies, but Islam promotes the idea of gender equity. The instructions given relate to the role of women in terms of their religious obligations, their rights and their position in society. While many verses honour and protect women, enshrining their legal rights, others imply a biological gender equity: '...He created for you from yourselves spouses so that you might find solace in them...' (30:21), and 'men and women are protectors of one another' (9:71).

HUMAN AGENCY

ISLAM TEACHES THAT HUMANKIND IS BOUND TO SERVE GOD BY A
PRIMORDIAL COVENANT, ENTERED WHEN ALL SOULS WERE CREATED,
PROMISING TO SUBMIT TO HIM AND BE HIS VICEGERENTS ON EARTH.

Human agency is based entirely on the idea of free will being exercised, for Islam teaches that God himself gave human beings the faculty of choice. However, in exercising their free will, individuals must recognize the responsibility of ensuring peace and goodness on earth, not oppression.

Muslims use the creation story of Adam to understand human agency and the purpose of humankind on earth. According to the Quran, after God created the physical form of Adam, he stroked his back and made all the souls who were to be born between then and the Day of Judgement to come out from between his back and loins. He then made all the souls stand before him, and asked them, 'Am I not your Lord?' (7:172). When they affirmed their choice, Allah took the primordial covenant with them, telling them that he was going to make the heavens and the earth a witness to their promise of recognizing him as Lord. The prophets, who were also among the souls, were then made to take a further covenant with God, with regard to their missions (33:7).

FREE CHOICE

The first thing this covenant clarifies is that humans are different from the animal world, not only because God breathed into them, but also because he allowed them to have choice. This free will to choose is interpreted by scholars as meaning that each person has an innate consciousness (*fitra*), which allows them to discriminate

Above A Saudi Arabian man stands alone in the desert. The Quran says that all souls took a covenant with God, recognizing him as worthy of worship.

between right and wrong. Whether individuals act according to that moral consciousness is another matter, but Islam asserts that at the time of taking the covenant, every man and woman clearly understood truth, falsehood and the importance of following God's laws.

ACCOUNTABILITY

In taking the covenant with God, men and women accepted the responsibility of being his earthly representatives. This involved being accountable for establishing peace and order, not being unjust toward anyone, ensuring through kind and gentle reminders that God was duly worshipped and protecting the existence and rights of all people, animals, plants and the earth at

Left According to the Quran, God first offered his covenant to the mountains and the skies, but they refused it, fearful of its consequences.

Left Islamic literature teaches Muslims what their role is on earth and how they are to represent God's plan for peace.

large. In turn, the whole of creation was made subservient to mankind (31:20). At the same time, in taking this covenant, humankind accepted the reality of free will. This was clearly a huge responsibility for men and women to undertake.

The Quran clarifies that God did not thrust this burden upon humankind: before making the covenant with all souls, he asked the heavens, the earth and, indeed, the mountains if they wanted this

responsibility (33:72). But according to the Quran, they all declined, because they did not want to have the choice of obeying or disobeying God but rather wanted to submit to his will at all times.

CHOOSING VICEGERENCY

In Islam, humanity is considered to be superior to the rest of the natural world, for men and women choose whether or not to obey God. This freedom to act is fundamental: there

are consequences of disobeying God, but individuals should always have the choice to act or not act.

Taking responsibility is seen as very noble: humankind was brave enough to accept God's vicegerency on earth. But at the same time, this choice has exposed humans to pressures that divert them from their original role. For this reason, the Quran describes humankind as unjust, claiming they took the covenant without reflecting fully on their new responsibility. The covenant is seen not as an ideal that cannot be fulfilled, but rather as one that must be borne with maturity and accountability.

Muslims believe that they have individually promised to worship God and represent him on earth. In practice, this means that they are bound to fulfilling the five pillars, protecting kith and kin, preserving the earth and spreading peace and harmony. In short, it means true, wilful submission: Islam.

Below A 15th-century miniature shows mystics engaged in discourse. Being God's vicegerent requires wisdom and justice.

THE MANTLE OF RESPONSIBILITY

'We did indeed offer the Trust to the heavens and the earth and the mountains, but they refused to undertake it, being afraid thereof: but man undertook it – he was indeed unjust and foolish.'

(33:72)

'When thy Lord drew forth from the children of Adam descendants from their loins, and He made them testify about themselves, "Am I not your Lord?", they said, "Yes! We do testify!" '

(7:172)

COMBATING THE EGO

WHILE ISLAM TEACHES THAT HUMAN NATURE IS BASICALLY GOOD, HUMANKIND MUST NEVERTHELESS ENDURE A STRUGGLE TO MASTER THE EGO-SELF (*NAFS*), WHICH WARS AGAINST THE SPIRITUAL SELF (*RUH*).

Muslim philosophers, and in particular Sufis, have argued consistently that humankind exists in two simultaneous and parallel realms. One is the physical, sensory and known world, referred to as the exoteric (*dhahir*), which is bound by natural laws and experienced realities. The other is the inner world of the unseen or spiritual, called the esoteric (*batin*). Both realms are clearly referred to in the Quran and hadith literature: 'God holds the unseen in the heavens and the earth, And unto him does every matter return, So serve Him and rely on Him, Your Lord is not unmindful of what you are doing' (11:123).

Muslims believe that the external world is ordered by divine instructions, laws and teachings, which are aimed at developing a cohesive and harmonized society. Similarly, the internal realm, which is comprehensively seen and known only by God, is believed to be subject to divine command: God instructs human beings to master or combat the ego and thereby elevate their souls.

BODY AND SOUL

Islamic theology teaches that the ego (*nafs*) and the soul (*ruh*) are essential components of humankind's metaphysical being. While both entities are believed to be contained within the physical being, the *nafs* and *ruh* have different constitutions. The *nafs* is a human being's physical, worldly nature, created from earth and clay and then given the 'breath of life' (literally, *nafas*) by God. Islam teaches that as God created and gave life to every individual, he also placed within each person something of himself. This divine presence that exists within all human beings is the *ruh*, or soul, and Muslims believe that it emanates from God's own essence, or divine light (*nur*).

Above *A Shiah man prays, holding a rosary, at the Imam Ali shrine. The lives of Muslim saints inspire many Muslims to live a virtuous life, free from the ego.*

This implies that man's nature is inherently good, rather than inclined to evil. Muslims believe that it is humankind's base and earthy physical nature that is at the root of his occasional succumbing to his own lower desires. The Quran explains that it is to the *nafs* that Satan whispers his temptations, in order to lead men and women away from their higher spiritual being and natural disposition of obedience to God. Each person therefore faces an internal battle between the earthly, sensory and pleasure-seeking self, or the ego, and the pure, spiritual soul, which desires only to be reunited to the one from whom it came.

SELF-STRUGGLE

Islamic mystics (Sufis) understand the internal struggle of ego and soul in terms of *tazkiyah*, or spiritual self-purification. *Tazkiyah* is the means by which all bad habits and

Left *Spiritual emotions run high as a Kashmiri Muslim woman prays in reverence at the shrine of the Sufi saint, Shaykh Hamza Makhdoomi.*

traits are tempered through worship of and devotion to God. In their desire to conquer their egos, some Sufis cut themselves off from the world, choosing a life of isolation and spiritual piety.

However, Muhammad advised his followers not to emulate the ascetic practices of the people of previous scriptures, but rather to live among people in order to spread goodness and serve humankind. His own methods of spiritual self-development included a number of specific forms of worship: a night prayer vigil (*tahajjud*), voluntary fasting, regular recitation of the Quran and remembrance of God (*dhikr*) and frequent charity.

The struggle between one's lower desires and the soul's yearning for a higher spiritual plain is a life-long endurance. Muslims view this striving for spiritual perfection as a test of belief, and the Quran offers encouragement in this struggle: 'And whoever desires the Hereafter and strives for it with due effort, and believes, those are the ones whose striving will be appreciated' (17:19).

INNER *JIHAD*

The word *jihad* actually means 'to struggle'. In the Islamic context, *jihad* signifies 'struggling in the way of God' and it covers all activities associated with the establishment of Islam or its defence. This extends from the individual's struggle for spiritual excellence to defending one's country, community or home from oppression and invasion.

At the individual level, the notion of *jihad* is concerned with combating the ego and submitting oneself sincerely to God. On one occasion, while returning from a battle against the pagan Arabs, Muhammad told the Muslims, 'we return from the lesser *jihad* to the greater *jihad*', explaining that 'greater *jihad*' was the constant struggle to combat the ego and lower desires.

Above Contemplation, or dhikr, *is an essential part of Muslim worship, which encourages spiritual self-development through remembrance of God's attributes.*

Below Offering night prayers, or tarawih, *at Ramadhan – here, shown at the al-Aqsa Mosque in Jerusalem – is one way in which Muslims honour the soul's yearning for spiritual perfection.*

JIHAD: A JUST WAR?

THE WORD *JIHAD* IS OFTEN MISINTERPRETED AS A 'HOLY WAR', BUT OCCASIONALLY FIGHTING TYRANNY AND AGGRESSION IS VIEWED AS A RELIGIOUS DUTY IN ISLAM. IT IS THEN UNDERSTOOD AS A 'JUST WAR'.

Historically, Western scholarship on Islam has tended to present Muhammad as a 'holy warrior', who sanctified violence and intolerance, spreading his religion by the sword to impose his beliefs on others. This misrepresentation has dominated non–Muslims' perception of Islam since the Middle Ages. But association of the term *jihad* with armed conflict has more to do with the hostilities of the medieval European crusades than with any true understanding of the word's multifarious meanings.

LESSER AND GREATER *JIHAD*

Jihad literally means 'struggle', and it implies a physical, moral, spiritual and intellectual effort. As the term *jihad* covers a wide range of activities relating to the struggles of faith, providing a precise definition for the term is difficult.

Islamic scholars identify two types of *jihad: al-jihad al-asghar*, or 'the lesser struggle', and *al-jihad al-akbar*, meaning the 'greater struggle'. *Al-jihad al-asghar* is concerned with the fight against oppression and tyranny, where armed conflict can result in loss of life. *Al-jihad al-akbar* is the internal battle waged by Muslims against their physical desires and baser instincts. It is perhaps because the enemy within, represented by the unfettered ego, is less discernible than one on the battlefield that Islam considers the internal struggle to be a greater *jihad*.

MILITARY *JIHAD*

The Quran states clearly the circumstances in which war is permitted, giving three major ones: Muslims are allowed to fight in defence of their freedom of religion; their country; and their community

Above *A 14th-century depiction of Averroes, who engaged with Aristotelian philosophy and published detailed legal treaties on the conduct of war.*

(22:39–40). Military *jihad* must also comply with conditions of Islamic law as contained in the Shariah, which details the moral duties and ethical actions of armed conflict.

The Quran refers to the defence of 'cloisters and churches and synagogues' (22:40), implying that religious freedom must be accorded to minority faith communities (*ahl al-dhimmah*) living in Muslim lands or under their protection. *Ahl al-dhimmah* are exempt from military *jihad* by payment of the *jizyah* (exemption tax).

ETHICS OF *JIHAD*

The Shariah contains a wide range of instructions and prohibitions relating to the ethics of *jihad*, and medieval Islamic scholars, such as Ibn Rushd and Ibn Khaldun, wrote detailed treatises on the ethics of military *jihad* and its permissibility.

According to the Quran, 'Permission to fight is given to those against whom war is being

Left *Artist Edwin Lord Weeks imagines the call to 'holy war' against Christians in this 19th-century representation of the Great Mosque of Córdoba, Spain.*

wrongfully waged, And God is indeed able to help them; those who have been unjustly driven out of their homes only because they said our Lord is God' (22:39–40). But the prohibition of aggression is unambiguously stated: 'Fight in the way of God against those who fight against you, but do not yourselves commit aggression; for behold, God does not love aggressors. And fight against them until there is no more persecution and people are free to worship God. But if they desist, then all hostilities shall cease, except against the oppressors…' (2:193)

The Prophet also gave explicit orders to Muslim soldiers in the theatre of war in order to prevent atrocities. He commanded them to seek permission from dependent parents before going to war, and he prohibited the molestation of harmless innocents and the weak and infirm, the demolishing of the dwellings or property of unresisting inhabitants and the destruction of their means of subsistence, such as livestock and agriculture, and of trees or date palms.

POLITICS OF *JIHAD*

Although the Quran interdicts Muslims from waging a war of aggression (2:190), the majority of scholars conclude that when the existence of the Muslim community or the borders of its lands are under attack, military *jihad* should be declared until all oppression has been abated. Conversely, if a Muslim political ruler declares an illegal war, the citizens of that state would be justified in disobeying a call to arms and becoming 'conscientious objectors'. However, if a declaration of hostilities is seen as a just war by the vast majority of religious scholars – and only a just war can be called a *jihad* – and if the state conforms to the principles and instructions of the Shariah, then every eligible Muslim must take up arms.

Above The Muslim ruler Timur, or Tamerlane, is depicted attacking a walled city in this 16th-century illustration. The Quran clearly states when war is justified.

Below Bosnian Muslims in training during the Bosnian War in the 1990s. Many Muslims defended their people and land from Serbian aggression.

Martyrdom and Suicide

SHAHADAH IS THE FIRST PILLAR OF ISLAM AND THE ARABIC WORD CARRIES THE SENSE OF BOTH 'TO BEAR WITNESS' AND 'MARTYRDOM', BUT IN ISLAM DYING FOR ONE'S FAITH DOES NOT INCLUDE SUICIDE.

Recent decades have witnessed a disturbing rise in the phenomenon generally described as 'Islamic fundamentalism'. The most obscene feature of this particular form of Muslim extremism is the alarming occurrences of terrorist suicide bombings and attacks. It is clear that there are many complex issues surrounding the political motivations for the use of violence, but the question remains: does Islam permit such indiscriminate acts of suicidal murder?

ISLAMIC MARTYRDOM
Islam has permitted war against tyranny and oppression through *al-jihad al-asghar*, or 'the lesser struggle', and recognizes those who die in such a 'just war' as martyrs. The Quran describes those fighting injustices as *mujahidun* (from the word *jihad*) and those who lose their lives in battle as *shuhadaa* (from *shahadah*, meaning 'martyrs').

Like the prophets, *shuhadaa* (sing. *shahid*) will not be brought to account on the Day of Judgement, and the Quran instructs believers to 'Think not of those who are slain in the way of God as dead, Nay, they are living, With their Lord they have provision. Jubilant (are they) because of that which God has bestowed upon them of His bounty, rejoicing for the sake of those who have not yet joined them but are left behind: that there shall no fear come upon them, neither shall they grieve' (3:169–70).

According to the Prophet, it is not only those who die in war

Left The iconography of martyrdom is illustrated in this fresco at the Martyrs Museum in Tehran, Iran. Shiahs revere martyrdom as exampled by Muhammad's grandson (d.680).

***Above** A coffin shroud bears the Muslim declaration of faith. Islam teaches that those who die fighting tyranny and oppression enter paradise as martyrs.*

who are considered martyrs, but also mothers who die in childbirth, victims of unjust killings through accident or murder and those who die as a result of severe illness, starvation or natural catastrophes.

MUSLIM FUNDAMENTALISM
The term 'fundamentalist' usually denotes someone who believes in the literal meaning of his or her religious scripture. In this sense, all Muslims might be understood as fundamentalist because they believe the Quran is literally God's word, but it would be wrong to assume that the majority of Muslims are literalistic in their interpretation and application of their scripture.

Nevertheless, there exists a minority of Muslims who insist on a single interpretation of the Quran that divides the world simplistically into two categories: believers (Muslims) and non-believers (*kuffar*). Some such literalists use extreme and violent means that are contrary to the teachings of Islam in an attempt to impose their restricted views upon the majority. Often motivated by fanatical political aims, these extremists employ distorted religious interpretations to justify acts of terrorism.

SUICIDE TERRORISTS

Certain of these extremist Muslim fundamentalist groups will even attack and kill innocent people in an attempt to further their political and religious aims. Such acts of terrorism are increasingly carried out in the name of Islam by Muslim 'suicide' attackers or bombers.

Such acts of violence are in opposition to Islam: the Quran stipulates that 'whosoever kills a human being for other than murder or corruption in the earth, it shall be as if he killed all humanity' (5:32), and the Prophet exhorted that there shall be no harming and no reciprocating of harm. The overwhelming majority of Islamic jurists conclude that Islam categorically forbids both the act of suicide and the killing of innocents or 'non-combatants'.

While there can never be a justification for such heinous and reprehensible crimes, a distinction needs to be made between the terrorist acts of individual Muslims,

Above A female suicide bomber poses with her son before blowing herself up and killing four Israelis at a checkpoint on the Gaza Strip in January 2004.

which are perpetrated in the name of their religion, and what Islam teaches and the Muslim community (*ummah*) believes and practises. Suicide bombings and killings are more symptomatic of the political, social and economic inequalities existing in a number of Muslim countries than of any inherent violence or aggression in Islam.

MODERATION IN ISLAM

Islam forbids both zealous fanaticism (*ghuluw*) and lapsed indifference (*dhalal*). To be Muslim is to belong to what the Quran describes as *ummatun wasata*, or 'the community of moderation', and to abide by the consensus (*ijma*) of the wider community, its scholars and leaders.

During times of fission and unity, where Muslim political and spiritual leadership is established, the *ummah* is able to identify both legitimate governance and religious orthodoxy. However, fragmentation and disunity can result in a shared loss of direction and even violence and extremism. Muhammad warned his followers about the decline of Muslim rule, advising them to always take the 'middle path' and remain faithful to the Quranic teachings and his example.

Below The Iran–Iraq war of the 1980s saw Muslims killing Muslims, leaving more than a million dead. Both sides claimed that those killed were martyrs.

ISLAMIC ETHICS

LAW AND ETHICS, THE PRECEPTS OF MORAL CONDUCT, ARE VERY
SIMILAR IN ISLAM: BOTH ARE ROOTED IN THE QURAN, AND MUSLIMS
ARE REQUIRED TO ACCOUNT TO GOD FOR THEIR FULFILMENT.

Islamic ethics are found not only in the Quran, but also throughout the entire records of Islamic history. In their personal moral behaviour and in relations with family, in business matters or when making political treaties, Muslims are exhorted to be just and merciful.

TEACHINGS OF THE QURAN

The Quran describes itself as the *furqan*, the criterion by which humankind can judge between right and wrong: 'Blessed is He who sent down the Criterion to His servant, that it may be an admonition to all creatures' (25:1). Later in this chapter 25, metaphors of light and darkness illustrate the Quran's claim that it alone can lead humankind to God's light, and thereby his blessings, and that a life away from this moral code leads one into darkness. The teachings of the Quran form the foundation for all social interaction for Muslims.

Muslim ethics are also based on the example of the Prophet, known as sunnah, and his fulfilment of the command to 'enjoin the good and forbid the evil' (3:104). The Quran and the sunnah are put into practice with the application of human 'reason', the faculty each person has to discern right from wrong, which is referred to more than 750 times in the Quran. Muslims believe that relying on a combination of all three sources promotes moral responsibility, the basis of ethics.

ETHICS AS *AKHLAQ*

The Arabic term for 'ethics' is *akhlaq*. In its singular form, the word means character trait, but in its plural, it carries the sense of morality or ethics. It is used to refer to good manners, politeness, justice and kindness. Islam teaches that only through personal reform and morality can a Muslim draw near to God and grow in his or her faith.

In a well-known hadith, the Prophet said, 'I was sent to perfect good character/ethics', thus placing ethics and morality at the centre of his prophetic mission. The Quran says of him '…you are

Above An Iraqi Mullah at Prayer*, by Konrad Filip, depicts an imam holding the Quran – the Muslim's criterion for judging right and wrong, which sets out a statement of ethics.*

indeed of an exalted character' (68:4). On many occasions, the Prophet asserted that the best Muslim, and the one dearest to Allah, is the one with the best moral character. Indeed, another oft-quoted hadith even claims that 'a person can reach a high status in the hereafter by his good conduct, though he may be weak in matters of worship, and he can also go down to the lowest part of hell by his wicked character'.

ETHICS IN PRACTICE

The Quran, sunnah, law and local customs have together shaped the whole body of rules known today as Islamic ethics. The first rule put into practice by the Prophet was dispensing with idol worship and focusing on monotheism. He then enjoined his followers to replace

Left These Saudi Arabian men are engaged in a business meeting. Moral and ethical conduct must be observed by Muslims at all times, whether in personal, social or business relations.

Right A 16th-century manuscript painting shows the Prophet's Night Journey, which is seen as an allegory for each Muslim's journey toward God, through worship and ethical conduct.

kinship and tribal bonds with the idea of a larger Muslim community, teaching that the hereafter is more important than ancestral legacies, and that humility and justice are of greater consequence than pride and image.

A STATEMENT OF ETHICS

Many scholars claim that the most detailed statement of Islamic ethics contained in the Quran is to be found in chapter 17, verses 22 to 39. The chapter opens with the Prophet's night journey to heaven, which is seen as an allegory for every Muslim's own journey toward God. It then outlines humankind's fall from God's grace before giving the good news of his guidance.

However, in order to receive this guidance, it states that human beings must fulfil a code of ethics. This requires them to worship God alone; to be kind to parents, particularly in their old age; to assist the wayfarer and those in need; to avoid squandering wealth, but without being niggardly; to speak kindly even to those with whom one disagrees; not to kill children out of fear of lack of provision; not to commit adultery; not to take life unlawfully; not to usurp the property of orphans; to measure and conduct business deals fairly; not to be idly curious; not to 'walk on the earth in arrogance'. This comprehensive charter of human ethical conduct has been compared with the Ten Commandments.

Right An Iraqi family is breaking its fast at sunset in Ramadhan, having fasted from dawn until dusk. Sharing meals, sitting and socializing together are all activities that the Shariah rules upon.

THE SANCTITY OF LIFE

ISLAM TEACHES THAT LIFE IS PRECIOUS AND GIVEN BY GOD, AND PROCREATION AND THE BLESSINGS OF CHILDREN ARE SEEN BY MUSLIMS AS A NATURAL CONSEQUENCE OF MARRIED LIFE.

Islam can be said to be generally pro-life, and any action that preserves, prolongs and protects life is encouraged, on condition that it conforms to the moral and ethical teachings of Islam as defined within the Quran and sunnah. Conversely, taking a life by any immoral or unethical means is expressly prohibited in Islam.

MARRIAGE
Islam prohibits fornication and adultery and carefully inhibits all pathways leading to them. Islam is also against celibacy and the suppressing of the sexual urge by castration or any other physical means. Instead, it encourages marriage as a means of living a wholesome and fulfilled life. Sexual relations within the sanctity of marriage are considered both a natural act and a blessing from God.

If a Muslim has the means to marry, then he or she should do so; and refraining from marriage in order to dedicate oneself to the worship and service of God by monasticism or renunciation of the world is discouraged. The Prophet forbade his companions from shunning marriage and withdrawing from the world, declaring such a lifestyle to be a deviation from Islam and a rejection of his sunnah.

BIRTH AND PATERNITY
Children are a natural consequence of marriage and are seen as a great blessing in Islam, and Muslims believe that God grants their sustenance. Female infanticide was a common practice among the pre-Islamic Arabs, but Islam prohibits the killing of one's children for fear of poverty or shame (17:31).

The right to family lineage and bloodline descent are often taken for granted, but many children do not know who one or other of their parents is. Muslims believe that God has ordained marriage in order that paternity can be established without ambiguity or doubt. Equally, a father is not allowed to deny his paternity of any child born within marriage.

Above Marriage is a sacred institution and the cornerstone of Muslim society. It has always been a cause for celebration in Islamic communities across the world.

Muhammad declared that 'every child is attributed to the one on whose bed it is conceived', by which he meant that every child is a product of a specific sexual relationship, whether or not the man and woman are married.

In exceptional circumstances, where infidelity and subsequent illegitimacy is suspected, an Islamic judge (*qadi*) can decide paternity either via blood tests or by *lian*, a process where both parties swear an oath against each other's accusations before divorcing (24:6–9). In such a case, the child will thereafter take the mother's name.

LEGAL ADOPTION
Just as it is prohibited for a man to deny his paternity of a child born in wedlock, so it is forbidden

Left Muslims believe all life to be sacred, and that the illegal taking of a single life is equal to killing the whole of humanity.

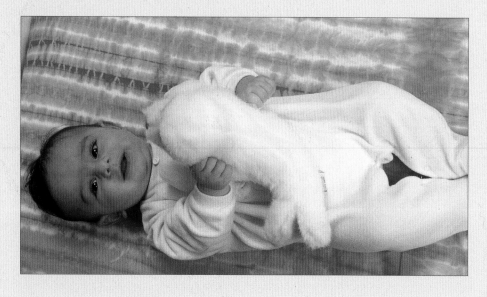

for him to legally claim that he is the father of any child he has not biologically conceived. In Muhammad's day, the pagan Arabs had a custom known as *tabanni* ('to make one's son'), whereby a child could be adopted by receiving the name and lineage of his or her adopting father. This practice was allowed even when the biological parents and family lineage of the child were known.

By contrast, the Quran states, 'Nor has He made your adopted sons your [real] sons, that is simply as saying from your mouths...call them by [the names of] their fathers, that is more just in the sight of God. But if you do not know their fathers, they are your brothers in faith and your wards' (33:4–5). Islam posits that the pronouncement

Right Marriage, and sexual relations within the marriage, are strongly encouraged in Islam.

of adopted children as one's own does not alter the biological and genealogical realities. Such a ruling safeguards lineage and protects any rights of inheritance. The Quran teaches that 'blood relatives are nearer to each other in the ordinance of God' (8:75). Legal adoption in expressed terms of claiming children who are not

Above A Qatari Arab Muslim with his daughter. Children are considered a great blessing from God in all Muslim societies.

biologically one's own is therefore forbidden. However, where the child's identity and paternity are presevered and protected, adoption and fostering is considered an extremely virtuous act in Islam.

ISLAMIC LAW

MUSLIMS BELIEVE THAT FULFILLING GOD'S WILL THROUGH UPHOLDING HIS LAWS LEADS TO A JUST AND SAFE SOCIETY. ISLAMIC LAW IS THE SYSTEM BY WHICH THE WILL OF ALLAH IS MADE MANIFEST.

Islamic law is often erroneously described as the Shariah, and presented as being fossilized and immutable. However, the Shariah is only that part of Islamic law which is derived from the two sacred primary sources: the Quran and sunnah. The rest of the body of law, known as *fiqh*, evolves as Islamic legal scholars arrive at new understandings of Shariah.

Muslims believe, however, that while God's laws need to be established on earth, God himself is the final judge, who will weigh all actions in his scale of justice.

SHARIAH
An Arabic word, Shariah means a 'path to a watering course'. Muslims believe that just as water sustains life, so, too, does Islam. A clear path is set before Muslims in the shape of the Shariah, which ensures that the principles and values laid out by God in the Quran are upheld with justice and compassion between individuals and the state.

Shariah forms the basic core of Islamic law, which is seen as eternal, for it is enshrined in the two primary sources: the Quran and the sunnah. Shariah contains core

Above A Shariah lecture at Khosrakh, Daghestan. The importance of the law and scholars learning from each other has always been a part of Islamic tradition.

principles to preserve life, and sets limits for human behaviour, thus ensuring that everyone's property and person remain sacred. It is worth noting, however, that of more than 6,000 verses in the Quran, only around 250 are legalistic, for while the law is important, it is only the basis of a godly Muslim life.

Muslims view the Prophet's life as the best example to follow in terms of his fulfilment and explanation of the law. Together with the divine revelation (the Quran), his sunnah provides a blueprint for Islamic law. These two sources together contain the few universal and concretized canonical laws that are at the heart of Shariah.

Eternally written principles are not problematic for Muslims, for they contain moral laws that are important for all times, such as just economic rules and control on crimes to make society safe.

PRINCIPLES OF LAW
Fiqh is an Arabic word that loosely translates as 'jurisprudence', but more literally means 'understanding and intelligence', and refers to

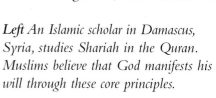

Left An Islamic scholar in Damascus, Syria, studies Shariah in the Quran. Muslims believe that God manifests his will through these core principles.

principles derived from Shariah by scholars reflecting on the application of the law. It is not eternally binding, but rather interprets and translates the few eternal principles.

There are several branches of *fiqh* that might find their way into the corpus of law. The first is *ijma*, the 'consensus of scholarly opinion': where a law is not clear from the Quran or sunnah, the views of scholars and their interpretations are taken into account. If there still is no clarity, or a new situation arises, then an analogy is drawn between the new case and a similar previous one, so that a new precedent can be created (*qiyas*). In another source of law, known as *ijtihad*, an individual scholar gives his opinion on a new situation in the spirit of the Quran and sunnah. Local norms and customs are also taken into account when applying and extending laws to new situations (*urf*).

Because *fiqh* evolves and changes, depending on the needs of time and place, there are several schools of law, all of which adhere to

Above The Grand Mufti of Egypt is one of the most important Islamic figures in the world and highly respected for his knowledge of law.

the divine laws but have slight differences in their interpretations. A growing number of scholars are of the opinion that it is now time for a further school of law to develop that will meet the needs of Muslims in the West.

Above At a conference in Baghdad in 2007, Shiah and Sunni clerics discuss Muslim unity and the application of Islamic law in Iraq.

GOD, THE INDIVIDUAL AND SOCIETY

The relationship between God, the individual and society can be viewed as a triangle where God is at the apex: his laws bind individuals in relationship with him through personal laws, *ibadat*, such as prayer and fasting, but he also links individuals with wider society through the *muamalat* laws, which protect public interest: for example, as in criminal law.

In Islamic law, actions are not simply viewed as either obligatory or forbidden. In fact, there are three degrees between these two extremes: actions may also be classified as being meritorious, permissible or reprehensible. For example, helping out at a local hospice may not be compulsory, but would be seen as meritorious, because the Prophet practised community care.

ESTABLISHING GOD'S WILL

MUSLIMS SEEK GUIDANCE AND ATTEMPT TO DETERMINE THE WILL OF ALLAH BY READING THE QURAN AND FOLLOWING THE SUNNAH, THE DEEDS AND SAYINGS OF THE PROPHET.

A Muslim's principal religious duty is to submit to and accept the will of Allah. The word Islam, which is usually translated as 'submission', derives from an Arabic root (s-l-m) that also suggests 'acceptance' and 'peace'.

In seeking and then attempting to follow Allah's will, Muslims believe that they can find equilibrium and inner peace and can begin to live in harmony with the laws of the created world as established by God. A Muslim's central source of guidance in determining Allah's will is the Quran and the sunnah, the traditions concerning the Prophet's words and deeds. By studying these sources, a Muslim is guided to be charitable and compassionate, to be trusting and sincere, to show fortitude and patience and always to be mindful of, and to fulfil, his or her personal commitments.

An oft-quoted verse in the Quran (2:177) offers a definition of 'righteousness' and suggests that a good Muslim life combines faith in God and religious observance with

Above Men read the Quran at the Great Mosque in Damascus, Syria. By following the word of God, Muslims believe they can be guided to inner peace.

Below Here, the teachings of the Quran provide guidance for Muslim women in the Jamia Mosque in Srinagar, northern India.

Right In Samarkand, Uzbekistan, a clock reminds the devout of the times for the five daily prayers. Religious observance is part of God's will.

being patient and displaying ethical behaviour, such as caring for travellers and the poor.

THE SUNNAH

Even before Muhammad's lifetime, the Arabic word 'sunnah' was in circulation and meant 'inherited customs and precedents'. Early in the history of Islam, Muslims began to use the term to refer to traditions relating to the Prophet's words and deeds. Hadith (sayings and reported actions of the Prophet) were collected by scholars dedicated to the purpose, and carefully identified by source. *Al-Sirah al-nabawiyyah*, or expanded and rather less strictly reliable narratives of Muhammad's life, also fed into the sunnah.

Muslims believe that the knowledge collected in the sunnah complements the Prophet's divinely inspired teachings, which are recorded in the Quran. Indeed, the Quran itself encourages Muslims to seek guidance in the example of the Prophet's life and actions: 'Verily in the messenger of Allah ye have a good example for him who looketh unto Allah and the Last Day, and remembereth Allah much' (33:21).

SHARIAH

In the early centuries of Islam, study of the sunnah and of the Quran fed into the developing Shariah ('pathway'), guidance on all aspects of how to live as a Muslim in the world. In some Muslim nations, Shariah developed into a legal system with courts and judges, and definitions provided by jurists (*fuqaha*), who were experts in the science of law (*fiqh*).

In the various Muslim traditions, the foundations of and authorities for *fiqh* were different. Shiah Muslims gave special authority to imams and those representing them. For Sunni Muslims, the basic sources for *fiqh* were the Quran and the sunnah, complemented by jurists' reasoning by analogy (*qiyas*) and the agreement of learned scholars and jurists (*ijma*).

For Muslims, Shariah is more than a legal system: it is a framework within which they can make a life in accordance with Allah's will, the basis of an individual's relationship with Allah and with others, and a framework for ethical decisions.

INNER GUIDANCE

Some Muslims believe that they can also find guidance in seeking the will of Allah within their own hearts, through their own inner leadings. A verse from the Quran quoted in support of this position is 6:125: 'And whomsoever it is Allah's will to guide, He expandeth their bosoms unto Islam', which suggests that Allah develops an individual's ethics and inner understanding so that they are guided through the process of surrender. The Quran praises 'he whose bosom Allah hath expanded for Al-Islam, so that he followeth a light from his Lord' (39:22).

Sufi Muslims consider that the most profound understanding of the will of Allah can be discerned through inner seeking by way of meditation and other spiritual disciplines, such as fasting. Sufis follow an inner path or 'way' (*tariqah*), led by a spiritual teacher, based around contemplation and meditation, often on verses from the Quran. This spiritual journey is believed by Sufis to culminate in an experience (*fana*) of the individual self being extinguished and united with its divine source in a deep experiential understanding of *tawhid* (the oneness of Allah).

Left A judge in a Shariah court. For Muslims, Shariah law provides guidance on how to live in accordance with God's will.

JUSTICE: APPLYING THE LAW

CIVIL ISLAMIC LAW IS CONCERNED WITH ASPECTS OF PROTECTING AN INDIVIDUAL'S RIGHTS IN A FAMILY LAW DISPUTE, AS WELL AS REGULATING CORPORATE CLIENTS IN BANKING LAWS.

Islamic law touches every aspect of Muslim life, and holds as central principles of freedom, equity and justice – social, political and economic. Promoting equality and the welfare of the community is a major task when enforcing the law. In civil law, this means ensuring justice both in the private sphere, such as family law, and in the public arena, such as business and banking law. The courts are expected to live up to the ideal of the law.

ECONOMICS

The right of the individual to pursue economic gain is recognized in Islamic law, but this must at all times be carried out in a permissible (*halal*) manner. Laws ensure that the world's wealth does not find its way into the hands of a few, and prevent the growth in disparity between the rich and the poor. The rich, therefore, are expected to pay *zakah* as a welfare system.

Economic and business systems are lawful only if they operate on principles of ethical and moral financing. Therefore, trade dealings with 'economic giants' who exploit poor countries through unfair trade practices are forbidden (*haram*).

Below An Islamic bank in Dubai. Ethical Islamic banking forbids the charging of interest, so interest-free loans and mortgages are arranged.

Above The headquarters of the Islamic Development Bank in Jeddah, Saudia Arabia. Under Islamic law, businesses must not exploit the poor.

ISLAMIC BANKING

One example of ethical economics law is banking: usury (*riba*) is not allowed in Islamic banking, because it takes advantage of people in a weak position. Because charging interest is considered unjust and inequitable, all Islamic banks loan money without demanding interest repayments, although they do apply administrative charges.

Islamic banking principles have been in force since the beginnings of the religion in the 6th century, because the taking of interest is forbidden in the Quran itself (2:275–6). But over the last few decades, Islamic banks have emerged as major international economic players.

Malaysia is a Muslim country that is leading the way in interest-free banking. In Britain, the HSBC bank began to offer Islamic mortgages in both Malaysia and Britain around 2003 and was surprised to find that half of its customers were not Muslim. Islamic economics thus benefits the whole of society.

Above Pregnancy outside marriage is seen as proof of adultery. Single Nigerian woman Safiya Hussaini was sentenced to death when pregnant with her daughter, but later acquitted.

FAMILY LAW AND DIVORCE

Fundamental aspects of civil law relating to the private sphere of domestic disputes are enshrined in the Quran. If a woman has been subjected to, or fears, cruel treatment at the hands of her husband, then she can ask for a *khul*, a divorce instigated by the wife (4:128). The parties can come to their own amicable settlement.

Fiqh rules have stipulated that a wife must apply to a court if she wishes to divorce her husband, and that she must return all her dowry in exchange for the divorce. However, if the divorce is requested on grounds of cruelty, the husband is legally obligated not to ill-treat his wife financially by demanding the dowry be repaid to him. He must also maintain her during the three-month separation period.

DIVORCE LAW IN MALAYSIA

Unfortunately, courts do not always apply the law justly. In a case recorded in Malaysia, a man caused such grievous bodily harm to his wife that he was imprisoned for ten years. Despite this, when the wife applied to the court for a divorce based on cruelty, her application was rejected. Instead, the husband agreed to divorce her on the undertaking that she would forego all rights to maintenance during the finalization of the divorce. Not only did the woman lose her legal right to a divorce, but the court also allowed her to be unfairly coerced into losing maintenance rights.

In order to try and redress this imbalance of justice against women, a judge pronounced during a maintenance dispute that the burden of proving that he is maintaining his wife should lie with the husband, not the wife. If the husband cannot produce such evidence of maintenance, then the wife is entitled to a divorce.

Above A Muslim man and woman sign a civil contract. Civil law gives women many legal rights, particularly in marriage and divorce laws.

CRIME AND PUNISHMENT

ALLAH FORBIDS INDIVIDUALS FROM TAKING AWAY THE FREEDOM AND RIGHTS OF ANOTHER. SUCH ACTS ARE SEEN AS CRIMINAL AND WORTHY OF PUNISHMENT, BUT THIS MUST BE METED OUT VERY CAREFULLY.

The purpose of criminal laws in the Quran is to give believers guidance based on spirituality, ethics and justice, so that life and property can be preserved and protected. The Quran lays down *hudud* (limits of human behaviour), which must not be transgressed, and also prescribes the punishments that are to be applied if these laws and precepts are broken.

CRIMINAL LAW

Because they are considered to be so significant in Islam, criminal laws have been enshrined in the Quran. These laws are of a universal moral nature, and many have been around for centuries in different societies.

Contrary to popular opinion, Islamic criminal law is not an expansive list of rules with stringent punishments for those who break them. In fact, only a few actions are viewed as criminal in the Quran. These include treason, murder, highway robbery, theft, slander and adultery and sexual offences. Such acts are criminalized in order to protect the individual and uphold the authority of the state with justice, compassion and reason.

In all cases, witness evidence to the act itself must be proved without any doubt. Circumstantial evidence in favour of the accused must also be taken into account. So, for example, the punishment for an accidental killing would be less severe than that for murder.

The criminal laws listed in the Quran have been enshrined there to prevent states from criminalizing or decriminalizing certain acts at whim, depending on their particular moral standpoint. Muslims believe that God alone is fit to decide what people can and cannot be allowed to do against others; to permit men and women to make such decisions is to invite subjectivity.

Islam's criminalizing of adultery provides a good example of Islamic law in practice. While Western

Above Iraqi former president Saddam Hussein, seen here on the first day of his trial, was executed in 2006 under Iraqi law for war crimes against humanity.

societies no longer view adultery as a crime but simply as a misconduct, Islamic law argues that the resulting breakdown of family and society justifies its criminalization. Proving adultery requires four eyewitnesses, however, and as this is so difficult, the law is rarely enforced. Rather, it is intended to act as a deterrent, to retain public morality in society. The fact that such cases rarely come to court can be seen as allowing scope for personal repentance and change.

PENAL POLICY

The few crimes listed in the Quran also carry divinely specified (*hudud*) punishments. The decision to take a criminal's life or liberty is a very grave undertaking, and Muslims believe it is one that cannot be left up to humankind: thus, God has prescribed appropriate punishments. Any Muslim can access this knowledge – it is not the sole domain of lawyers, rulers and law

Left Iranian dissident Hashem Aghajari, left, defends himself during his trial for apostasy. His original death sentence was eventually reduced to imprisonment. A fair trial is fundamental in Islamic law.

books. However, the laws must be administered by recognized Shariah courts with fully trained Islamic judges, because the responsibility of enforcing divine law is great.

Islamic penal policy, which includes the death sentence for murder and amputation of a limb for theft, has been criticized by many people for being too harsh. However, punishments are rooted in *adl*: justice and compassion must prevail at all times. According to a hadith, Allah has made his mercy predominate over his judgment, or wrath. Therefore, judges, although they must be firm, are also required to be clement. The law allows for flexibility in penal policy and judges have licence to pronounce a range of punishments for a given crime.

It is also important that the victim (or the victim's family) feels that justice has been done. While there are prescribed punishments for particular crimes, the victim (or family) can choose to be merciful.

Above A young woman receives a public caning in Aceh Province, Indonesia, after being found having illegal sex with her boyfriend at her house.

For example, in a murder case, the victim's family may choose to dispense with a death sentence, opt for compensation instead, or as the Quran advises, they may forgive (5:45). In practice, a judge may rule that some form of punishment is needed for a serious crime.

In theft cases, amputation of limbs is not mandatory. If the theft was due to poverty, for example, then blame lies with the failure of the state's welfare system rather than with the accused. Judges may also choose to imprison an offender, or try to rehabilitate him. Fear of amputation can be a deterrent to

Right A Muslim prisoner reads the Quran on his bunk. Imprisonment is meant to reform, and spiritual support is provided to facilitate reflection.

crime: in some Muslim countries where amputation for theft is the law, many a shopkeeper will leave his shop unattended to go and pray in the mosque without fear of theft. In this respect, the laws fulfil a fundamental purpose of providing a safe society with a low crime rate.

SHARIAH RULE

IN RECENT TIMES, THE APPLICATION OF SHARIAH AND ISLAMIC LAW HAS RAISED CONTROVERSIES. IN THEORY, THE RULES TO BE FOLLOWED BY THE COURTS AND JUDGES ARE VERY CLEAR, BUT PRACTICE VARIES.

Islam is a way of life that is rooted in hope and mercy. Islamic laws reflect this: they are not intended as literal pronouncements, but should convey a spirit of hope and stability in their application. To this end, trained and impartial legal judges are given licence in interpretation and enforcement of Shariah.

The Quran is emphatic that witnesses must stand up for justice, even if they have to give testimony against relatives, and that judges (*qadis*) must be utterly impartial, regardless of whether the accused is rich or poor (4:135). God is seen as the law-maker, while the Muslim community, acting through the judges, is the law enforcer.

Judges are expected to be just, impartial and upright in their personal practice of Islam and to have a deep understanding of the laws. They should not pass judgements in anger and, according to a hadith, should refrain from pronouncing *hudud* (divinely ordained) punishments (for crimes such as theft and adultery) as far as possible, especially where there is the slightest doubt in evidence.

THE FIRST JUDGES

The Prophet enforced the law by judging in disputes brought before him, as instructed in the Quran (4:105). He also set a precedent for appointing judges, by installing Ali (his cousin) as a judge in Madinah and Muadh ibn Jabal in Yemen.

After the Prophet's death, the first four caliphs arbitrated in cases brought before them, but as the Muslim empire began to expand, they also appointed judges in various areas: the second caliph, Umar, is known to have appointed Abu

Above *Brass scales represent the scales of justice. Muslims believe that on the Day of Judgement, their actions will be weighed in scales before God.*

Darda in Madinah and Shurayh in Basra and placed a female judge in charge of the markets. He also advised his judges to take evidence on oath and retract a judgement if a *qadi* later felt it was wrong. He encouraged the use of the judge's own reason (*ijtihad*) where necessary, and, above all, he advised patience.

DIFFERENT COURTS

Today, Shariah courts are found in many Muslim countries: in some, for example Pakistan, they run in conjunction with a semi-secular legal system. In others, such as Saudi Arabia, they are the only form of judiciary. In non-Muslim countries, such as the UK, Shariah courts deal largely with personal and domestic matters. Often, Shariah courts uphold the law, but on occasions they fall foul of the Islamic ideal.

In Pakistan, the legal system is built on a combination of Islamic laws and the legacy of the Anglo–Muhammadan laws of the British empire. However, Shariah law is invoked in religious matters,

Left *A* qadi, *Islamic judge, Khartoum, Sudan, late 19th century.* Qadis *are expected to be just, impartial and upright, with a deep understanding of the laws.*

such as blasphemy. Several years ago, an Islamic judgement ruled that two Christians could not be charged with defaming and blaspheming against the Prophet, on the grounds that Islamic law cannot be applied to non-Muslims. The judge upheld a basic Islamic legal principle, much to the dismay of the populace.

In Saudi Arabia, the application of Shariah responds to the times. A traditional ruling that the meat from the sacrificial animals during *Hajj*, must be distributed among family and the poor of Makkah has been sensitively updated, as there is no longer poverty in Makkah: various Saudi scholars have ruled that the meat may be processed, canned and distributed outside Makkah, in countries where there is a dire need for food.

In Britain, the Shariah court in London hears cases of domestic disputes. Although it cannot replace the English court system and

law, the court helps parties to reach legal settlements regarding matrimonial disputes, gives advice relating to reconciliation and issues *talaq* (Islamic divorce), where necessary.

Above A Pakistani legislator in Peshawar in 2006 protests the proposed establishment of an Islamic accountability bureau to suppress vices. Here she is returning a copy of the Accountability Bill to the assembly speaker.

Above Indonesian protestors at a rally in Makassar, South Sulawesi, in 2004 call for implementation of Shariah law.

IS SHARIAH LAW RELEVANT TODAY?

The purpose of the law is to protect the rights of individuals, but, unfortunately, not all Muslim states apply Islamic law fairly and consistently. Some scholars argue that where there is no real Islamic state, then the *hudud* rulings must be suspended, for they should never be applied with force and without justice.

Furthermore, where Muslims live as a minority in a non-Muslim land, they cannot enforce Shariah in public matters and are obliged to follow the law of that land, provided that they are not forced to contravene Islam.

WOMEN'S RIGHTS UNDER SHARIAH

IN ISLAMIC SOCIETY, THE POSITION OF WOMEN IS OFTEN HOTLY DEBATED, BUT, IN FACT, AS MOTHERS AND WIVES, WOMEN APPEAR TO BE GIVEN MANY MORE RIGHTS THAN MEN UNDER SHARIAH LAW.

A close examination of the Quran reveals many divinely enshrined rights for women. Although the Quran addresses both men and women as believers, encouraging them to lead a godly life to attain Allah's reward (33:35), there are also verses that specifically relate to women: for example, regarding their rights of inheritance (4:7-12). Women also have political rights to vote and rights to education, as prescribed by hadiths. These are modern rights, given the political struggles of women in Europe during the last century.

MARRIAGE

As the family is central to Islamic life, many laws relating to women pertain to marriage. In Islam, marriage is considered a civil contract between two sane adults with free choice. Certain blood relations prohibit a marriage, and a Muslim woman may only marry a man who is also a Muslim. She receives a dowry, and her husband has full financial responsibility; he is considered the maintainer of the family (4:34). But any income that a Muslim woman has is entirely her own; that is, she is not obliged to contribute financially to the family.

Interestingly, the only legal requirement of a Muslim wife is to fulfil her conjugal role: she is not compelled by divine law to cook, clean or, indeed, rear her children. If she chooses to do so out of a sense of love, compassion or ethical duty, then she will find her reward with God. She is also not required to change her name on marriage: her independent identity is God-given and ought to be preserved.

The marital relationship is described in the Quran in sublime metaphors. One passage states: 'And among His signs is that He created for you mates…so that you may dwell in tranquillity with them, and He has put love and mercy between your hearts' (30:21). These attributes

Above In pledging his daughter Fatimah in marriage to his cousin Ali, Muhammad can be seen to be encouraging marriage as a way of life.

of love and mercy are suggestive of privacy and sacredness. Just as one covers the body with clothes for privacy and beautification, so, too, according to the Quran, '(Your wives) are a garment to you and you are a garment to them' (2:187).

In spiritual matters, husband and wife are equal before God (33:35). In fact, the most noble is believed to be whoever is more God-conscious (49:13). As another verse from the Quran says, 'The best garment is the garment of God-consciousness' (7:26).

Islam recognizes that human relationships can fail. It therefore permits divorce, but reconciliation must first be sought (4:35).

ONE WIFE OR MANY?

Patriarchy was the norm in the Middle East in the 7th century, but it was not created by Islam; rather it was endorsed as the existing system.

Left A qadi examines the case of a young couple wishing to divorce. Divorce forms the bulk of the work of the Shariah courts in Iran.

Right An Iranian female athlete, participating in a cycling competition, is shown having fun and enjoying sports while still observing Shariah dress codes.

Measures were put in place to curtail certain patriarchal practices that had gone unchecked, such as polygyny. The verse in the Quran allowing a man to have four wives put a restriction on the unlimited polygyny of the time: 'and if you fear that you will not deal fairly by the orphans, marry of the women who seem good to you, two, or three or four: and if you fear that you cannot do justice then (only) one' (4:3). As a subsequent verse proposes that a man could *not* treat all four wives equally; however, only one is usually allowed: 'you will not be able to deal equally between your wives, however much you wish' (4:129).

MOTHERHOOD

Although only one facet of most women's lives, motherhood is elevated beyond all relationships: well-known hadiths state that paradise lies under a mother's feet and that a mother has three times more right than a father to be served. The Quran is emphatic that pregnancy and weaning are difficult, and, therefore, people should show gratitude to their parents (31:14).

VEILING

The Quran requires men and women to observe dress codes. For women, this is interpreted in different ways in different countries and sects. Many women cover their hair and entire body, apart from face and hands. The laws state that covering is so women are known as believers and are protected from men's lusts.

Right Young girls at a Quran class in a women's madrasa in Pakistan. Most madrasas *provide free religious education for girls from poor families.*

LAWS ON PURITY

Purity laws and cleanliness are central to Muslim life. Quranic references to menstruation are a natural acceptance of, and engagement with, bodily functions: 'They will ask you concerning the monthly course: say it is a hurt, so go apart from women during the monthly period and do not approach them until they are purified' (2:222). Some commentators have translated 'hurt' as a 'pollution' and interpret the exclusion of women from religious rites – prayer and fasting – during menstruation as unfair, but many women believe that such verses show a respectful acknowledgement of the female body and are grateful for the dispensation from prayer and sexual intercourse that allows a woman to 'take it easy'.

CHAPTER 7

UNITY AND DIVISION

There is a surprising unity among the global Muslim community, where fraternity extends beyond nations and cultures. However, although core Islamic beliefs remain the same everywhere, Muslims in various parts of the world interpret and practise their faith in different ways.

Muslims are no longer under the rule of a caliphate but are members of nation states, so they live under different political authorities. How they organize themselves politically remains a contentious issue. Although the majority of Muslims are Sunni, ten per cent of the global community are Shiah, and their concept of political authority differs from that of the Sunnis, as do their schools of law.

Religious practice also varies immensely: some Muslims stress the importance of adhering to laws and ritual, while others, such as the Sufis, lay greater emphasis on the esoteric nature of their faith. Together, these different expressions of Islam make up the body of the Muslim *ummah*.

Opposite An Afghani man prays at the Blue Mosque of Ali ibn Abu Talib at Mazar-e Sharif. The global Muslim community shares fundamental beliefs, but is very diverse in culture and practice.

Above Pilgrims from all over the world pray as they arrive at the Mount of Mercy at the centre of the plain of Arafah, near Makkah. Here on the Hajj, Muslim unity outweighs diversity.

THE *UMMAH*: ISLAMIC UNIVERSALISM

THE MUSLIM *UMMAH* IS A COMMUNITY BOND OF FAITH THAT LINKS MUSLIMS THROUGHOUT THE WORLD TOGETHER, DESPITE THEIR DIFFERENCES IN GEOGRAPHY, CULTURE AND LANGUAGE.

Muslims are estimated to make up approximately 20 per cent of the world's population, and the religion is represented globally. Although Islam sprang up in what is now called Saudi Arabia, the current population of the country, estimated to be 100 per cent Muslim, is only 28 million, whereas there are more than 120 million Muslims in Bangladesh, 160 million in Pakistan and 200 million in Indonesia. As minorities, Muslims number 1.6 million in Britain, and approximately 150 million in India.

Widespread geographically, the global Muslim community is also very diverse in terms of culture and language. The one uniting factor is its belief system: all Muslims have a strong sense of belonging to a single brotherhood of believers.

MUSLIM UNITY

Umm in Arabic means 'mother', and *ummah*, derived from it, means the 'mother source'. In Islam, *ummah* refers to the primary group to which a Muslim belongs ideologically. The word appears more than 60 times in the Quran, where all prophets are said to have had their own *ummah* (10:47) and Muslims are described as *ummatun wasata*, or moderate community (2:143).

Ummah does not replace other identities of tribe, culture or language, but it certainly takes priority over them. Some scholars have argued that this makes the concept of nations virtually redundant, for while people are divided and defined by state identity, as Muslims, they surpass geographical boundary limitations

Above Although this young girl learning in Brunei is reading the Quran in Arabic, her daily language is Malay.

by a sense of belonging to a wider ideological community, regardless of language and culture.

The originator of the *ummah*, or universal Muslim community, was the Prophet Muhammad himself: after he migrated to Madinah, a constitution was signed by the indigenous Madinans and the new migrants, stating that Muhammad and his followers constituted one single *ummah*. Belonging to the *ummah*, therefore, means belonging to the *ummah* of the Prophet.

Beyond time and space, then, all Muslims – past, present, and future – are seen as belonging to one community. Islam is a universal religion and its fellowship is open to all people, regardless of their race, ethnicity, culture or economic status. Each member is equal: the only distinction in God's eyes is made on the basis of piety. Indeed, the Prophet Muhammad's last sermon at *Hajj* is a testimony to what *ummah* means in practice as a universal brotherhood.

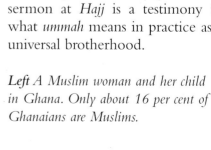

Left A Muslim woman and her child in Ghana. Only about 16 per cent of Ghanaians are Muslims.

Above A Russian man prepares to kill a sheep for a feast to mark Eid ul-adha. *There are 20 million Muslims in Russia.*

CULTURAL DIVERSITY

As Muslims spread into new places, indigenous peoples often accepted Islam as a belief system. However, the new converts did not reject their traditional languages and cultures but, rather, Islamized them. Therefore, Muslims in different parts of the world have a great diversity in dress, language and ethnicity. These differences, which often give varied expressions to Islamic practice and interpretation, are celebrated in the Quran (49:13).

Muslims claim that Islam is a missionizing religion, but only to the extent that Muslims follow a mission of *daawah* – 'inviting' people to the peace of Islam. This invitation carries no obligation: those invited have a fundamental right to accept or refuse the offer, as 'there is no compulsion in religion' (2:256). For this reason, Islam insists that people of other faiths living under Islamic rule must be given legal rights and protected as part of the Muslim polity.

Right The 'burqini' worn by this Australian woman was specially designed for female Muslim lifesavers.

THE UNIVERSAL BROTHERHOOD OF ISLAM

'O mankind! We created you from a single pair of a male and a female, and made you into nations and tribes, so that you may know each other. Verily the most honoured of you in the sight of Allah is the most righteous. And Allah has full knowledge of things and is most discerning.'

(The Quran, 49:13)

'All mankind is from Adam and Eve: an Arab has no superiority over a non-Arab nor a non-Arab over an Arab; also a white person has no superiority over a black person nor does a black person have any superiority over a white person, except by piety and good action. Learn that every Muslim is a brother to each other and that Muslims constitute one brotherhood...Do not, therefore, do injustice to yourselves.'

(The Prophet's Last Sermon)

RELIGIOUS AND POLITICAL AUTHORITY

ISLAMIC AUTHORITY IS FORMULATED ON THE VALUES AND CONCEPTS CONTAINED IN THE QURAN, WHICH TEACHES THAT MAN IS GOD'S CALIPH, OR VICEGERENT, ON EARTH.

Islam teaches that the laws prescribed for human conduct and social interaction have been set by God through the Shariah. As God's caliphs, Muslims have a duty to establish divine law and moral order as exampled in the first Muslim community at Madinah.

GOD'S VICEGERENTS

In Islam, men and women are seen as God's earthly representatives and are therefore instructed to rule in accordance with his laws (24:55). A Muslim ruler (caliph) is answerable both to God and to the Muslim community: he must ensure, therefore, that he rules by Shariah and with the community's consent (ijma). If he does not, then he can be removed from office and even punished for any misdemeanours. The preconditions of the caliph's rule are that he must be a Muslim, possess qualities of justice, virtue and piety and have knowledge of

the Shariah and principles of *fiqh* (jurisprudence). The political and religious caliph is usually a man.

To ensure that the caliph fulfils his divine obligations, the institution of *shura* (consultation) exists as a means of mutually agreeing the correct application of Shariah and assuring the interests of the whole community (42:38). Through the process of *shura*, the head of state is chosen and executive state decisions are agreed. Although the Shariah does not dictate the exact nature of state institutions, the general principles (*maqasid*) encourage the common good (*istislah*) of the community through good council and fair representation.

THE ISLAMIC STATE

While the Prophet Muhammad's city of Madinah is seen as the paradigm for all Muslim societies and modern ideas regarding the 'Islamic State', the Quran and

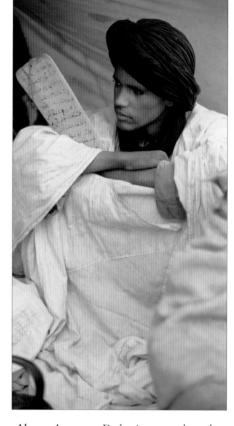

Above A young Bedouin nomad reads the Quran, written in ink on a wooden slab. Muslims believe that authority lies in God's divine words.

hadith do not, in fact, offer much detail regarding a specific design of government or rule.

After Muhammad's death, the first four caliphs were elected by due process; therefore, a democratic model is endorsed. (Although the caliph was elected for life, he could be removed for misconduct.) There is also an absence of detail relating to definitions of Islamic nation states or sovereign countries. Nevertheless, the increase in religious identity and the mobilization of Islamic political parties mean that debates and theories regarding the precise nature and political shape of the 'Islamic State' are ongoing.

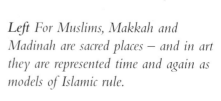

Left For Muslims, Makkah and Madinah are sacred places – and in art they are represented time and again as models of Islamic rule.

Some consensus has been reached on the general principles upon which an Islamic state should be founded; in particular, the religious or devotional aspects of community life and practical social matters (*din wa dunya*), which are concerned with the common good or the collective enforcement of public morals (*istislah*). This general accord has led to greater acceptance of the need for unity of both religious and political authority as a practical application of God's laws administered by humankind.

MODERN ISLAMIC STATES

A number of Muslim countries – Iran, Morocco, Pakistan, Saudi Arabia and Sudan – have declared themselves Islamic states, based on the principles of both Shariah and sunnah. Not surprisingly, these countries differ from each other, but there are some similarities in their prohibition of *riba* (usury) and application of the *hudud* (punishment laws) of the Shariah.

Constitutionally, too, these countries differ greatly – from those with hereditary monarchical systems of rule to those that have a democratically elected president with a limited term of office.

POLITICAL DIVERSITY

These variations indicate that while all Islamic states lean toward the adoption and implementation

Above Muslims in Tehran, Iran, hold aloft posters of Ayatollah Khomeini, who believed political authority was the domain of religious scholars.

of the Shariah in areas relating to moral and social issues, their governmental structures, forms of leadership, specific political features and social and economic orientations are quite disparate.

MODERN ISLAMIC POLITICAL THOUGHT

Some Muslim thinkers argue that there is indeed a distinct model of the Islamic state and Muslim government referred to in the Quran, which, they claim, condemns those who do not judge by what God has revealed (5:44).

Some modern political Islamists see the caliph and *shura* style of government as a 'theodemocracy' – a theory propagated by Abul Ala Maududi (1903–79). Others, notably Sayyid Qutb (1906–66), view Muslim government as a 'social contract'.

Few, however, with the exception of Ayatollah Khomeini (1902–89), have envisaged caliph and *shura* as being the exclusive domains of the *ulama* (religious scholars). Thus, the 'Islamic State' was presented in Iran as the establishment of God's sovereignty, as governed, and even legislated, by man, with religious law guiding society along the 'straight path' (1:5–7).

THE *MADHHABS*: SCHOOLS OF LAW

POLITICAL AND RELIGIOUS AUTHORITY WAS AT FIRST UNITED, BUT AS DYNASTIC RULE WAS ESTABLISHED, SCHOLARS AND JURISTS – PEOPLE WHO INTERPRETED ISLAMIC LAW – BECAME MORE IMPORTANT.

As Islam spread rapidly into new territories, Muslims came into contact with different cultures and contexts. In the absence of specific answers from the Quran and sunnah to unprecedented problems, new legal rulings became necessary. This meant that well-known scholars passing such judgements eventually became the main authoritative voice of Islamic law in different areas of the Muslim world, thus giving rise to different madhhabs, or schools of law.

EXPLAINING ISLAM
The jurists' task was to explain Islam to ordinary Muslims, so that they could best apply the rules of the Quran and sunnah to their own lives. According to traditions, the Prophet had already started training some of his companions during his lifetime to use reasoned judgement (*ijtihad*) in reaching just conclusions in new circumstances.

The first four caliphs set a precedent for problem-solving by first referring to the Quran: in the absence of an answer there, they would examine the Prophet's sunnah. If that, too, failed to provide an explicit solution, they would try to come to a unanimous agreement (*ijma*). Where they were unable to reach such a consensus, they would form their own opinion through *ijtihad*, often by applying analogical

Above A 16th-century illustration shows a Mongol ruler holding court, listening to petitioners, while outside Islamic law is upheld, with thieves being punished.

reasoning (*qiyas*). Later jurists followed this same pattern when applying and explaining the law in new circumstances.

Thus, while the politicians took care of governance, jurists took care of souls through religious laws. Very often, they rejected the patronage of the ruling Umayyad and Abbasid caliphs, which in many cases resulted in bouts of imprisonment, but this independence guaranteed their impartiality.

THE MAIN LAW SCHOOLS
There were many schools of law in the early centuries of Islam, as many able scholars gave *fatwas*: al-Awzai, al-Layth, al-Thawri, to name but a few. The great number of early schools shows that scholars were responding to the needs of their community by formulating laws

Left The ornate calligraphy of this 17th-century Shiah legal text is a testament to the importance of Islamic law.

Right In the mosque of Sultan Hassan in Cairo, the complex courtyard allowed for the study of Islamic law from all four schools: each occupied a separate recess.

through *ijtihad*. Over time, some of these schools disappeared, while others consolidated.

There are four main Sunni law schools, which are followed in and around those parts of the world where they developed. All are named after their founding scholars, who followed the same primary sources but gave different weighting to secondary sources. Each scholar held the others in mutual respect and said that his own opinion should be disregarded if proved wrong by a hadith. There was thus no rigidity of outlook in these schools; their aim was to respond to the needs of their people and places. In their support of this diversity, scholars referred to a prophetic hadith, which claimed that difference among the scholars was a mercy for the *ummah*.

IMAM MALIK (717–801) believed that the consensus of the scholars of Madinah, where he was born, was a most important source of law. However, he refused to have his seminal work, *al-Muwatta*, imposed as unifying state law by the Abbasids on Muslims in other regions, whom he believed were entitled to come to their own reasoned conclusions. Today, the Maliki School is mostly followed in North and West Africa and the Gulf States.

IMAM ABU HANIFAH (730–67) was born in Kufa, Iraq. He valued consensus and local customs (*urf*), which gave rise to a multicultural and diverse practice of Islam. The Hanifi School operates today in and around Iraq, the Indian sub-continent and Turkey.

Right The Al-Azhar University in Cairo, Egypt, is perhaps the most prestigious school of Islamic law.

IMAM ASH-SHAFII (769–820), who was originally from near Gaza in Palestine, travelled to Madinah to study with Imam Malik. In Iraq, he studied Hanifi law before moving to Egypt, where he remained until his death. His juristic opinions combined the Maliki and Hanifi rulings while he was in Iraq, but in Egypt, faced with new hadiths and legal reasonings, he developed a new school of thought. He is known mostly for his work, *al-Risalah*, on the fundamentals of *fiqh*. Today, the Shafii School is followed in Egypt, Yemen and South-east Asia.

IMAM IBN HANBAL (778–855) was born in Baghdad, Iraq, and studied Hanifi law. He is well known for his *Musnad*, a collection of hadiths. Hanbal taught that only the consensus of the *sahaba* (the companions of the Prophet) was authentic. The Hanbali School is followed today in Palestine and Saudi Arabia.

PROMISED REFORMERS: THE MAHDI AND JESUS

MAJORITY SUNNI DOCTRINE CLAIMS THAT JESUS WILL RESTORE ORDER ON EARTH, BUT SOME SUNNIS AND ALL SHIAHS NAME THE PROPHET'S DESCENDANT, KNOWN AS AL-MAHDI, AS THE REFORMER.

Belief in the hereafter is a fundamental article of Muslim faith, but, according to hadiths, the afterlife will be preceded by the Day of Judgement, a final reckoning of all souls, who will collectively stand before God. Islam teaches that this last day will follow a series of apocalyptic events that

will centre around two main figures in hadith literature: the Mahdi and Jesus.

THE END OF TIME
Hadith collections give extremely detailed predictions of events on earth before the end of time. Some scholars believe that these hadiths should be understood literally, whereas others assert that they are metaphorical in nature. They envision, for example, the sun rising from the West, devastating earthquakes occurring with

Below The Al-Askari Mosque in Samarra, Iraq, is dedicated to the 12th imam, whom Shiahs believe to be the promised reformer. The mosque also houses the tombs of the 10th and 11th imams.

Above Alexander the Great builds a wall between the fighting Gog and Magog. Muslims believe that these warring tribes are eschatological, not just historical, and that Jesus will eventually destroy them.

Above *One of the signs of the end of time, according to Islamic eschatology, is a change in the weather systems and an increase in natural disasters – such as the earthquake here.*

increasing frequency, time passing more quickly than usual and afflictions appearing from the East.

Hadiths also claim that there will be widespread moral decadence, which will manifest itself in unjust rulers oppressing people's rights, miserliness, sexual immorality and killing. At this point, they foretell, the Mahdi, and later Jesus, will enter the apocalyptic scene, and through them, Islam and peace will be re-established on earth.

It is said that some time after the Mahdi, the Antichrist, Dajjal, will appear as a young man from between Syria and Iraq. He will be blind in his right eye and will terrorize people, and he will also have miraculous control over fire and water. Setting up camp outside Madinah, he will kill a man, then will bring him back to life. Thus ensuring his might and power, he will call people to a false religion. However, the prophecies claim, Jesus will fight the Dajjal and will vanquish his rule of tyranny.

THE REFORMER MAHDI

The Mahdi, meaning 'the guided one', is believed to be Muhammad Ahmad bin Abdullah, a descendant of the Prophet. According to Shiah belief, he is the 12th imam, currently in occultation, who will come to earth before the end of time to lead a battle of good forces against evil.

This idea is also found to varying degrees in Sunni Islam, for though not clearly formulated in Sunni theology, it has a significant hold on popular beliefs. Some scholars claim that ascetics and Sufis introduced the messianic figure to Sunni thought, while others still claim that the Mahdi and Jesus figures are eschatological, not just historical.

The Prophet Muhammad is reported to have said that when oppression covers the earth, a member of his tribe, bearing his name, will appear and will be guided to fight injustice. However, his rule will be short, and will be followed by the return of Christ.

JESUS RETURNS

Many hadiths claim that as, according to Islam, Jesus has not yet died, he has yet to return to earth. It is said that this will happen at the end of time, and that he will destroy all false claims to religion. Once the Dajjal appears, Jesus will reportedly descend in Damascus. He will search for and kill the Dajjal, after which he will slay the evil forces of Gog and Magog. After these great trials, hadiths claim, peace will reign, and Jesus will marry, have children, die a natural death and be buried in Madinah beside the Prophet. It is after the second coming of Jesus that life on earth as we know it will end, and God's final judgement will take place.

ORTHODOXY VERSUS HETERODOXY

Various figures have appeared throughout Islamic history and cultures claiming to be promised reformers. However, there also exist some differences in religious belief among Muslims, particularly between Shiahs and Sunnis. Within these two main groups, there are further distinctions in doctrine.

Such 'diversity', however, has its limits: many splinter factions claim to be adherents of Islam, yet the majority of the Muslim community considers them to be outside orthodox Islam. The Ahmadiyyas from India and the Druze, who exist mainly in Lebanon, are two such heterodox groups. The former do not consider that revelation and prophethood are final, while the Druze believe that individuals of unusual spiritual attainment can manifest divine attributes.

Above *The Druze, an offshoot of the Ismaili Shiah branch of Islam, are found mostly in Lebanon, Syria and Israel. They are considered to be heretical due to their incorporation of gnostic and neo-platonic philosophies into their faith.*

SHIAHS: THE PARTY OF ALI

THE MUSLIM COMMUNITY IS SPLIT INTO TWO MAIN THEOLOGICAL CAMPS: THE LARGEST, REPRESENTING 90 PER CENT OF THE WORLD'S MUSLIMS, IS SUNNI; THE REMAINDER ARE SHIAH.

Muhammad's death around 632 not only deprived the nascent Muslim community of its temporal and spiritual leader, but it also threw his followers into a quandary about who the next leader ought to be. The Quranic revelation dictated democracy, which meant that Muslims were free to debate, differ about and elect a leader (4:59, 42:38). However, nobody could have predicted that this one event – the election of a successor to Muhammad – would lead to such a serious divide in the Muslim community.

ELECTING A SUCCESSOR

Hadith accounts relate that when Muhammad passed away, his family and companions gathered outside his house. Ali ibn Abu Talib, his son-in-law and cousin, withdrew to his own house with a few others, but the majority of people began to elect a leader. Umar and Abu Bakr learned of this and joined them.

Abu Bakr persuaded the people that it would be best for a member of the Quraysh tribe to lead the community because of their central position among the Arabs. Umar immediately elected Abu Bakr, on the grounds that he had been appointed by Muhammad to lead prayers at the end of his life, and because he had been mentioned in the Quran (9:40). The whole congregation pledged allegiance to Abu Bakr as their leader – all, that is, except Ali.

THE DISSENSION OF ALI

Ali's position, and that of the *Ahl al-Bayt*, members of the Prophet's family, is unique in Islam because hadiths record Muhammad as having extolled their importance. Indeed, Muslims send peace and blessings on a daily basis on the Prophet and his descendants.

For some members of the early community, this meant that Ali was the natural successor to the Prophet. Not only was he a member of Muhammad's family, but he had also become a Muslim at the age of ten, had been trusted by Muhammad with special missions and was renowned for his bravery and justice. As a direct relative, he was entrusted with the responsibility of preparing Muhammad's body for burial, and lowering it into the grave. Indeed, no one could doubt the importance of Ali.

Above A Turkish painting depicts Muhammad and his cousin Ali, who is for Shiahs the true successor to the Prophet.

Above Arabic calligraphy with the names of Muhammad and his family members. Reverence for the Ahl al-Bayt, house of the Prophet, is central to Shiah belief.

However, most members of the *ummah* believed that succession should not be based on blood ties, and that an elected elder would be a better leader. Not until months later, after his wife Fatimah's death, did Ali express his dissatisfaction with the electoral process to Abu Bakr. His objection was that as everybody had rallied around Abu Bakr, without taking absentees into account, no one was given the right to dissent and choose a different leader. Nevertheless, he now pledged allegiance to the new caliph.

SUPPORT FOR ALI

The matter did not come to an end, however, for there was still a minority of people who were

rallying support for Ali, believing that succession ought to remain with the Prophet's descendants. Indeed, they claimed that at the last pilgrimage, at Ghadir Khumm, Muhammad himself had designated Ali as his successor.

Eventually, the Shiah, 'party' of Ali, was appeased when he became the fourth caliph. But his murder five years later again plunged the community into a dilemma about succession. This time, however, neither those who proposed an elected leader nor those who wanted a direct descendant of the Prophet succeeded: instead, power was vested in a politically and militarily strong might, Muawiyah, the governor of Syria, who then established a dynastic line.

SUNNIS VERUS SHIAHS
While the early differences between the two factions may seem to have been largely political, they were fraught with religious tensions, too, for Islam did not (and does not) make a division between the social, political and religious. The choice

Right A Pakistani Shiah Muslim procession during Ramadhan marks the anniversary of Imam Ali's martyrdom.

of a suitable leader was thus a deeply religious matter. This conflict continued down the centuries.

The emerging Sunni Muslims were those who believed they were following the Prophet's sunnah (hence their name). Their faith was patronized by the rulers, but scholars did not necessarily either trust or support these rulers. The dissenting Shiahs became a minority who stood up against the

Above Shiahs make up well over half the population of Iraq. Here, Shaykh Muhammad al-Gharawi addresses a Shiah conference in Baghdad.

state-patronized religion and continued their loyalty to the Prophet's family. For them, Ali would remain the exemplary ruler: a blood relative loved by the Prophet, who was brave, humble, spiritual and literarily accomplished.

THE SHIAH IMAMS

SHIAH ISLAM DEVELOPED SOPHISTICATED THEOLOGY REGARDING THE SUCCESSION AND LEADERSHIP OF THE COMMUNITY VIA DIVINELY APPOINTED 'IMAMS', WHO WERE DESCENDANTS OF THE PROPHET.

After Muhammad's death, those who supported Ali believed that succession should be via the Prophet's male descendants: as he had no surviving sons, this would be through his daughter Fatimah's marriage to Ali. The Shiah imams, of whom there are 12 in total, are all descendants from Fatimah and Ali's marriage. Over time, the deeply rooted differences between Sunni and Shiah Islam, originally political, became theological.

HISTORICAL DEVELOPMENT

Shiah Islam is a highly organized branch of the faith, which, unlike Sunni Islam, has a clergy. As the first division in Islam occurred over the issue of leadership of the *ummah*, a central tenet of Shiah thought is that authority must be lawfully and divinely vested in leaders.

For Shiahs, the term 'imam' refers to those of Muhammad's descendants who are believed to have been divinely designated by God as the Prophet's heirs. Each imam appointed his successor before his death and Shiahs believe that he was inspired by God in this choice.

Early divisions increased with the establishment of the Umayyad dynasty, which was seen as corrupt and tyrannical, not upholding the values of Islam. Dissension was therefore viewed as a religious act. After Ali's death, his followers turned their attention to his son Hassan, and recognized him as imam. Hassan was very quietist, whereas his brother Hussain, the third imam, became a pivotal public figure in the development of Shiah Islam with his martyrdom at Karbala in 680. After Karbala, the Sunni–Shiah divide took on further theological shape.

THEOLOGY OF THE SHIAH

Shiah theology developed over time to claim that as God is merciful and just – *rahman* and *adl* – he would not leave his creation without guidance. As prophethood was now closed, Shiahs asserted that God would guide humankind through divinely appointed imams. Imams are therefore viewed by Shiah Muslims as *ayat-Allah*, signs of God's mercy, and as *hujjat-Allah*, proof of God.

Shiahs also believe that these imams were created from the same light as Muhammad and Fatimah, thereby making them *masum*, sinless and hence infallible. The role of

Left A scene from the Battle of Karbala showing Hussain's brother being attacked. The Prophet and Ali are depicted looking on from heaven.

Above Ali Zayn al-Abidin, the 4th imam and the son of the martyred Hussain, preaches in a mosque in defence of his father.

these imams was simply to elucidate the inner meanings of the Quran. According to the Shiahs, the ruling imam would be imbued by God with full knowledge, which he would pass on to his chosen successor just before his death.

Eleven imams lived earthly lives. However, since the death of the 11th, the 12th imam is believed by Shiahs to have gone into hiding, or occultation (*ghaybah*), as a child, to reappear at an apocalyptic time near the ending of the world. In the meantime, Shiah governments have been legitimized by claiming to be 'caretaker' governments in the 12th imam's absence; such is the case in Iran, for example.

Shiahs have their own hadith collections of the teachings of the imams, which explain the Quran's esoteric meanings, and the Prophet's life example. *Nahjul Balaghah* is an important collection of Ali's sermons, in which he elucidates the faith in the light of the Quran and prophetic teachings.

THE TWELVE IMAMS

1 Ali (d.660)
2 Hassan (d.670)
3 Hussain (d.680)
4 Ali Zayn al-Abidin
  (d.712)
5 Muhammad al-Baqir
  (d.743)
6 Jafar al-Sadiq (d.765)
7 Musa al-Kazim (d.799)
8 Ali al-Rida (d.818)
9 Muhammad Jawad al-Taqi
  (d.835)
10 Ali Hadi al-Naqi (d.868)
11 Hassan al-Askari (d.874)
12 Muhammad al-Mahdi
  (went into hiding 941)

Above An Iraqi Shiah woman lights a candle in Karbala as part of festivities to mark the birthday anniversary of the 12th imam, Muhammad al-Mahdi.

Different branches of Shiah Islam developed because of disputes over the persona of the imams. The Twelvers evolved largely in urban Iraq and believe in the 12 imams listed above. The Ismailis lived in rural North Africa, leading to the formation of the Fatimid dynasty in Egypt. They believe Ismail ibn Jafar was the rightful seventh imam.

Twelver Shiahs represent the largest Shiah group, with a majority in Iran and southern Iraq and a significant minority in Lebanon, Kuwait, Pakistan and India. Ismailis form the second largest group and exist mainly in India and East Africa.

Zaydis, the third largest Shiah group, are found mainly in Yemen. Zaydis believe that an imam did not have to be a direct descendant of Ali and Fatimah: it would be sufficient for him to be the son of the ruling imam, albeit from a wife whose genealogy could not be traced to Fatimah. On these grounds, they rejected Muhammad al-Baqir for his brother Zay.

Below Some 6,000 members of the Nizari Ismaili sect of Shiah Islam pray as they wait for the arrival of their leader, Aga Khan IV.

SHIAH PILGRIMAGES

IRAN AND IRAQ ARE KEY PLACES OF PILGRIMAGE FOR SHIAHS. IRAQ CONTAINS HOLY SHRINES IN KARBALA, NAJAF AND SAMARRA, WHILE IRAN HAS MASHHAD AND THE CENTRES OF SHIAH LEARNING AT QOM.

The world's principal pilgrimage site is the same for Shiah and Sunni Muslims: Makkah in Saudi Arabia, the destination for the *Hajj*, which is compulsory once in a lifetime for all able-bodied Muslims who can afford it. Like their Sunni counterparts, Shiah Muslims travel to the Great Mosque and make seven circuits of the sacred *Kaabah*.

The other main destination for Muslim pilgrims in Saudi Arabia, Madinah, has special significance for Shiahs as the site of shrines to the second and fourth imams, Hassan ibn Ali and Ali Zayn al-Abidin.

KARBALA AND NAJAF

After Makkah and Madinah, the most sacred place for Shiahs is Karbala in Iraq. Karbala is the site of the battle in which Hussain ibn Ali, grandson of the Prophet, was killed on 10 Muharram 680. Around one million Shiahs travel as pilgrims to Karbala to commemorate his death in the month of Muharram.

South-east of Karbala is the holy Shiah city of Najaf, site of the tomb of Ali ibn Abu Talib, the first Shiah imam. Pilgrims visit the Imam Ali Mosque and the Wadi as-Salam, a cemetery nearby that contains the graves of many holy men of the Shiah faith. Najaf is also a great centre of Shiah scholarship.

SAMARRA

Another centre for Shiah pilgrims in Iraq is the city of Samarra, which was the capital of the Sunni Muslim Abbasid caliphate (833–92). It contains the extraordinary Great Mosque of Samarra, built by Caliph al-Mutawakkil (reigned 847–61), but its main significance for Shiah Muslims lies in its being the place where, they believe, the 12th imam, Muhammad al-Mahdi, was miraculously hidden by Allah in a process known as occultation. Pilgrims visit a shrine marking the place at which al-Mahdi was last seen before his occultation.

***Above** Pilgrims gather at the Jamkaran Mosque near Qom, Iran, where the hidden imam, al-Mahdi, is said once to have made a miraculous appearance.*

Samarra is also the site of shrines to the 10th and 11th imams, Ali al-Hadi al-Naqi and Hassan al-Askari. All three are contained within the Al-Askari Mosque, built in 944, which also houses the tombs of Ali Hadi al-Naqi's sister, Hakimah Khatun, and the hidden imam's mother, Narjis Khatun. The mosque once had a dazzling golden dome, 68 metres (223 feet) across, and two golden minarets, each 36 metres (118 feet) tall, but both dome and minarets were destroyed in bomb attacks attributed to Sunni militants in February 2006 and June 2007.

Shiahs also visit the Iraqi capital, to make devotions at the shrines to the seventh and ninth imams, Musa al-Kazim and Muhammad Jawad al-Taqi, in Kazimayn, now a suburb of Baghdad. The shrine to the imams was built by Shah Ismail I (reigned 1502–24) of the Safavid dynasty.

***Left** Thousands of Shiah pilgrims gather at the Imam Ali shrine in Najaf, Iraq, just before dawn to celebrate the birthday of the hidden imam, al-Mahdi.*

Right The tomb of Hussain ibn Ali at
the Imam Hussain Shrine in Karbala,
Iraq, is topped with a golden dome 27
metres (89 feet) high.

MASHHAD AND QOM

In Iran, the principal pilgrimage
destination for Shiah Muslims is the
city of Mashhad. It contains the
shrine of Ali al-Rida, the eighth
Shiah imam, who is said to have
been poisoned by Abbasid caliph
al-Mamun (reigned 813–33) and is
viewed as a martyr. A domed shrine
was built over this tomb as early as
the 9th century, but this has been
rebuilt several times since. The
tomb of Abbasid caliph Harun
al-Rashid (reigned 786–809) stands
opposite the shrine to Ali al-Rida.
Mashhad became a major place of
pilgrimage under the Safavid
dynasty, and Shah Abbas I (reigned
1588–1629) walked there as a
pilgrim from Esfahan.

Qom, the principal centre for
Shiah scholarship in the world and
the place where Ayatollah Khomeini
trained, is another Iranian pilgrimage
site for Shiahs. Qom is considered a
holy city because it contains the
shine to Fatema Masume, sister of
Ali al-Rida. Pilgrims also make
their way to the Jamkaran Mosque

on the outskirts of the city.
According to tradition, the 12th,
and hidden, imam, Muhammad
al-Mahdi, miraculously appeared at
the mosque and pilgrims there
make intercessions to him at a
sacred well, from which it is said he
will one day emerge. In 2005, the
Iranian government reportedly
donated US$20 million to develop
Jamkaran Mosque into a major
Shiah pilgrimage centre.

*Left In Mashhad, the faithful draw
inspiration from an image of Ayatollah
Khomeini, Supreme Leader of Iran, and
his successor, Ayatollah Khameini.*

TASAWWUF: SUFISM

THE MATERIALISM OF THE ISLAMIC EMPIRES LED TO MANY MUSLIMS SEEKING AN ASCETIC AND DERVISH LIFE, REMEMBERING GOD THROUGH SIMPLE LIVING, AWAY FROM THE OSTENTATION OF SOCIETY.

Sufism, which can be described loosely as Islamic mysticism, is concerned with the search for deep spirituality, an inner journey that is undertaken by some Muslims to achieve closeness to God. Its main feature is *tazkiyah*, or purification of the soul. Sufis claim that the roots of their way of life lie in the example of the Prophet and his companions, and that while observation of the laws is important, inner development of the soul is paramount.

According to Sufi thought, to follow the law literally, without regard for the essence of matters and without paying due attention to nurturing the soul, would leave a Muslim leading a partial life.

Left A Prince visits an ascetic, from The Book of Love *(16th century). The nobility were believed to visit ascetics to attain spiritual guidance and blessings.*

THE MEANING OF SUFISM

The word Sufism is thought to derive from the Arabic term *tasawwuf*, which means 'to wear woollen garments', a reference to the coarse woollen clothes worn by early ascetics as a sign of their simplicity of life and their rejection of the world. (Sufism, which is taken to mean mysticism, literally means 'wearing wool'.)

Others claim, however, that the word originates from *ahl-al-suffah* (literally, 'the people of the platform'), the name given to those indigent Muslims who devoted themselves to seeking knowledge, learning and living on a raised platform in the Prophet's Mosque. Abu Hurayrah, a well-known companion of the Prophet, was one of the *ahl-al-suffah*, which gives weight to the claim that Sufism's origins date to the time of the Prophet himself.

THE ROOTS OF SUFISM

One of the early treatises explaining Sufism was the *Kashf al-Mahjub* (Unveiling of the Veiled), written in the 11th century by Ali al-Hujwiri. He quoted a 10th-century Sufi as saying that in the time of the Prophet, Sufism as a name did not exist but was part of the life of every Muslim. Thus, the first mystics were

Above A funerary stele is inscribed with the Quranic 'verse of light' (24:35). This verse is often recited by Sufis in an attempt to attain nearness to God.

the Prophet, with his exemplary contemplative and ascetic lifestyle, and his companions.

Indeed, Sufi goals are derived from the Quran and sunnah, especially the verse of light (24:35): 'Allah is the light of the heavens and the earth...'. Many hadiths relate to the remembrance of God, *dhikr*, a central Sufi practice, and exhort self-development and purification. These hadiths also show that Muhammad encouraged inner development of the soul, as did his companions, especially Abu Bakr and Ali.

ZUHD: ASCETICM

What is now known as Sufism first exhibited itself as *zuhd* (asceticism). Seeing the material development that accompanied the expansion of Islam, certain Muslims became concerned that a desire for the trappings of the world was taking precedence over the Quran's warnings against greed. They believed that the only way to fortify themselves against this was to become 'inward looking' and to exert themselves in acts of worship and ascetic piety. However, a rigorous regime of self-control did not mean denying the world entirely to live in celibate seclusion. Rather, following the example of the Prophet, such ascetics married, had families and lived within society, but as though they were not part of it, detached from its desires.

SUFISM DEVELOPS

From the 10th century onward, such expressions of individual asceticism began to find form as organized mysticism. Rules and methods were explained to followers that would help them not simply to focus on their inward lives, but rather to turn that attention toward God, with gnosis (*marifah*), knowledge of the eternal, as their main goal. According to Sufism, this could not be achieved alone; the seeker must attach himself to a Sufi teacher (*murshid*).

While the *ulama* (religious scholars) studied the exoteric Shariah, the *murshids*, or spiritual guides, were concerned with the esoteric *tariqah* (path of spirituality). This path led off the main road (Shariah) and was thus embedded in observing the law, but focused on

Left A 19th-century engraving, Dervishes of Khiva, *depicts members of a Sufi Muslim order. Their ragged dress and single possession – a cooking pot – shows their unworldly lifestyle.*

observing the spirit, not merely the letter of the law, and on following God's will. For Sufis, seeking God's pleasure is more important than anything else.

Sufis who followed the same sorts of observances and practices eventually organized themselves into orders, known as *tariqahs*. Today, well-known Sufi orders include the Naqshbandi, Chishti, and Shadhili, all of which are named after their founders. These orders now operate globally and have millions of affiliated members.

Below Shaykh Nazim al-Haqqani leads members of the Naqshbandi-Haqqani Sufi order in Lefka, Northern Cyprus. The Naqshbandi order numbers thousands worldwide.

MAULANA RUMI AND HIS *MATHNAWI*

JALAL-UD-DIN RUMI (1207–73) IS THE MOST CELEBRATED MYSTICAL POET AND TEACHER IN MUSLIM HISTORY, AND HIS MAGNUM OPUS, *MATHNAWI*, IS ONE OF THE GREAT CLASSICS OF SUFI LITERATURE.

Above *A common representation of Rumi: his size denotes his importance. In reality, however, he was known to be a slight man, much given to fasting.*

While scholars used Arabic as their literary language, Sufis wrote their poetry and treatises in the vernacular. This use of local languages, especially Persian, became legendary in Rumi's epic *Mathnawi* (meaning 'couplet'), a six-volume poem with more than 25,000 verses of parables, metaphors and tales about prophets and saints.

RUMI'S LIFE

According to his biography, Rumi was born in Persian Khorasan (now in Afghanistan) in 1207. His family moved to Rum in Anatolia around 1222 and to Konya in 1229. Rumi's father was a scholar and Rumi took his place as a teacher at the *madrasa* in Konya, after the latter's death in 1231. Here, his new teacher, Burhanuddin, instructed him in Sufism and sent him to Aleppo and Damascus for further study. Rumi returned to teach in Konya again when he was 30 years old.

Rumi was already accomplished as a jurist and Sufi when, in 1244, he met Shams Tabrizi, an Iranian Sufi mystic, on his way home from teaching. The meeting changed Rumi's life – it is said that he fainted after the spiritual and verbal exchange that took place – and after this time, he neglected his teaching duties to devote himself to Sufi development under the guidance of Shams.

Only 15 months later, however, Shams disappeared. Rumi, despondent and dejected, poured his anguish into verse. Shams did return but disappeared again only a few months later. Legend has it that the teacher was murdered by Rumi's son Ala-uddin. More rational accounts claim that Shams, a highly evolved soul, sought like-minded men to train further in God's way, and that once his task was complete, he would leave so that their great work on earth could begin. Certainly,

Left *Rumi holds court and warns his son, Sultan Walad, against sin in this manuscript painting from* The Legend of Maulana Jalal ud-Din Rumi *(1599).*

it was after Shams' disappearance that the now mature and refined Rumi wrote his major works.

Rumi died in 1273, after a short illness. It is recorded that people of all races and religions attended his funeral, which took place in Konya. To this day, his burial place is a pilgrimage site for his many devotees. Rumi is fondly known throughout the Muslim world as Maulana, 'our teacher', from which the Mevlevi (whirling dervishes) Sufi order, founded by his son Sultan Walad, takes its name.

THE *MATHNAWI*

Rumi began writing and dictating the *Mathnawi* in 1260 and the work continued until his death. Its many verses teach that although scholars and theologians are important, they lost their way in the depths of books and laws, and that the spirit of God is of paramount importance and knowing him the aim of life.

Left Rumi's mausoleum in Konya, Turkey, attracts thousands of visitors each year, and to this day, Konya remains an openly spiritual city.

The work opens with 'The Poem of the Reed', a lament by a reed when it is cut off from the reed-bed. The poem is a metaphor of human anguish: pain emanates from the fact that humankind is cut off from God since being rejected from heaven and longs to return to him.

The Mathnawi combines hadiths and Quranic verses with parables, anecdotes, paradoxes and moral teachings. These elements often flow naturally, while at other times a narrative is resumed after interruption by another.

While as an accomplished Sufi, Rumi no longer experienced a separation of the temporal and spiritual realms, he acknowledged that most people did. He is also said to have been very conscious of the limitations of words to describe the divine and the spiritual. Perhaps it is for this reason that he often uses very bawdy, coarse language and imagery to portray spiritual truths.

EXCERPTS FROM THE *MATHNAWI*:

'Listen to the reed how it tells a tale, complaining of separations – saying "ever since I was parted from the reed-bed, my lament has caused man and woman to moan.

I want a bosom torn by severance, that I may unfold the pain of love-desire.

Every one who is left far from his source wishes back the time when he was united with it…"' *(The Poem of the Reed, vol. 1)*

'When the mirror of your heart becomes clear and pure, you will behold images from beyond this world of water and clay.

You will behold both the image and the image-Maker, both the carpet and the carpet-Spreader.

The image of the beloved is like Abraham – outwardly an idol worshipper, inwardly an idol-breaker.'

(The Prophet Abraham, vol. 2)

Above Whirling dervishes dance in the Maulana hall at Rumi's mausoleum. Murids, or seekers, are not admitted to the dance until they have attained certain stations in their spiritual quest.

SUFISM IN PRACTICE

SUFI PRACTICE IS BASED ON THE IDEA THAT GOD IS LOVE, AND
THEREFORE THE ONLY AIM OF THE SUFI IS TO LOVE GOD, OTHERS
AND HIMSELF. WELL-KNOWN SUFI MAXIMS ELABORATE THIS BELIEF.

Sufism can be summed up as the fulfilment of the Quran and sunnah so that the exoteric laws are understood through esoteric dimensions. This emphasis on inner spirituality was ardently promoted by some Sufis, who insisted that Sufis should not wear noticeably different clothes, because outward appearance should not be the hallmark of a Sufi.

According to various treatises, Sufis are seekers of gnosis (*marifah*), or knowledge of spiritual mysteries, which cannot be attained until the ego has been fully controlled through prescribed practices.

BODY AND SPIRIT

An interesting tension exists between the body and the spirit in Islam: while humankind is both, the body is understood, in Sufi terms, to be that earthly element (*al-nafs al-ammarah*), which distances man from God. Sufis therefore believe that a rigorous programme of worship, night vigils and fasting is necessary in order to starve the ego and body

and purify the soul. Only in this way, they claim, can the 'ever-reproachful soul' (*al-nafs al-lawwamah*) become the 'contented soul' (*al-nafs al-mutmainnah*).

Sufis teach that constant recitation of God's divine names and praises will purify the heart until it is ready to receive divine grace. For Sufis, the legal injunctions of Islam are valid only if performed with God's presence and pleasure in mind.

THE STATIONS AND STATES

For Sufis, knowing God is such a serious business that it cannot be achieved without a teacher. The Prophet, himself the guide (*murshid*) who showed the way to God, is cited as the precedent for this practice. Sufis believe that God bestows this task on pious souls who themselves have travelled the same journey. These teachers are usually affiliated to Sufi orders (*tariqahs*), and trace their chain of authority (*silsilah*), to the Prophet and his companions. They are seen as God's friends, or *awliya* (10:62).

Above Dhikr, *remembrance of God, is
a Sufi practice that takes different forms.
Members of the Qadriyya sect, like this
Sudanese Sufi, whirl rapidly in prayer.*

Each Sufi, then, is required to attach himself to such a teacher, who will give him or her various spiritual and physical exercises to perform. The stages of Sufi development are described as *maqamat*, or stations, and include repentance, patience, gratitude, acceptance, trust and love. The paradigmatic journey to God was the Prophet's ascent to heaven (*Miraj*). While on the path, a Sufi is believed to experience various transcendent states (*ahwal*), such as fear and hope. Imam al-Ghazali asserted that the stations are permanent changes gained through acts of devotion, whereas states are temporary, dependent on the grace and favour of God.

Finally, through the stations of love and gnosis, the Sufi is said to reach the position of *fana*, or

*Left Depicted here at his execution,
al-Hallaj was thought to have blasphemed
by claiming to have attained union with
God, a controversial theme in Sufism.*

Above An illustration from a manuscript by the renowned Persian Sufi poet, Farid-ud-Din Attar.

SUNNI AND SHIAH SUFI ORDERS

Sufis believe that a network of teachers operates under God's instructions to bring peace and love to the world. These teachers are believed to hold different ranks with God – some are thought to be nearer to him than others – and adhere to organized *tariqahs*. All these *tariqahs* have their own lodges (*zawiyahs* or *khanqahs*) and welcome any seeker at their door.

In North Africa, the Shadhili order originated in Tunisia but now has a large following in the West, too. In Turkey, the Mevlevi order, following the teachings of Jalal-ud-Din Rumi, is renowned for its whirling dervishes. The Chishti order, which converted masses of Hindus in India, is well known for its *qawwali* devotional music. The Naqshbandi order spread from Daghestan, in the Caucus, to India and Turkey and is famous for its silent meditation. Among the Shiahs, the Nimatullahi is the best-known Sufi order.

self-annihilation, where he can then exist and dwell (*baqa*) wholly in God. Such ideas, alluding to union with God (*wahdat-ul-wujud*), have been very controversial, often resulting in what appear to be blasphemous statements: Mansur al-Hallaj (d.922) was eventually executed in Baghdad for having uttered, 'I am the Truth'. In an attempt to defend and clarify this union with God, several Sufi writings explain that the Sufi becomes one with the divine will, rather than actually joining with the essence of God.

CELEBRATING THE DIVINE

Sufis celebrate the divine in many different ways. While some have very puritan rituals, such as silent meditation, others have produced trancelike dance movements (whirling dervishes), music (Abida Perveen's *qawwalis* in Pakistan), poetry (Bulleh Shah) and literature (al-Ghazali, Jalal-ud-Din Rumi's *Mathnawi*, Farid-ud-Din Attar's *Conference of the Birds*).

Above Sufis pray at the tomb of Shaykh Salim Chishti, at Fatehpur Sikri in Uttar Pradesh, India. The Chishti is a very influential Sufi order in India.

RABIAH AL-ADAWIYYAH

RENOWNED FOR HER WISDOM AND LOVE OF GOD, RABIAH AL-ADAWIYYAH (717–801) IS OFTEN DESCRIBED AS THE FIRST SUFI WOMAN BECAUSE OF HER FAR-REACHING INFLUENCE.

In the 8th and 9th centuries, Basra (in present-day Iraq) was a great centre of asceticism, where women ascetics, in particular, flourished. It is here that Rabiah spent her life, giving advice and moral teachings and introducing pure love in mysticism. Sufism is often more inclusive of women than ritual Islam, and Rabiah is seen as the model of female sainthood.

Rabiah is so important in Sufi thought that she is cited by later seminal historical treatises, such as those by Al-Sulami (d.1021) and Farid-ud-Din Attar (d.1229). Al-Sulami begins his work on women Sufi saints with Rabiah, not because she was the first, but because her influence was so profound and far-reaching. Attar, her main biographer, describes her as a 'man' in appreciation of her status and achievements.

RABIAH'S LIFE

It is thought that Rabiah was born in Basra and sold into slavery as a young girl. The story tells that following her conversion to Islam, Rabiah was observing all-night devotions after having worked all day. Her master saw her and was so amazed that he set her free. She is said to have spent the rest of her life as an ascetic, never marrying, despite receiving numerous proposals.

Various sayings and anecdotes have been attributed to Rabiah, both about her love for God and relating her intellectual debates. She reportedly defeated the old jurist Hassan al-Basra in many intellectual contests, for unlike him, she managed to synthesize theology with the practice of self-discipline in her debates. Her thinking and approach was to pave the way for later Sufism.

Above This 16th-century Persian-style manuscript painting depicts a Sufi preaching in a mosque.

LOVING GOD

Rabiah is well known for having explained the concept of *sidq*, or sincerity with God. Brutally critical of those who claimed to be ascetic, she argued that if they had truly shunned the world, then they ought to be so consumed with affirming God that there would be no scope in their life to shun anything. In other words, detachment from the world was not a verbal confession, but a state of being.

Linked with this was her most famous argument: that believers should be so truthful and devout to God that notions of hell and heaven, despite being present in the Quran, would cease to matter. The goal of worship, she asserted, was not heaven but nearness to God and his pleasure (*rida*). There are famous legendary accounts of her running down a street with fire in one hand and water in the other, because she wanted to burn heaven and douse hell so that people would love God, heedless of reward or punishment.

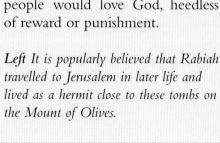

Left It is popularly believed that Rabiah travelled to Jerusalem in later life and lived as a hermit close to these tombs on the Mount of Olives.

Above Women members of a Sufi order at the festival of Sboue in the oasis town of Timimoun in Algeria. The festival is in honour of the Prophet's birthday.

This sincere love (*mahabba*), was so crucial to her that she is said to have exclaimed that she could not hate Satan, for she had no need to think of him, nor could she love the Prophet, with all due respect, for she was too busy loving the One God. This was the epitome of her trust (*tawakkul*), in Allah, for her life consisted of turning exclusively to him.

CATALOGUE OF MIRACLES

Rabiah is said to have annihilated her ego to such an extent that her life became a catalogue of miracles. One story tells that when she went on pilgrimage to Makkah, the *Kaabah* came to greet her rather than her visiting it. It is told that she was thoroughly disappointed by this, for unlike others, she had not travelled to visit the *Kaabah*, but rather its Master.

Below A woman whirling dervish in Istanbul. Women are very visible in Sufi orders, sometimes even leading them.

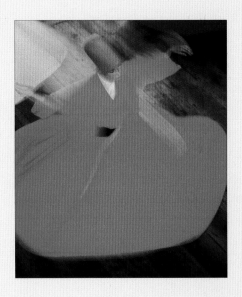

SAYINGS OF RABIAH

Scholar Sufyan al-Thawri visited Rabiah and said, 'Oh God, grant me safety', at which she wept and said, 'Have you not learned that true safety from the world is to abandon all that is in it? So how can you ask such a thing when you are still soiled by the world?'

Rabiah once said, weeping, 'I ask God's forgiveness for my lack of truthfulness and sincerity in saying "I ask God's forgiveness".'

Salih al-Murri, a Sufi and well-known scholar in Basra, once said in the presence of Rabiah, 'He who continues to knock on the door will have it opened for him.' She replied, 'The door is [already] open: but the issue is, who wants to enter it?'

Glossary

ADHAN the call to prayer signalling the congregational times of the five daily prayers. *See also muadhdhin.*

ADL justice, equity or equality.

AHL AL-BAYT 'the people of the house', the immediate family of the Prophet, namely Muhammad, Fatimah, Ali, Hassan and Hussain. Significant in Shiah theology.

AHL AL-DHIMMAH religious minorities living under Muslim rule.

AHWAL (singular *hal*) the different temporary states of spirituality experienced through Sufi practice.

AKHLAQ morality and ethics. In its singular form, the word means character, manners and etiquette.

AL-BURAQ the winged, horselike beast that Muslims believe carried Muhammad to Jerusalem and then to heaven on the *Isra* and *Miraj*.

AL-DAJJAL the Antichrist who it is said will appear before the end of times, wreak havoc on earth and be killed by Jesus after his second coming.

AL-GHAYB the unseen world; a created reality but not seen with the human eye (for example, *jinn*, or heaven).

AL-MAHDI literally 'the guided one', a descendant of the Prophet Muhammad, who Muslims believe will appear at the end of time and establish peace on earth. In Shiah theology, he is the 12th awaited imam, the 'hidden imam'.

AL-MASIH literally 'the anointed one', referring to Jesus.

AL-MUHADDITHUN scholars of hadith and Islamic jurists.

AL-SIRAH AL-NABAWIYYAH biographical accounts of the Prophet's life.

AL-YAWM AL-AKHIR the Last Day or Day of Judgement.

AMIR the leader of a Muslim community.

AQD a legal contract or agreement.

ARAFAH the valley plain near Makkah where *Hajj* pilgrims spend the day in repentance and prayer.

ASR the third prayer of the day, offered in late afternoon.

AYAH a verse from the Quran.

BATIN the hidden or esoteric.

BURQA a long overgarment, usually black, covering the entire body of a Muslim woman. Also usually covers face with a veil. *See also niqab.*

CALIPH the appointed leader of the Muslim community in early Islamic history until the Ottoman times.

DHAHIR the manifest and known, or the physical and tangible world.

DHIKR remembrance of God through spiritual practices of repeating his name and praises.

DHUHR the second prayer of the day, offered early in the afternoon.

DIN religion, a way of life.

DUNYA earthly existence.

EID the celebration at the end of Ramadhan (*Eid ul-fitr*) and *Hajj* (*Eid ul-adha*).

ESCHATOLOGY branch of theology concerning the final events in the history of the world or humankind.

FAJR the first prayer of the day, offered just before sunrise.

FAQIH (plural *fuqaha*) a Muslim scholar of Islamic religious law.

FARD an obligatory action that must be performed by every sane, healthy adult.

FATWA a religious edict; a legal opinion, issued by a *mufti* (legal expert), although it is not binding in nature.

FIQH body of jurisprudential principles derived from Shariah by legal scholars exercising their understanding of the law.

FITRA the state of natural or primordial disposition.

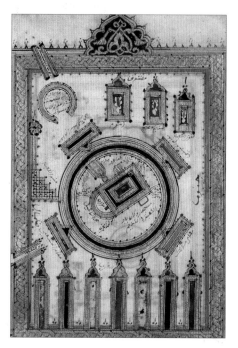

Above An 18th-century plan of the Sacred Mosque in Makkah. Muslims believe that the original mosque was built by Ibrahim and Ismail.

FURQAN 'the criterion', referring to the Quran as the measure of what is right and wrong.

GHULUW excessiveness, extremism.

GHUSL ritual bath to attain purification, a state that is compulsory before offering prayers.

HADITH the sayings and narrations of the Prophet.

HAJJ pilgrimage to the *Kaabah* in Makkah: the fifth pillar of Islam.

HANIF (plural *hunafa*) a believer in one God but without any professed or formal religion.

HARAM actions that are forbidden/unlawful under Islamic law.

HIJAB a headscarf worn by women to cover all the hair.

HIJRAH the Prophet Muhammad's migration from Makkah to Madinah in 622CE.

IBADAH (plural *ibadat*) an act of worship. This forms the 'personal' part of Islamic law.

IFTAR the meal taken at sunset to break the fast during Ramadhan.

IHRAM the simple two-piece (usually) white cloth worn by pilgrims on *Hajj*.

IJMA the majority consensus of Muslim scholars.

IJTIHAD exerted effort by the use of analogy to arrive at an Islamic legal opinion.

IMAM In Shiah theology, the leader of the Muslim community from the descendants of the Prophet. In Sunni practice, the religious leader of the mosque community.

ISHA the fifth prayer of the day, offered at nightfall.

ISLAM as a verb, wilful submission to God; peace. As a noun, the faith of Islam as taught by the Prophet Muhammad.

ISNAD the chain of hadith transmitters connecting directly to the Prophet Muhammad.

ISRA the Prophet's night journey with Archangel Jibril to Jersualem from Makkah on al-Buraq.

JAHANNAM hellfire.

JAHILIYYAH ignorance; a term used to described the state of polytheist pre-Islamic Arabia.

JIHAD (verb) to struggle. Usually refers to the 'greater' self-struggle of purifying the soul from earthly desires, but also means physical/military struggle (which is known as the 'lesser' *jihad*).

JINN creatures of the unseen who, like humans, have been endowed with free will.

JIZYAH the exemption tax paid by religious minorities under Muslim rule.

JUMUAH Friday, the day of congregational prayer.

JUZ (plural *ajza*) one portion of the Quran divided into 30 parts.

KAABAH the cubelike edifice in

Right A battle scene from the Suleymanname, *an illustrated history of the life of Suleyman the Magnificent, dating from the 16th century.*

the Haram Mosque, Makkah, which is considered to be the first house of worship.

KAFIR (plural *kuffar*) a theological definition of a non-believer.

KALAM the rhetorical expositions of philosophers.

KUFR disbelief.

LIAN a particular oath relating to alleged infidelity and taken in a divorce petition.

MADHHAB Islamic jurisprudential school or developed method of legal interpretation.

MADINAH the city of Yathrib, which became known as 'the city of the Prophet'.

MADRASA a school/seminary/college/class for learning the Quran and Islam, usually attached to a mosque.

MAGHRIB the fourth compulsory prayer of the day at sunset.

Above Now a Christian church, the Mezquita of Córdoba was originally built by Abd al-Rahman I in 784 and remained a mosque until 1236.

MAKKAH Muhammad's birth city and the place of Ibrahim's ancient temple, the *Kaabah*.

MALAK (plural *malaaikah*) an angel.

MAQAM (plural *maqamat*) different stations on the Sufi path that are experienced on the journey toward God (for example, repentance and gratitude).

MAQASID established principles or reasons for Islamic rulings and interpretations.

MATN used in relation to hadith interpretation, meaning the hadith's content or principle.

MAWLID the Prophet's birthday celebration; also known as *Milad*.

MIHRAB arched niche in the mosque from where the imam leads congregational prayers.

MINBAR pulpit to the right of the *mihrab* with a flight of stairs leading to the top, from where the imam delivers his sermons.

MIRAJ the Prophet's Night Journey to heaven, on al-Buraq. *See also* Isra.

MIZAN scales or balance.

MUADHDHIN the caller who recites the *adhan*, to call believers to the ritual prayers.

MUAMALAT those aspects of Islamic law dealing with social relations and interactions.

MUFTI an Islamic jurist qualified to give a legal ruling.

MUHARRAM the first month of the Islamic calendar, also the month in which Hussain, the Prophet's grandson, was martyred at Karbala.

MUJAHID (plural *mujahidun*) a Muslim engaged in physical *jihad*.

MURSHID a Sufi master, attached to a *tariqah* (Sufi order), who guides his/her disciples. Also known as a *shaykh*.

MUSALLAH 'a place of prayer'. Refers both to the physical place of prayer and a prayer mat.

MUSLIM one who submits his or her will to worshipping one God: a follower of the religion of Islam.

MUWAHHIDUN unitarian belief stressing the oneness of God, and used as a self-label by those more usually called 'Wahhabis' by critics. *See also* Wahhabism.

NABI a prophet of Allah.

NAFS the ego encompassing human virtues and desires.

NIKAH the marriage contract, detailing an offer by the groom, acceptance by the bride, witnessed by two people.

NIQAB face veil.

QADI an Islamic judge, who presides over legal matters and proceedings.

QADAR God's divine measure, decree or predestination.

QIBLA the direction of prayer facing toward the *Kaabah* in the city of Makkah.

QIYAM-UL-LAYL night of devotional prayer to achieve nearness to God, through either formal prayer or recitation of the Quran and *dhikr*.

QIYAS analogous reasoning used in applying Islamic jurisprudence.

QURAN the book of divine revelations that Muslims believe was revealed by God to the Prophet Muhammad via Archangel Jibril.

QURAYSH the ruling Arab tribe of Makkah during the pre-Islamic period of Muhammad's era.

RAMADHAN the ninth month of the Islamic calendar, during which Muslims fast. *See also sawm.*

RASUL God's messenger.

RIBA usury. The taking or giving of interest in economic transactions is forbidden by Islam because it is considered to be unjust.

RISALAH divine messengership. Denotes the messenger bringing a divine text, such as the Quran and Torah, to humankind.

RUH the spirit or the soul.

SALAH (plural *salawat*) formal ritual prayer, offered in Arabic, reciting verses from the Quran and other prayers, toward the direction of the *Kaabah*. Apart from the five compulsory prayers, *salah* can also be extra optional units of prayer. *Salah* is the second pillar of Islam.

SAWM fasting in the month of Ramadhan, the fourth pillar of Islam. Usually begins with *suhur* (a meal taken before sunrise).

SHAHADAH the first pillar of Islam; the declaration of faith that there is no god but the one God and that Muhammad is his prophet.

SHAYKH An elder, leader or teacher. *See also murshid.*

SHAYTAN Satan, the devil. Also known as Iblis.

SHIAH a Muslim who follows the minority political and theological system that recognizes Ali and his descendants as the rightful heirs and leaders of the Muslim community.

Above *A detail of the exquisite tiling on the vaulted ceiling of the traditional Nasir al-Mulk Mosque in Shiraz, Iran, completed in 1888.*

SHIRK polytheism, or the sin of associating partners with God.

SHURA consultation, or the act of seeking council by the caliph from learned advisors.

SILSILAH Sufi chain or order of spiritual authority.

SIRAH the biography or historical account of the Prophet Muhammad.

SUFISM/*TASAWWUF* mysticism, spiritual inner journey where remembrance and love of God, together with purification of the heart, is emphasized more than outer dimensions of faith.

SUNNAH the 'way' or life example of the Prophet Muhammad.

SUNNI a term used to describe the overwhelming majority of Muslims, who adhere to the teachings and life example of the Prophet.

SURAH a chapter from the Quran.

TAFSIR exegesis or explanation and interpretation of the Quran.

TAJWEED the art of reciting the Quran.

TALBIYAH 'I am at your command O Allah, I am at your command', the prayer recited by pilgrims throughout the *Hajj*.

TAQLID adherence to established Islamic legal rulings.

TAQWA an all-encompassing awareness of God.

TARAWIH the extra optional night prayer offered in congregation during Ramadhan.

TARIQAH a Sufi order of brotherhood, organized with a spiritual guide (*murshid*) helping his or her disciples (*murids*) on their inner journey to God.

TAWBAH repentance. The process of asking God for forgiveness to attain purity of faith.

TAWHID God's oneness or unicity.

TAZIYAH passion plays and models of Hussain's mosque, carried in processions to commemorate his martyrdom in Muharram.

TAZKIYAH purification of the soul. A deeply spiritual exercise.

ULAMA Islamic religious scholars.

UMMAH the universal Muslim community.

UMMATUN WASATA the Muslim nation as a community of moderation.

VICEGERENT a deputy or steward to God on earth.

WAHHABISM the name often given to the puritanical reform movement founded by Muhammad ibn Abd al-Wahhab in the 18th century, adopted by the ruling family in Saudi Arabia.

WUDU ritual ablutions to prepare for prayer.

YAWM AL-QIYAMAH the Day of Resurrection.

ZAKAH the required Islamic principle of giving alms to the poor. The third pillar of Islam.

ZAMZAM, WELL OF the well in Makkah that, according to Islam, sprang up when Ismail's mother, Hajar, searched for water in the barren valley to quench his thirst.

INDEX

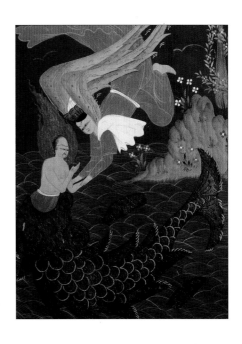

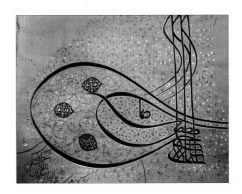

This edition is published by
Hermes House
an imprint of Anness Publishing Ltd,
Blaby Road,
Wigston,
Leicestershire
LE18 4SE

Email: info@anness.com

Web: www.hermeshouse.com;
www.annesspublishing.com

© Anness Publishing Ltd 2011

*Produced for Hermes House
by Toucan Books*

Anness Publishing has a new picture
agency outlet for images for publishing,
promotions or advertising. Please visit
our website www.practicalpictures.com
for more information.

All rights reserved. No part of this
publication may be reproduced, stored
in a retrieval system, or transmitted in
any way or by any means, electronic,
mechanical, photocopying, recording
or otherwise, without the prior written
permission of the copyright holder.

A CIP catologue record for this book
is available from the British Library.

ETHICAL TRADING POLICY
Because of our ongoing ecological
investment programme, you, as our
customer, can have the pleasure and
reassurance of knowing that a tree
is being cultivated on your behalf to
naturally replace the materials used to
make the book you are holding. For
further information about this scheme,
go to www.annesspublishing.com/trees

For Anness Publishing Ltd:
Publisher: Joanna Lorenz
Editorial Director: Helen Sudell

For Toucan Books:
Managing Editor: Ellen Dupont
Editor: Anne McDowall
Project Manager: Hannah Bowen
Designer: Ralph Pitchford
Picture Researchers: Tam Church,
 Mia Stewart-Wilson
Proofreader: Marion Dent
Indexer: Jackie Brind
Cartography by Cosmographics, UK

PUBLISHER'S NOTE
Although the advice and information
in this book are believed to be accurate
and true at the time of going to press,
neither the authors nor the publisher
can accept any legal responsibility or
liability for any errors or omissions that
may have been made nor for any
inaccuracies nor for any loss, harm or
injury that comes about from following
instructions or advice in this book.

PICTURE CREDITS

The publishers have made every effort
to trace the photograph copyright
owners. Anyone we have failed to
reach is invited to contact Toucan
Books, 89 Charterhouse Street,
London EC1M 6HR, United
Kingdom.

akg-images front cover tml, back
cover bml, 3b, 20t, 21t, 25t, 29, 33t,
34t, 56b, 65b, 82b, 83t, 84b, 86b, 117b,
130t, 142b, 143b, 146t, 147b, 173b,
234b, 236.
Alamy back cover tc, 4br, 8t, 26t, 48t,
69t, 75t, 82t, 98b, 106, 157t, 175t, 196,
201t, 211t, 231, 241t.
Ancient Art & Architecture 1, 2, 3t,
4bml, 5br, 11r, 56t, 64t, 66, 71b, 75b,
77b, 87t, 88t, 92b, 96t, 98t, 101b, 171b,
204t, 255.
The Art Archive front cover flap, 4bl,
5bml, 10, 11l, 15b, 16t, 17, 18t, 20b,
23t, 26b, 27b, 28t, 30b, 36t, 42b, 45b,
46t, 48b, 50b, 51t, 52t, 65t, 66, 69mr,
70b, 71t, 72b, 73t, 74t, 76, 77t, 78t, 79b,
80, 81t, 84t, 87b, 89b, 99b, 100t, 101t,
102, 103b, 104t, 115, 119b, 121, 124t,
126t, 128, 129, 131b, 132, 133t, 137,
138b, 142t, 144t, 145l, 146b, 160t,
182b, 188t, 191t, 194bl, 195, 198b,
201b, 205t, 209t, 210t, 222t, 232t, 242,
245t, 246t, 251, 253, 254.
Art Directors 4bmr, 12, 14, 16b, 19t,
21b, 46b, 47t, 51b, 57t, 59t, 60t, 61t,
72t, 81b, 93b, 100b, 107, 108t, 109b,
112b, 116, 117t, 118b, 120, 122t, 125,
130b, 135t, 140t, 152t, 154t, 155b,
158b, 177, 178b, 182t, 184b, 185t, 189t,
194br, 200, 208b, 216b, 220t, 224, 228b,
229, 232b, 239t, 239b, 240t.
The Bridgeman Art Library 11m,
22b, 25b, 30t, 38, 42t, 58t, 61b, 62t, 64b,
67t, 83b, 85b, 86t, 133b, 136b, 138t,
143t, 145r, 150b, 194t, 204b, 212t, 234t,
240b, 244b, 248.
CORBIS front cover tl, tmr, tr, ml and
bl, back cover tl, tr, bl, bmr and br,
spine t, 5bl, 9b, 27t, 31b, 35, 36b, 37,
39b, 43b, 44b, 47b, 49t, 53t, 55, 58b,
62b, 67b, 70t, 78b, 79t, 85t, 90t, 91, 92t,
103t, 104bl, 112t, 113b, 118t, 119t,
127b, 135b, 140b, 143, 151br, 153b, 155t,
156t, 157b, 158t, 159, 161b, 162b, 163t,
166, 168t, 169t, 174, 175mr, 176, 179b,
181, 185b, 186t, 187t, 188b, 192b, 193,
202, 203t, 205b, 207t, 208t, 209b, 211b,
214b, 217, 218t, 219, 221b, 222b, 223,
225, 237b, 238b, 241b, 243, 244t, 256.
Getty Images front cover tc and br,
back cover tml, tmr and bc, spine b,
back cover flap, 7, 9t, 13, 15t, 18b, 23b,
24b, 40t, 44t, 50t, 90b, 94t, 108b, 110t,
111t, 114, 123b, 134b, 136t, 139, 149,
150t, 153t, 156b, 164t, 167t, 168b,
169b, 170, 172b, 173t, 186b, 187b, 192t,
197, 199b, 203b, 206b, 207b, 210b,
213t, 215b, 218b, 221t, 226, 227, 228t,
230b, 233t, 235b, 237t, 246b, 252.
Imagestate 40b, 41t, 134t, 152b, 163b,
178t.
NASA 123t.
Peter Sanders 22t, 32t, 33b, 39t, 49b,
104br, 151bl, 154b, 161t, 165, 198t,
199t, 206t.
Photolibrary 6b, 19b, 31t, 45t, 52b,
53b, 54, 57b, 59b, 60b, 63, 68b, 74b,
88b, 89t, 93t, 94b, 95t, 96b, 97, 99t, 105,
109t, 111b, 113t, 124b, 131t, 147t,
160b, 171t, 172t, 212b, 220b, 233b, 250.
Photoshot 24t, 167b, 179t, 180, 190,
191b.
Reuters 247t.
Rex Features Ltd 148, 162t, 164b,
213b, 214t, 216t, 238t, 235t.
Robert Harding 68t, 95b, 122b, 184t,
245b.
Shutterstock 43t, 183, 189b. **Sonia
Halliday** 249.
TopFoto 5bmr, 41b, 73b, 215t.
Werner Forman Archive 6t, 28b,
34b, 126b, 127t, 144b, 230t.
**Zeynep Mufti/
photographersdirect.com** 247b.